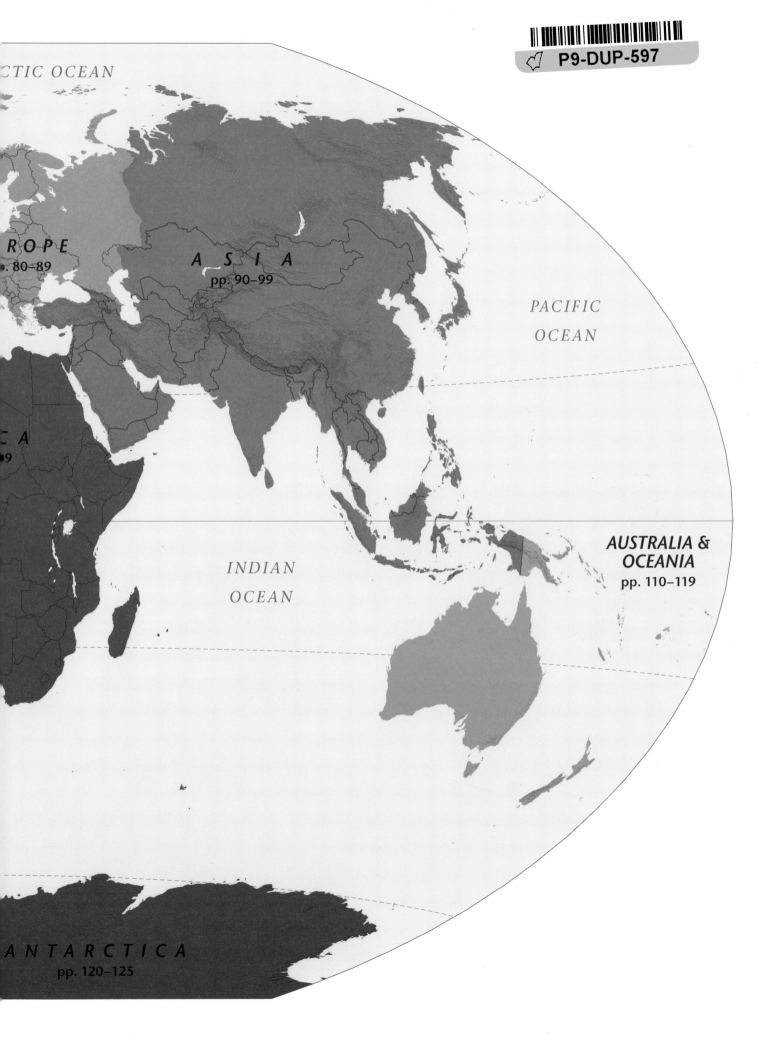

CTIC OCEAN

ROPE
80–89

ASIA
pp. 90–99

PACIFIC
OCEAN

CA
9

INDIAN
OCEAN

AUSTRALIA &
OCEANIA
pp. 110–119

ANTARCTICA
pp. 120–125

STUDENT
WORLD
ATLAS

NATIONAL GEOGRAPHIC
WASHINGTON, D.C.

Table of Contents

North America:
Floods, page 68

South America: Three-toed sloth,
page 78

Europe:
Hungarian
Parliament,
page 89

Mercury

Venus

Earth

Mars

Ceres

Sun

Jupiter

Saturn

Uranus

Neptune

Pluto

Haumea

Makemake

Eris

🌑 **EIGHT PLANETS** and at least five dwarf planets orbit the sun, held in place by its gravitational field. Tiny Mercury's orbit is the shortest: 88 Earth days, while Neptune takes almost 169 Earth years to complete its journey around the sun.

Art shows relative size of the sun and planets, but distances are not to scale.

Earth in Space

At the center of our solar system is the sun, a huge mass of hot gas that is the source of both light and warmth for Earth. Third in a group of eight planets that revolve around the sun, Earth is a terrestrial, or mostly rocky, planet. So are Mercury, Venus, and Mars. Earth is about 93 million miles (150 million km) from the sun, and its orbital journey, or revolution, around the sun takes 365¼ days. Farther away from the sun, four more planets—Jupiter, Saturn, Uranus, and Neptune (all made up primarily of gases)—plus at least five dwarf planets (Ceres, Pluto, Haumea, Makemake, and Eris) complete the main bodies of our solar system. The solar system, in turn, is part of the Milky Way galaxy.

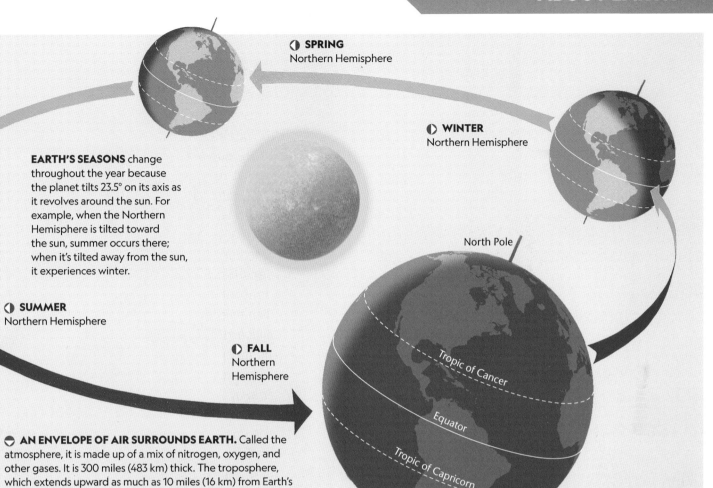

SPRING
Northern Hemisphere

WINTER
Northern Hemisphere

EARTH'S SEASONS change throughout the year because the planet tilts 23.5° on its axis as it revolves around the sun. For example, when the Northern Hemisphere is tilted toward the sun, summer occurs there; when it's tilted away from the sun, it experiences winter.

SUMMER
Northern Hemisphere

FALL
Northern Hemisphere

North Pole

Tropic of Cancer

Equator

Tropic of Capricorn

South Pole

AN ENVELOPE OF AIR SURROUNDS EARTH. Called the atmosphere, it is made up of a mix of nitrogen, oxygen, and other gases. It is 300 miles (483 km) thick. The troposphere, which extends upward as much as 10 miles (16 km) from Earth's surface, is called the zone of life. The combination of gases, moderate temperatures, and water in this layer supports plants, animals, and other forms of life on Earth.

EARTH ROTATES WEST TO EAST on its axis, an imaginary line that runs through Earth's center from pole to pole. Each rotation takes 24 hours, or one full cycle of day and night. One complete rotation equals one Earth day. One complete revolution around the sun equals one Earth year.

Map Projections

Maps tell a story about physical and human systems, places and regions, patterns and relationships. This atlas is a collection of maps that tell a story about Earth.

Understanding that story requires a knowledge of how maps are made and a familiarity with the special language used by cartographers, the people who create maps.

Globes present a model of Earth as it is—a sphere—but they are bulky and can be difficult to use and store. Flat maps are much more convenient, but certain problems result from transferring Earth's curved surface to a flat piece of paper, a process called projection. There are many different types of projections, all of which involve some form of distortion in area, distance, direction, or shape.

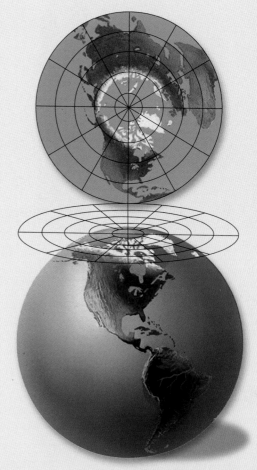

AZIMUTHAL MAP PROJECTION. This kind of map is made by projecting a globe onto a flat surface that touches the globe at a single point, such as the North Pole. These maps accurately represent direction along any straight line extending from the point of contact. Away from the point of contact, shape is increasingly distorted.

MAKING A PROJECTION. Imagine a globe that has been cut in half as this one has. If a light is shined into it, the lines of latitude and longitude and the shapes of the continents will cast shadows that can be "projected" onto a piece of paper, as shown here. Depending on how the paper is positioned, the shadows will be distorted in different ways.

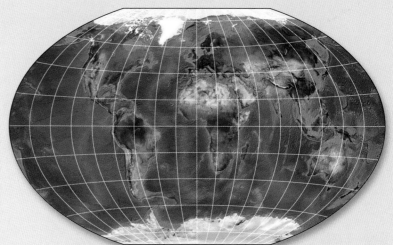

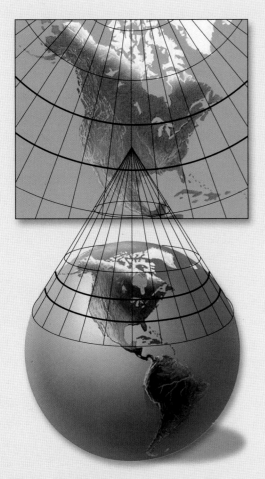

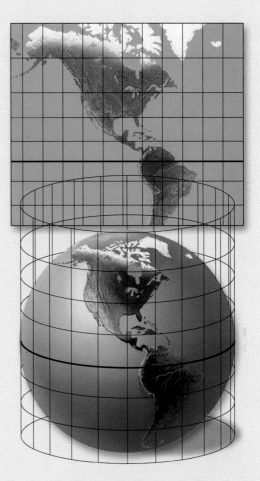

◔ **CONIC MAP PROJECTION.** This kind of map is made by projecting a globe onto a cone. The part of Earth being mapped touches the sides of the cone. Lines of longitude appear as straight lines; lines of latitude appear as parallel arcs. Conic projections are often used to map mid-latitude areas with great east-west extent, such as North America.

◔ **CYLINDRICAL MAP PROJECTION.** A cylindrical projection map is made by projecting a globe onto a cylinder that touches Earth's surface along the Equator. Latitude and longitude lines on this kind of map show true compass directions, which makes it useful for navigation. But there is great distortion in the size of high-latitude landmasses.

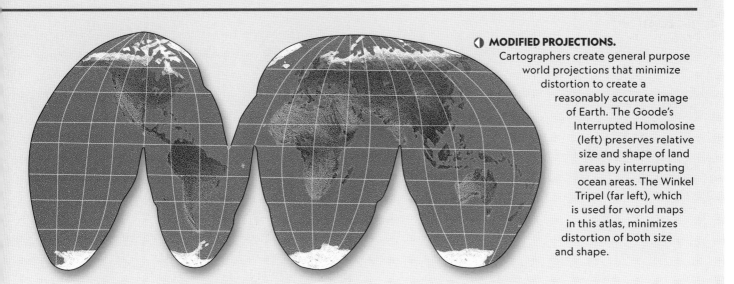

◑ **MODIFIED PROJECTIONS.**
Cartographers create general purpose world projections that minimize distortion to create a reasonably accurate image of Earth. The Goode's Interrupted Homolosine (left) preserves relative size and shape of land areas by interrupting ocean areas. The Winkel Tripel (far left), which is used for world maps in this atlas, minimizes distortion of both size and shape.

Reading Maps

People can use maps to find locations, to determine direction or distance, and to understand information about places. Cartographers rely on a special graphic language to communicate through maps.

An imaginary system of lines, called the global grid, helps us locate particular points on Earth's surface. The global grid is made up of lines of latitude and longitude that are measured in degrees, minutes, and seconds. The point where these lines intersect identifies the absolute location of a place. No other place has the exact same address.

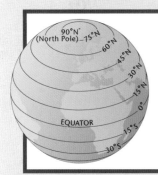

LATITUDE. Lines of latitude—also called parallels because they are parallel to the Equator—run east to west around the globe and measure location north or south of the Equator. The Equator is 0° latitude.

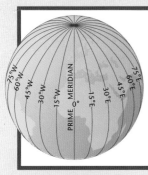

LONGITUDE. Lines of longitude—also called meridians—run from pole to pole and measure location east or west of the prime meridian. The prime meridian is 0° longitude, and it runs through Greenwich, near London, England.

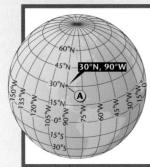

GLOBAL GRID. When used together, latitude and longitude form a grid that provides a system for determining the exact, or absolute, location of every place on Earth. For example, the absolute location of point A is 30°N, 90°W.

DIRECTION. Cartographers put a north arrow or a compass rose, which shows the four cardinal directions—north, south, east, and west—on a map. On the map above, point **B** is northwest (NW) of point **A**. Northwest is an example of an intermediate direction, which means it is between two cardinal directions. Grid lines can also be used to indicate north.

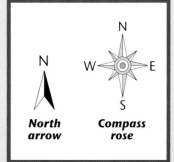

North arrow   **Compass rose**

SCALE. A map represents a part of Earth's surface, but that part is greatly reduced. Cartographers include a map scale to show what distance on Earth is represented by a given length on the map. Scale can be graphic (a bar), verbal, or a ratio. To determine how many miles point **A** is from point **B**, place a piece of paper on the map above and mark the distance between **A** and **B**. Then compare the marks on the paper with the bar scale on the map.

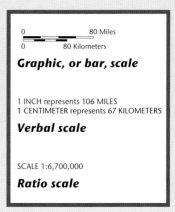

Graphic, or bar, scale

1 INCH represents 106 MILES
1 CENTIMETER represents 67 KILOMETERS

Verbal scale

SCALE 1:6,700,000

Ratio scale

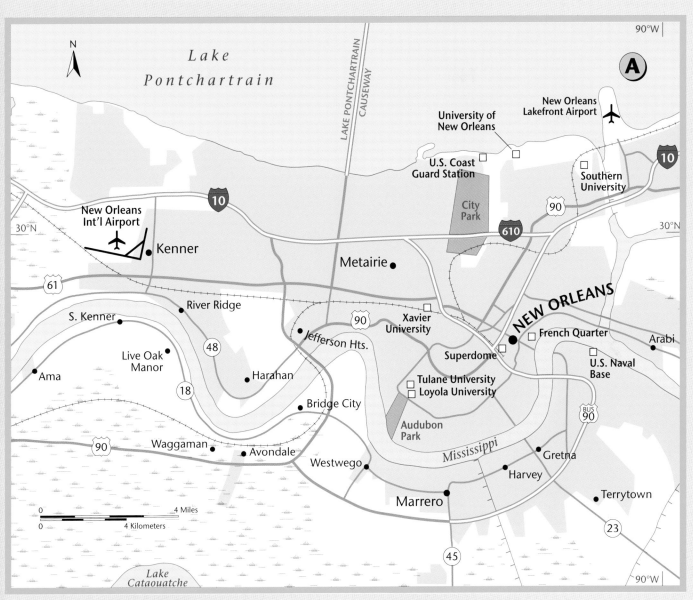

SYMBOLS. Finally, cartographers use a variety of symbols, which are identified in a map key or legend, to tell us more about the places represented on the map. There are three general types of symbols:

● ● **POINT SYMBOLS** show the exact location of places (such as cities) or their size (a large dot can mean a more populous city).

⊢⊢⊢⊢ **LINE SYMBOLS** show boundaries or connections (such as roads, canals, and other trade links).

▢ **AREA SYMBOLS** show the form and extent of a feature (such as a lake, park, or swamp).

Additional information may be coded in color, size, and shape.

PUTTING IT ALL TOGETHER. We already know from the map on page 8 which states A and B are located in. But to find out more about city A, we need a larger-scale map—one that shows a smaller area in more detail (see above). The key below explains the symbols used on the map.

MAP KEY

▢	Metropolitan area	──	Road
▢	Lake or river	⊢⊢⊢⊢	Railroad
▢	Park	⊲	Runway
▢	Swamp	✈	Airport
⊢⊢⊢	Canal	▢	Point of interest
══	Highway	●●●	Town

Types of Maps

This atlas includes many different types of maps so that a wide variety of information about Earth can be presented. Three of the most commonly used types of maps are physical, political, and thematic.

A **physical map** identifies natural features, such as mountains, deserts, oceans, and lakes. Area symbols of various colors and shadings may indicate height above sea level or, as in the example here, ecosystems. Similar symbols could also show water depth.

A **political map** shows how people have divided the world into countries. Political maps can also show states, counties, or cities within a country. Line symbols indicate boundaries, and point symbols show the locations and sometimes sizes of cities.

Thematic maps use a variety of symbols to show distributions and patterns on Earth. For example, a choropleth map uses shades of color to represent different values. The example here shows the main economic activity as a percentage of gross domestic product. Thematic maps can show many different things, such as patterns of vegetation, land use, and religions.

A **cartogram** is a special kind of thematic map in which the size of a country is based on some statistic other than land area. In the cartogram at far right, population size determines the size of each country. This is why Nigeria—the most populous country in Africa—appears much larger than Algeria, which has more than double the land area of Nigeria (see the political map). Cartograms allow for a quick visual comparison of countries in terms of a selected statistic.

PHYSICAL MAP

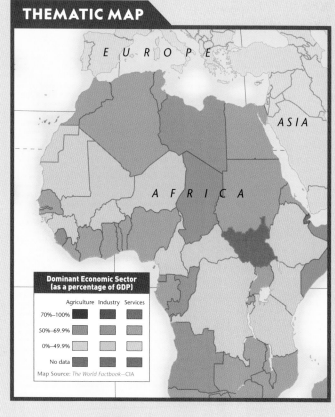

THEMATIC MAP

Dominant Economic Sector
(as a percentage of GDP)

Agriculture Industry Services

70%–100%

50%–69.9%

0%–49.9%

No data

Map Source: *The World Factbook*—CIA

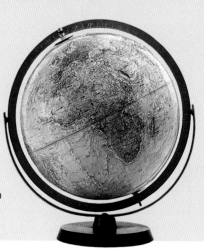

THIS GLOBE is useful for showing Africa's position and size relative to other landmasses, but very little detail is possible at this scale. By using different kinds of maps, mapmakers can show a variety of information in more detail.

POLITICAL MAP

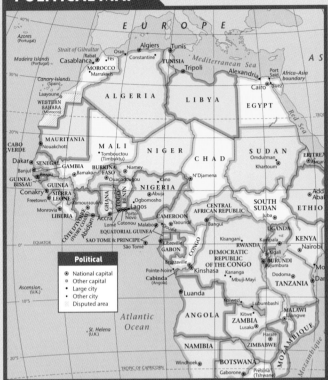

Political
- ⊛ National capital
- ⊙ Other capital
- • Large city
- • Other city
- ▦ Disputed area

CARTOGRAM

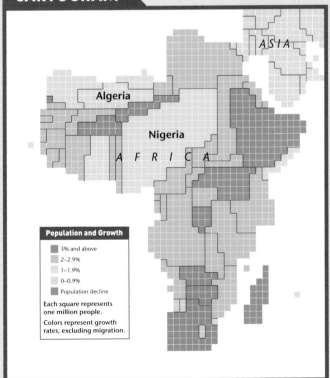

Population and Growth
- ▦ 3% and above
- ▦ 2–2.9%
- ▦ 1–1.9%
- ▦ 0–0.9%
- ▦ Population decline

Each square represents
one million people.

Colors represent growth
rates, excluding migration.

SATELLITE IMAGE MAPS

Satellites orbiting Earth transmit images of the surface to computers on the ground. These computers translate the information into special maps (below) that use colors to show various characteristics. Such maps are valuable tools for identifying patterns or comparing changes over time.

⬡ CLOUD COVERAGE

⬡ TOPOGRAPHY/BATHYMETRY

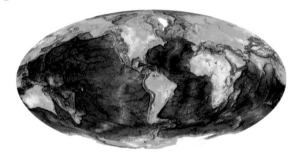

⬡ SEA LEVEL VARIABILITY

⬡ SEA SURFACE TEMPERATURE

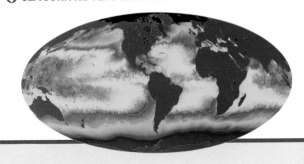

Time Zones

The *Fiji Times*, a newspaper published in Suva, capital of the Fiji Islands, carries the message "The First Newspaper Published in the World Every Day" on the front page of each edition. How can this newspaper from a small island country make such a claim? Fiji lies just west of the date line, an invisible boundary designated to mark the beginning of each new day. The date line is part of the system we have adopted to keep track of the passage of days.

For most of human history, people determined time by observing the position of the sun in the sky. Slight differences in time did not matter until, in the mid-19th century, the spread of railroads and telegraph lines changed forever the importance of time. High-speed transportation and communications required schedules, and schedules required that everyone agree on the time.

In 1884, an international conference, convened in Washington, D.C., established an international system of 24 time zones based on the fact that Earth turns from west to east 15 degrees of longitude every hour. Each time zone has a central meridian and is 15 degrees wide, 7½ degrees to either side of the named central meridian.

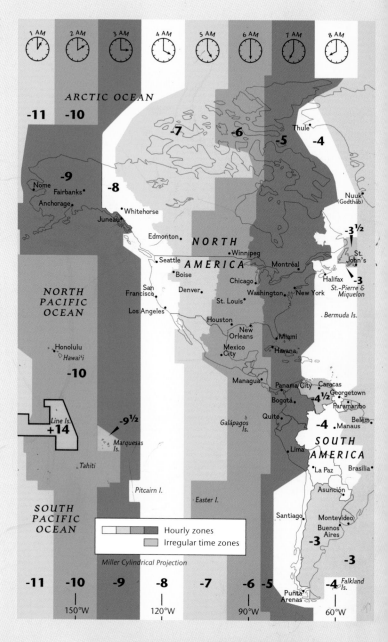

Hourly zones
Irregular time zones

Miller Cylindrical Projection

◑ WORLD TIME CLOCK, on Alexanderplatz in Berlin, Germany, features a large cylinder that is marked with the world's 24 time zones, as well as major cities found in each zone. The cylinder rises almost 33 feet (10 m) above the square and weighs 16 tons (14.5 t).

◒ A SYSTEM OF STANDARD TIME put trains on schedules, which helped reduce the chance of collisions and the loss of lives and property caused by them.

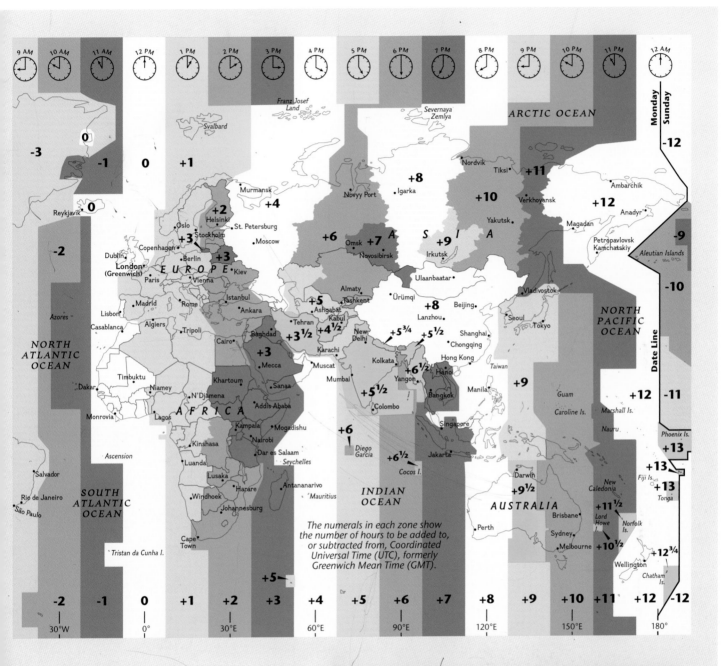

9 AM 10 AM 11 AM 12 PM 1 PM 2 PM 3 PM 4 PM 5 PM 6 PM 7 PM 8 PM 9 PM 10 PM 11 PM 12 AM

Monday
Sunday

Franz Josef Land
Svalbard
ARCTIC OCEAN

-3
0
-1
0
+1

Reykjavik
0
-2

Murmansk
+4
+2
Helsinki
St. Petersburg
Oslo
Stockholm
+3
Moscow
Copenhagen
Berlin
+3
Dublin
London (Greenwich)
EUROPE
Kiev
Paris
Vienna

+6
Omsk
+7
A S I A
Novosibirsk

+8
Igarka
Novyy Port

Nordvik Tiksi
+11
Verkhoyansk
+10
Yakutsk
Magadan
+12
Anadyr'
-9
Petropavlovsk Kamchatskiy
Aleutian Islands

Severnaya Zemlya

+9
Irkutsk

Ulaanbaatar
Madrid
Rome
Istanbul
Ankara
Lisbon
Azores
Casablanca
Algiers
Tripoli

Almaty
Tashkent
+5
Ashgabat
Kabul
+4½
New Delhi
Tehran
+3½
Baghdad
Cairo
+3
Mecca
Khartoum
Sanaa
Timbuktu
Dakar
Niamey
N'Djamena
Lagos
Monrovia
AFRICA
Addis Ababa
Kampala
Nairobi
Mogadishu
Kinshasa
Dar es Salaam
Luanda

Karachi
Mumbai
Kolkata
+5¾
+5½
+6½
Yangon

Ürümqi
+8
Lanzhou
Beijing
Chongqing
Shanghai
Hong Kong
Taiwan
Hanoi
Bangkok
Manila

Vladivostok
Seoul
Tokyo

NORTH PACIFIC OCEAN

Date Line

-10

-11
+12

+9

Guam
Caroline Is.
Marshall Is.
Nauru

Phoenix Is.
+13
+13
+13
Fiji Is.
Tonga

NORTH ATLANTIC OCEAN

+5½
Colombo
+6
Diego Garcia
+6½
Cocos I.

Singapore
Jakarta

INDIAN OCEAN

Darwin
New Caledonia
+9½
AUSTRALIA
Perth
Brisbane
+11½
Lord Howe Is.
Sydney
Melbourne
+10½
Norfolk Is.

Ascension
Luanda
Lusaka
Harare
Antananarivo
Mauritius
Seychelles
Windhoek
Johannesburg
Salvador
Rio de Janeiro
São Paulo
SOUTH ATLANTIC OCEAN
Cape Town
Tristan da Cunha I.

+5

The numerals in each zone show the number of hours to be added to, or subtracted from, Coordinated Universal Time (UTC), formerly Greenwich Mean Time (GMT).

Wellington
+12¾
Chatham Is.

-2 -1 0 +1 +2 +3 +4 +5 +6 +7 +8 +9 +10 +11 +12 -12
30°W 0° 30°E 60°E 90°E 120°E 150°E 180°

THE DATE LINE (180°) is directly opposite the prime meridian (0°). As Earth rotates, each new day officially begins as the 180° line passes midnight. If you travel west across the date line, you advance one day; if you travel east across the date line, you fall back one day. Notice on the map how the line zigs to the east as it passes through the South Pacific so that the islands of Fiji will not be split between two different days. Also notice that India is 5½ hours ahead of Coordinated Universal Time (UTC) (formerly Greenwich Mean Time, or GMT), and China has only one time zone, even though the country spans more than 60 degrees of longitude. These differences are the result of decisions made at the country level.

The Physical World

Realms of land and water make up the physical world. More than two-thirds of Earth's surface is covered by water: oceans, lakes, and rivers. The rest is land: continents and islands. Every continent is permanently inhabited except Antarctica, which lies frozen beneath a vast ice sheet at Earth's South Pole. Each continent is unique, but all show evidence of dynamic forces at work. Some forces build up mountains such as the Rockies, the Andes, and the Himalaya; other forces wear down Earth's surface, creating vast sedimentary plains and lowlands. Powerful rivers such as the Mississippi, the Congo, and the Yangtze (Chang) cut through the land and empty billions of gallons of freshwater into the oceans and seas each day.

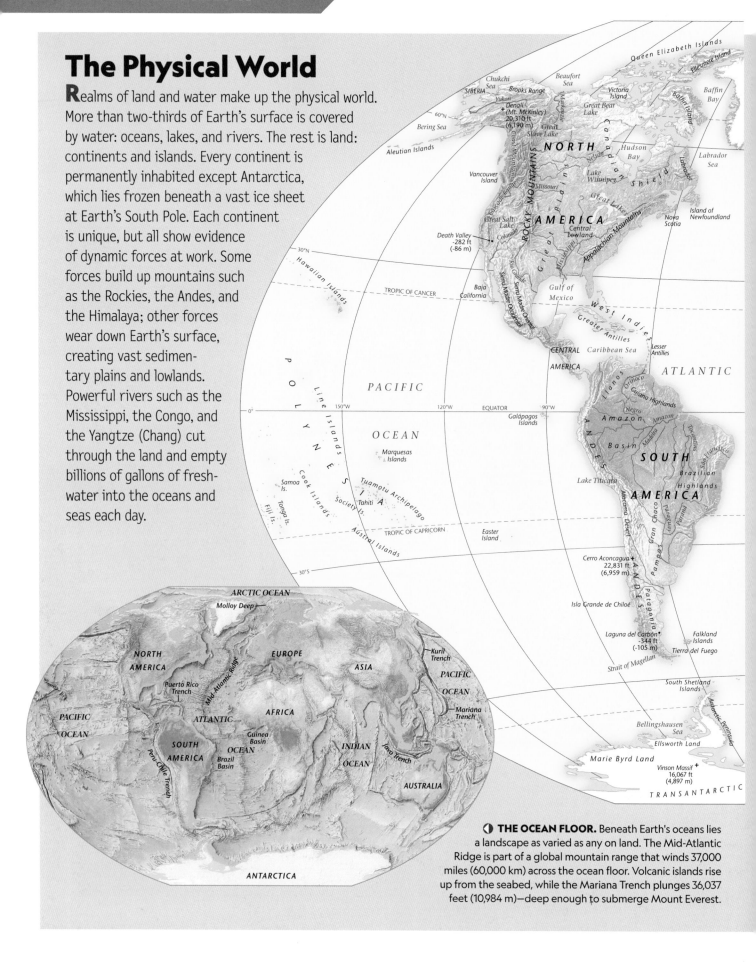

◖ THE OCEAN FLOOR. Beneath Earth's oceans lies a landscape as varied as any on land. The Mid-Atlantic Ridge is part of a global mountain range that winds 37,000 miles (60,000 km) across the ocean floor. Volcanic islands rise up from the seabed, while the Mariana Trench plunges 36,037 feet (10,984 m)—deep enough to submerge Mount Everest.

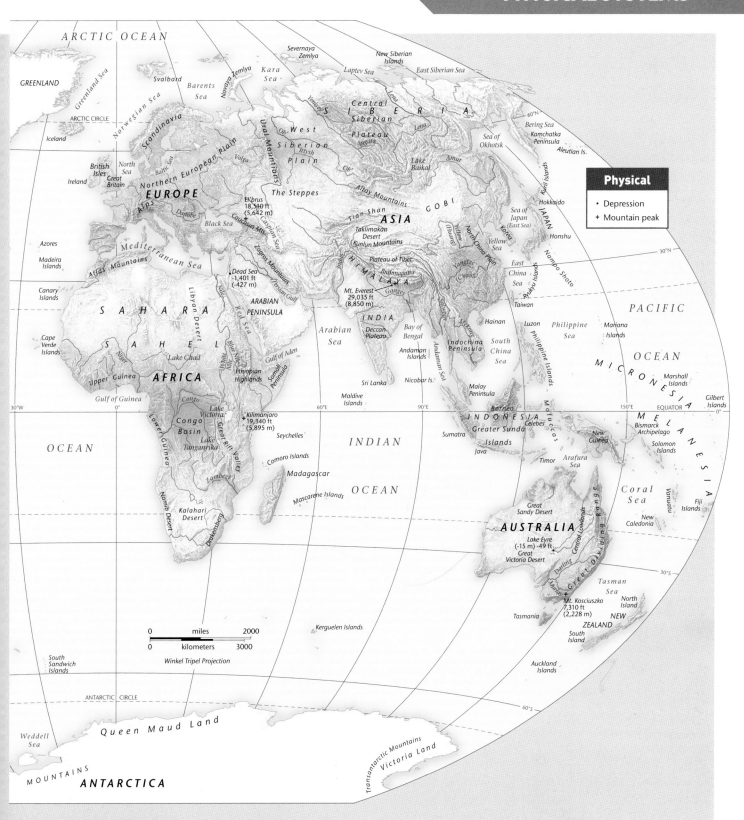

Physical

- • Depression
- + Mountain peak

ARCTIC OCEAN

GREENLAND

Greenland Sea

Svalbard

ARCTIC CIRCLE

Iceland

Norwegian Sea

Scandinavia

Baltic Sea

Barents Sea

Novaya Zemlya

Kara Sea

Severnaya Zemlya

New Siberian Islands

Laptev Sea

East Siberian Sea

CENTRAL SIBERIAN PLATEAU

Ob'

Yenisey

Lena

Angara

Lena

60°N

Bering Sea

Kamchatka Peninsula

Aleutian Is.

Sea of Okhotsk

British Isles

North Sea

Great Britain

Ireland

Northern European Plain

Ural Mountains

West Siberian Plain

Irtysh

Ob'

Lake Baikal

Amur

Kuril Islands

Hokkaido

EUROPE

Alps

Danube

Volga

El'brus 18,510 ft (5,642 m)

The Steppes

Altay Mountains

GOBI

Sea of Japan (East Sea)

Korea

JAPAN

Honshu

Black Sea

Caucasus Mts.

Caspian Sea

Tian Shan

ASIA

North China Plain

Yellow (Huang)

Yellow Sea

30°N

Azores

Mediterranean Sea

Zagros Mountains

Taklimakan Desert

Kunlun Mountains

Plateau of Tibet

Yangtze (Chang)

East China Sea

Ryukyu Islands

Nampo Shoto

Madeira Islands

Atlas Mountains

Dead Sea -1,401 ft (-427 m)

Persian Gulf

HIMALAYA

Brahmaputra

Mt. Everest 29,035 ft (8,850 m)

Ganges

Taiwan

PACIFIC

Canary Islands

SAHARA

Libyan Desert

Nile

Red Sea

ARABIAN PENINSULA

Arabian Sea

INDIA

Deccan Plateau

Mekong

Salween

Hainan

Luzon

Philippine Sea

Mariana Islands

OCEAN

Cape Verde Islands

SAHEL

Blue Nile

Ethiopian Highlands

Somali Peninsula

Gulf of Aden

Bay of Bengal

Andaman Islands

Andaman Sea

Indochina Peninsula

South China Sea

Philippine Islands

MICRONESIA

Upper Guinea

White Nile

Niger

Lake Chad

AFRICA

Sri Lanka

Nicobar Is.

Malay Peninsula

Marshall Islands

Gilbert Islands

Gulf of Guinea

0°

Lake Victoria

Kilimanjaro 19,340 ft (5,895 m)

Maldive Islands

60°E

90°E

150°E

EQUATOR

0°

30°W

Congo

Seychelles

INDONESIA

Greater Sunda Islands

Borneo

Celebes

Moluccas

New Guinea

Bismarck Archipelago

MELANESIA

OCEAN

Congo Basin

Lower Guinea

Great Rift Valley

Lake Tanganyika

INDIAN

Sumatra

Java

Timor

Arafura Sea

Solomon Islands

Zambezi

Comoro Islands

Madagascar

OCEAN

Coral Sea

Vanuatu

Fiji Islands

Namib Desert

Kalahari Desert

Drakensberg

Mascarene Islands

Great Sandy Desert

AUSTRALIA

Central Lowlands

Great Dividing Range

New Caledonia

30°S

South Sandwich Islands

Lake Eyre (-15 m) -49 ft

Great Victoria Desert

Darling

Murray

Tasman Sea

North Island

0 miles 2000

0 kilometers 3000

Kerguelen Islands

Mt. Kosciuszko 7,310 ft (2,228 m)

NEW ZEALAND

Winkel Tripel Projection

Tasmania

South Island

Auckland Islands

ANTARCTIC CIRCLE

60°S

Weddell Sea

Queen Maud Land

Transantarctic Mountains

Victoria Land

MOUNTAINS

ANTARCTICA

⬭ **THE PHYSICAL WORLD.** Great landmasses called continents break Earth's global ocean into four smaller ones. Each continent is unique in terms of the landforms and rivers that etch its surface and the ecosystems that lend colors to it, ranging from the deep greens of the tropical forests of northern South America and southeastern Asia to the browns and yellows of the arid lands of Africa and Australia. Most of Antarctica's features are hidden beneath its ice sheet.

Earth's Geologic History

Earth is a dynamic planet. Its outer shell, or crust, is broken into huge pieces called plates. These plates ride on the slowly moving molten rock, or magma, that lies beneath the crust. Their movement constantly changes Earth's surface. Along one convergent boundary—a place where two plates meet—the Indian Plate moves northward, colliding with the Eurasian Plate and heaving up the still growing Himalaya. Along another convergent boundary, the Nasca Plate dives beneath the South American Plate—a process called subduction that can trigger volcanoes, underwater earthquakes, and giant ocean waves called tsunamis. Along transform faults, such as California's San Andreas Fault, plates grind past each other, resulting in destructive earthquakes. Along divergent boundaries, plates are pushed apart, as in the Mid-Atlantic Ridge, where the ocean floor is spreading apart, allowing molten rock to rise, and Africa's Great Rift Valley, where the continental plate is separating.

🌐 **OUR CHANGING PLANET.** The Latin phrase *terra firma* implies planet Earth is solid and unchanging. However, Earth's surface has been anything but unchanging. Geologic evidence suggests that moving plates have collided and moved apart more than once over the course of the planet's long history. As the main map shows, the forces of change show no signs of stopping.

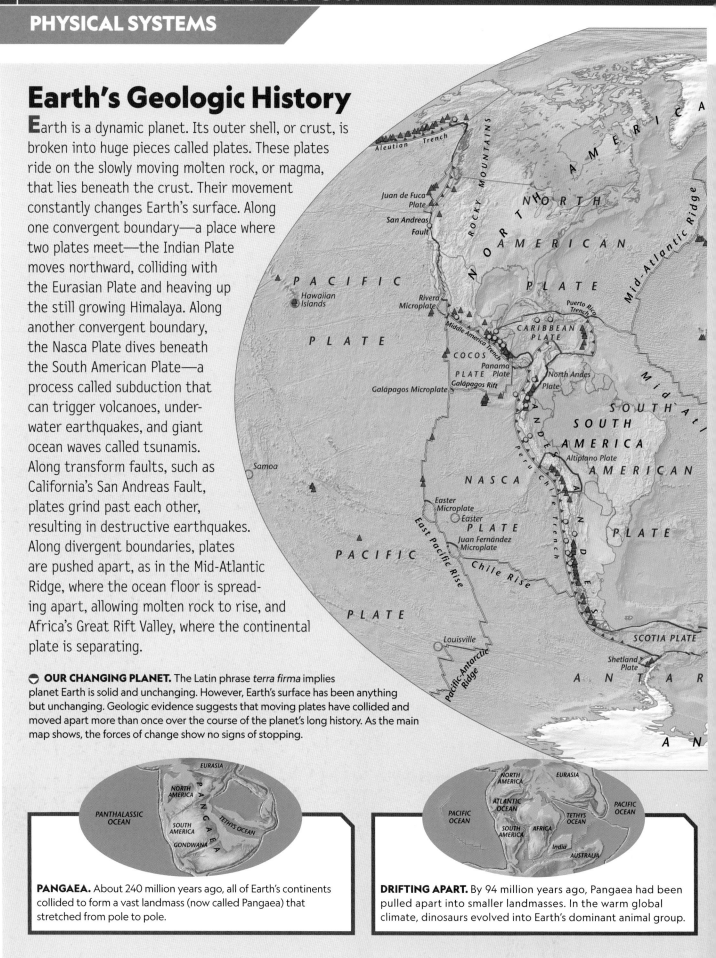

PANGAEA. About 240 million years ago, all of Earth's continents collided to form a vast landmass (now called Pangaea) that stretched from pole to pole.

DRIFTING APART. By 94 million years ago, Pangaea had been pulled apart into smaller landmasses. In the warm global climate, dinosaurs evolved into Earth's dominant animal group.

Gakkel Ridge

NORTH AMERICAN PLATE

Location Uncertain

Iceland

A S I A

EUROPE

E U R A S I A N   P L A T E

OKHOTSK PLATE

AMUR PLATE

Kuril Trench

ALPS

Anatolian Plate

Aegean Sea Plate

Plateau of Tibet

H I M A L A Y A

YANGTZE PLATE

Okinawa Plate

Mariana Trench

ARABIAN PLATE

A F R I C A

INDIAN PLATE

PHILIPPINE PLATE

Philippine Trench

NUBIA PLATE

Burma Plate

SUNDA PLATE

CAROLINE PLATE

PACIFIC PLATE

Great Rift Valley

AFRICAN PLATE

SOMALI PLATE

PLATE

Mid-Indian Ridge

Molucca Sea Plate

Banda Sea Plate

Java Trench

North Bismark Plate

South Bismark Plate

Solomon Sea Plate

Birds Head Plate

Timor Plate

Belmoral Reef Plate

Woodlark Plate

Samoa

Réunion

CAPRICORN PLATE

Location Uncertain

New Hebrides Plate

antic Ridge

Tristan da Cunha

Southwest Indian Ridge

A U S T R A L I A N

AUSTRALIA

PLATE

Conway Reef Plate

Kermedic Plate

Tonga Plate

South Sandwich Plate

Southeast Indian Ridge

PACIFIC PLATE

C T I C   P L A T E

	miles	
0		2000
0	kilometers	3000

Winkel Tripel Projection

T A R C T I C A

Plate Tectonics

— Convergent boundary

▲▲▲ Subduction zone (triangles indicate direction of subduction)

— Divergent boundary

— Oceanic spreading boundary

— Transform fault

- - - Diffuse plate boundary (may be more than 100 mi [161 km] across)

◉ Earthquake with more than 1,000 deaths or greater than magnitude 8.5, 1900–2016

▲ Volcanic eruption, 1900–2016

○ Selected hot spot

Map Sources: USGS; Smithsonian Institution

◖ **TECTONIC BOUNDARIES** mark areas of geologic change in ocean floors, along continental margins, and even through continents, as in East Africa's Great Rift Valley. Clusters of volcanoes and frequent earthquakes signal areas of instability.

MASS EXTINCTION. By 65 million years ago, continents were moving toward their current positions. Dinosaurs died out, likely due to the impact (∗) of an asteroid in the Gulf of Mexico.

DEEP FREEZE. By 18,000 years ago, the continents resembled their current shapes. A great ice age had the far northern and southern regions locked under huge ice sheets.

Earth's Land & Water Features

The largest land and water features on Earth are the continents and the oceans, but many other features—large and small—make each place unique. Mountains, plateaus, and plains give texture to the land. The Rockies and the Andes rise high above the lowlands of North and South America. In Asia, the Himalaya and the Plateau of Tibet form the rugged core of Earth's largest continent. These features are the result of powerful forces within Earth pushing up the land. Other landforms, such as canyons and valleys, are created when weathering and erosion wear down parts of Earth's surface.

Dramatic features are not limited to Earth's continents. Deep beneath the surface of Earth's oceans, submarine mountains appear like pale blue threads in the dark blue water on the satellite map at right. These mountain chains rise from the seafloor and trace zones of underwater geologic activity where plates converge. Deep trenches form in subduction zones where one plate dives beneath another.

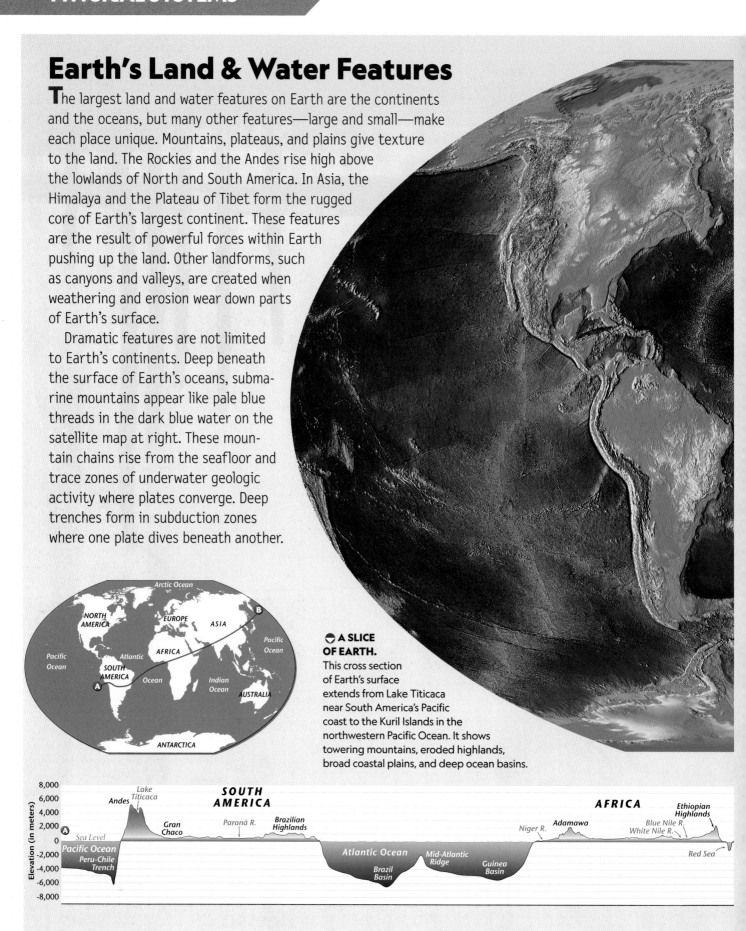

⬤ A SLICE OF EARTH.

This cross section of Earth's surface extends from Lake Titicaca near South America's Pacific coast to the Kuril Islands in the northwestern Pacific Ocean. It shows towering mountains, eroded highlands, broad coastal plains, and deep ocean basins.

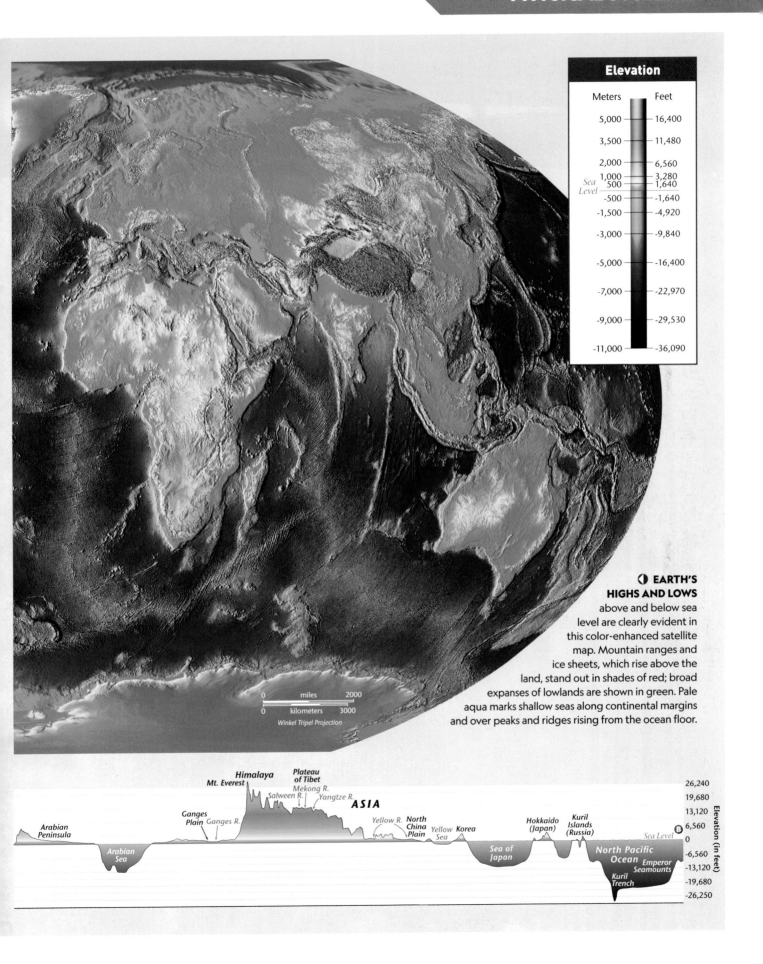

Elevation

Meters		Feet
5,000		16,400
3,500		11,480
2,000		6,560
1,000		3,280
500		1,640
Sea Level		
-500		-1,640
-1,500		-4,920
-3,000		-9,840
-5,000		-16,400
-7,000		-22,970
-9,000		-29,530
-11,000		-36,090

0   miles   2000
0   kilometers   3000
Winkel Tripel Projection

◖ EARTH'S HIGHS AND LOWS above and below sea level are clearly evident in this color-enhanced satellite map. Mountain ranges and ice sheets, which rise above the land, stand out in shades of red; broad expanses of lowlands are shown in green. Pale aqua marks shallow seas along continental margins and over peaks and ridges rising from the ocean floor.

Himalaya
Mt. Everest
Plateau of Tibet
Mekong R.
Salween R.
Yangtze R.
Ganges Plain
Ganges R.
ASIA
Yellow R.
North China Plain
Yellow Sea
Korea
Hokkaido (Japan)
Kuril Islands (Russia)
Arabian Peninsula
Arabian Sea
Sea of Japan
North Pacific Ocean
Emperor Seamounts
Kuril Trench
Sea Level

Elevation (in feet)
26,240
19,680
13,120
6,560
0
-6,560
-13,120
-19,680
-26,250

Earth's Climates

Climate is not the same as weather. Climate is the long-term average of conditions in the atmosphere at a particular location on Earth's surface. Weather refers to the momentary conditions of the atmosphere. Climate is important because it influences vegetation and soil development. It also influences people's choices about how and where to live.

There are many different systems for classifying climates. One commonly used system was developed by Russian-born climatologist Wladimir Köppen and later modified by American climatologist Glenn Trewartha. Köppen's system identifies five major climate zones based on average precipitation and temperature, and a sixth zone for highland, or high elevation, areas. Except for continental climate, all climate zones occur in mirror image north and south of the Equator.

CLIMATE GRAPHS. A climate graph is a combination bar and line graph that shows monthly averages of precipitation and temperature for a particular place. The bar graph shows precipitation in inches and centimeters; the line graph shows temperature in degrees Fahrenheit and Celsius. The graphs below (keyed to map colors) are typical for places in the climate zone represented by their background color. The seeming inversion of the temperature lines for Alice Springs, in Australia, and McMurdo, in Antarctica, reflects the reversal of seasons south of the Equator, where January is midsummer. The abbreviations for months are across the bottom of each graph.

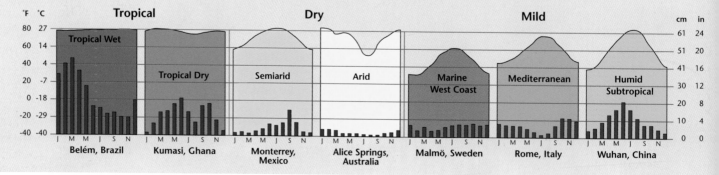

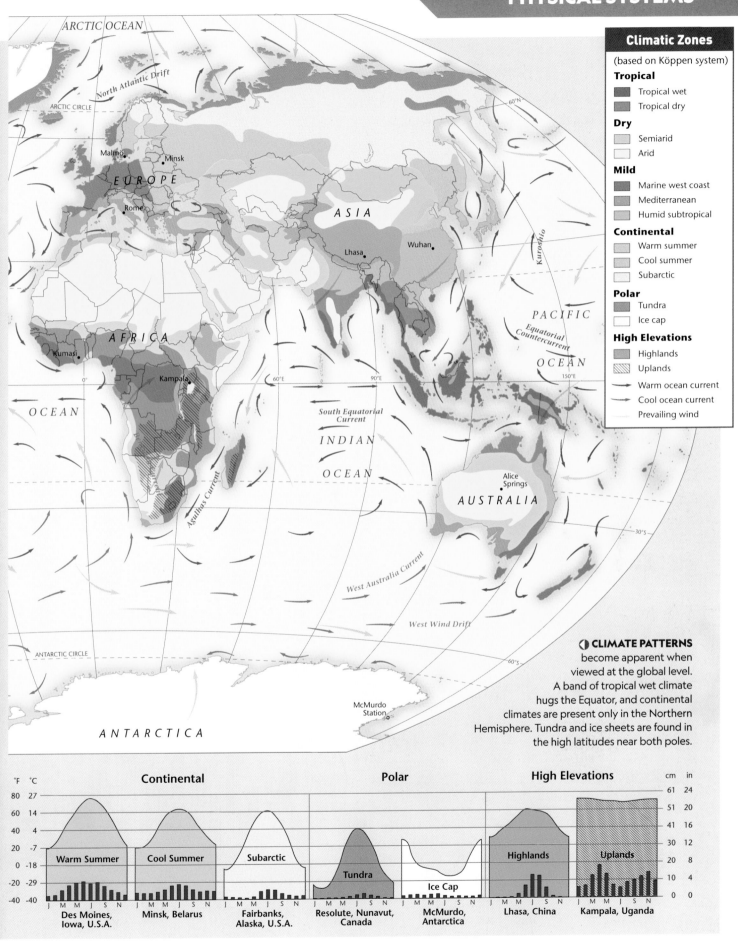

ARCTIC OCEAN

North Atlantic Drift

ARCTIC CIRCLE

60°N

Malmö
Minsk

EUROPE

Rome

ASIA

Lhasa
Wuhan

Kuroshio

AFRICA

Kumasi

Kampala

0°

60°E

90°E

150°E

PACIFIC

Equatorial
Countercurrent

OCEAN

OCEAN

South Equatorial
Current

INDIAN

OCEAN

Agulhas Current

AUSTRALIA

Alice
Springs

30°S

West Australia Current

West Wind Drift

60°S

ANTARCTIC CIRCLE

McMurdo
Station

ANTARCTICA

Climatic Zones
(based on Köppen system)

Tropical
- Tropical wet
- Tropical dry

Dry
- Semiarid
- Arid

Mild
- Marine west coast
- Mediterranean
- Humid subtropical

Continental
- Warm summer
- Cool summer
- Subarctic

Polar
- Tundra
- Ice cap

High Elevations
- Highlands
- Uplands
- → Warm ocean current
- → Cool ocean current
- Prevailing wind

CLIMATE PATTERNS become apparent when viewed at the global level. A band of tropical wet climate hugs the Equator, and continental climates are present only in the Northern Hemisphere. Tundra and ice sheets are found in the high latitudes near both poles.

Continental	Polar	High Elevations

°F °C
80 27
60 14
40 4
20 -7
0 -18
-20 -29
-40 -40

cm in
61 24
51 20
41 16
30 12
20 8
10 4
0 0

Warm Summer

Cool Summer

Subarctic

Tundra

Ice Cap

Highlands

Uplands

J M M J S N J M M J S N J M M J S N   J M M J S N J M M J S N   J M M J S N J M M J S N

Des Moines,
Iowa, U.S.A.

Minsk, Belarus

Fairbanks,
Alaska, U.S.A.

Resolute, Nunavut,
Canada

McMurdo,
Antarctica

Lhasa, China

Kampala, Uganda

Climate Controls

The patterns of climate vary widely. Some climates, such as those near the Equator and the poles, are nearly constant year-round. Others experience great seasonal variations, such as the wet and dry patterns of the tropical dry zone and the monthly average temperature extremes of the subarctic.

Climate patterns are not random. They are the result of complex interactions of basic climate controls: latitude, elevation, prevailing winds, ocean currents, landforms, and location.

These controls combine in various ways to create the bands of climate that can be seen on the world climate map on pages 20–21 and on the climate maps in the individual continent sections of this atlas. At the local level, however, special conditions may create microclimates that differ from those that are more typical of a region.

ELEVATION

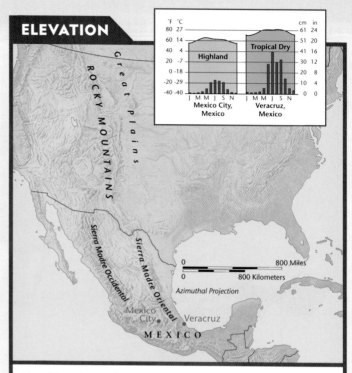

Not all locations at the same latitude experience similar climates. Air at higher elevations is cooler and holds less moisture than air at lower elevations. This explains why the climate at Veracruz, Mexico, which is near sea level, is warm and wet, and the climate at Mexico City, which is more than 7,000 feet (2,100 m) above sea level, is cooler and drier.

LATITUDE

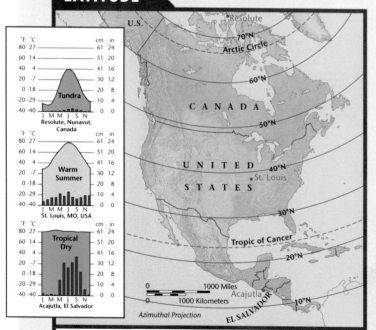

Latitude affects the amount of solar energy received. As latitude (distance north or south of the Equator) increases, the angle of the sun's energy becomes increasingly oblique, or slanted. Less energy is received from the sun, and annual average temperatures fall. Therefore, the annual average temperature decreases as latitude increases from Acajutla, El Salvador, to St. Louis, Missouri, U.S.A., to Resolute, Canada.

LANDFORMS

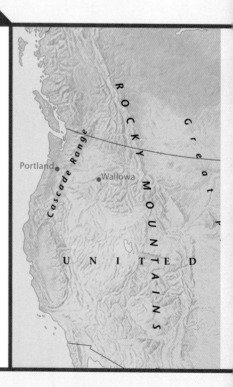

When air carried by prevailing winds blows across a large body of water, such as the ocean, it picks up moisture. If that air encounters a mountain when it reaches land, it is forced to rise and the air becomes cooler, causing precipitation on the windward side of the mountain (see Portland graph). When air descends on the side away from the wind—the leeward side—the air warms and absorbs available moisture. This creates a dry condition known as rain shadow (see Wallowa graph).

PREVAILING WINDS AND OCEAN CURRENTS

Earth's rotation, combined with heat energy from the sun, creates patterns of movement in Earth's atmosphere called prevailing winds. In the oceans, similar movements of water are called currents. Prevailing winds and ocean currents bring warm and cold temperatures to land areas. They also bring moisture or take it away. The Gulf Stream and the North Atlantic Drift, for example, are warm-water currents that influence average temperatures in eastern North America and northern Europe. Prevailing winds—trade winds, polar easterlies, and westerlies—also affect temperature and precipitation averages.

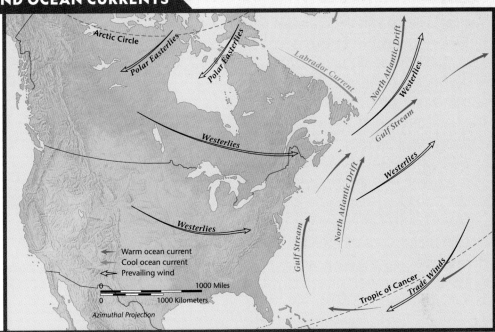

LOCATION

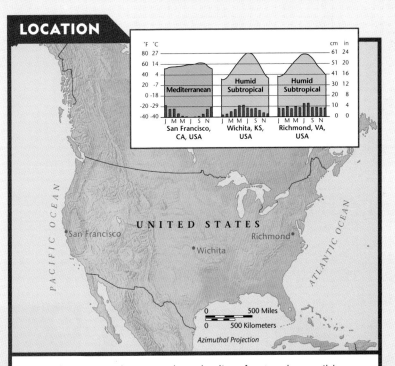

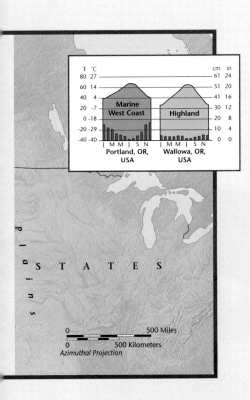

Marine locations—places near large bodies of water—have mild climates with little temperature variation because water gains and loses heat slowly (see San Francisco graph). Interior locations—places far from large water bodies—have much more extreme climates. There are great temperature variations because land gains and loses heat rapidly (see Wichita graph). Richmond, which is relatively near the Atlantic Ocean but which is also influenced by prevailing westerly winds blowing across the land, has the moderate characteristics of both conditions.

Earth's Natural Vegetation

Natural vegetation is plant life that would be found in an area if it were undisturbed by human activity. Natural vegetation varies widely depending on climate and soil conditions. In rain forests, trees tower as much as 200 feet (60 m) above the forest floor. In the humid mid-latitudes, deciduous trees shed their leaves during the cold season, while coniferous trees remain green throughout the year. Areas receiving too little rainfall to support trees have grasses. Dry areas have plants such as cacti that tolerate long periods without water. In the tundra, dwarf species of shrubs and flowers are adaptations to harsh conditions at high latitudes and high elevations.

Vegetation is important to human life. It provides oxygen, food, fuel, products with economic value, even lifesaving medicines. Human activities, however, have greatly affected natural vegetation (see pages 28–29). Huge forests have been cut to provide fuel and lumber. Grasslands have yielded to the plow as people extend agricultural lands.

TYPES OF VEGETATION. Vegetation creates a mosaic of colors and textures across Earth's surface. Grasslands dominate in places where there is too little precipitation to support trees. In the wet conditions of the tropics, rain forests and mangroves flourish. Desert shrubs are adapted to dry climates, and tundra plants survive a short growing season. These photographs show some of the plants found in various vegetation regions. Each is keyed to the map by color and number.

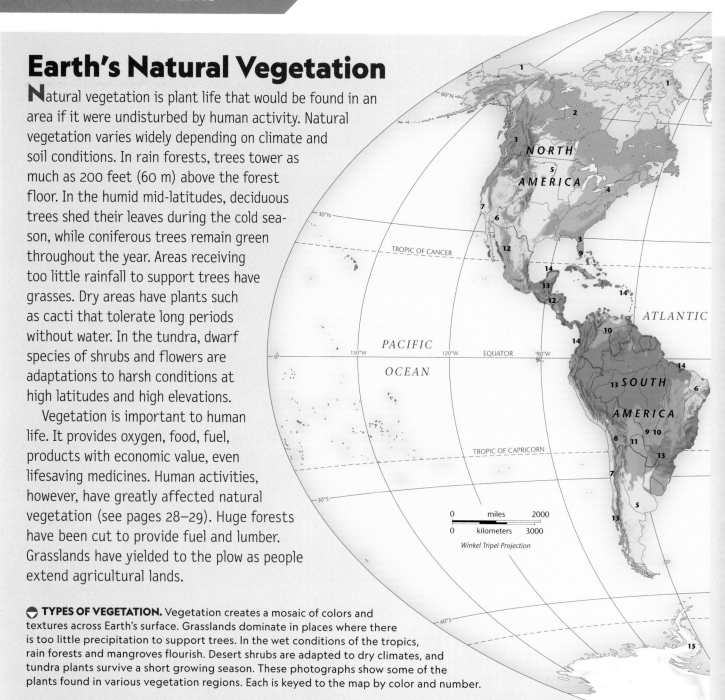

Winkel Tripel Projection

TUNDRA

NORTHERN CONIFEROUS FOREST

TEMPERATE BROADLEAF FOREST

TEMPERATE GRASSLAND

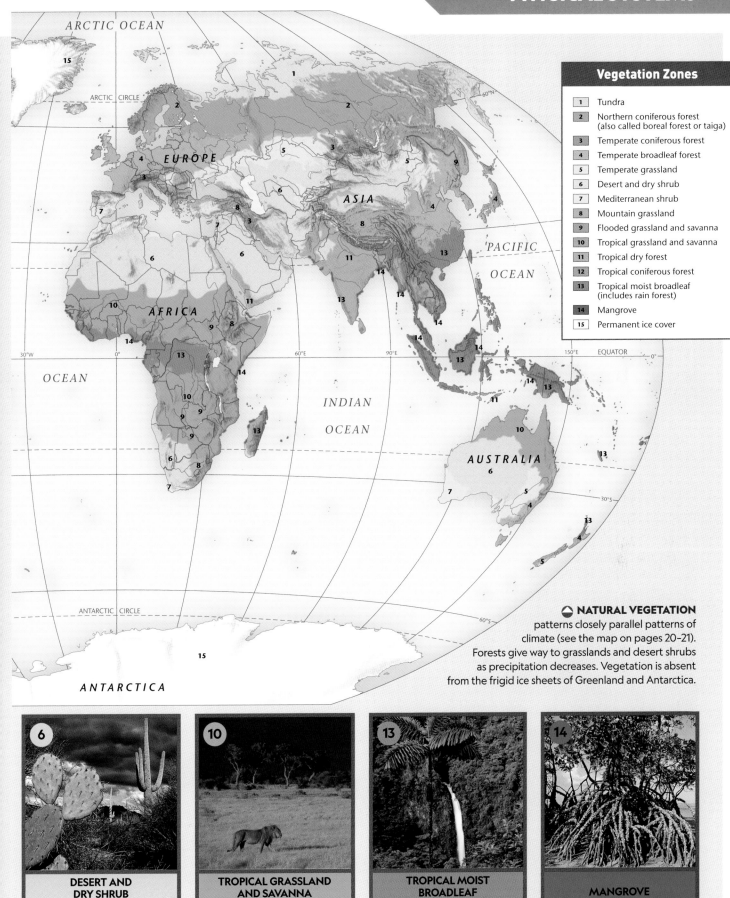

ARCTIC OCEAN

ARCTIC CIRCLE

EUROPE

ASIA

PACIFIC OCEAN

AFRICA

OCEAN

INDIAN OCEAN

EQUATOR

AUSTRALIA

ANTARCTIC CIRCLE

ANTARCTICA

Vegetation Zones

1	Tundra
2	Northern coniferous forest (also called boreal forest or taiga)
3	Temperate coniferous forest
4	Temperate broadleaf forest
5	Temperate grassland
6	Desert and dry shrub
7	Mediterranean shrub
8	Mountain grassland
9	Flooded grassland and savanna
10	Tropical grassland and savanna
11	Tropical dry forest
12	Tropical coniferous forest
13	Tropical moist broadleaf (includes rain forest)
14	Mangrove
15	Permanent ice cover

NATURAL VEGETATION patterns closely parallel patterns of climate (see the map on pages 20–21). Forests give way to grasslands and desert shrubs as precipitation decreases. Vegetation is absent from the frigid ice sheets of Greenland and Antarctica.

6 DESERT AND DRY SHRUB

10 TROPICAL GRASSLAND AND SAVANNA

13 TROPICAL MOIST BROADLEAF

14 MANGROVE

Earth's Water

Water is essential for life and is one of Earth's most valuable natural resources. It is even more important than food. More than 70 percent of Earth's surface is covered with water in the form of oceans, lakes, rivers, and streams, but most of this water—about 97 percent—is salty and without treatment is unusable for drinking or growing crops. The remaining 3 percent is fresh, but most of this is either trapped in glaciers or ice sheets or lies too deep underground to be tapped economically.

Water is a renewable resource that can be used over and over because the hydrologic, or water, cycle purifies water as it moves through the processes of evaporation, condensation, precipitation, runoff, and infiltration. However, careless use can diminish the supply of usable freshwater when pollution results from industrial dumping, runoff of fertilizers or pesticides from cultivated fields, or discharge of urban sewage. Like other natural resources, water is unevenly distributed on Earth. Some regions, such as the eastern United States, have sufficient water to meet the needs of the people living there. But in other regions, such as large areas of Asia, the demand for water places great stress on available supply (see the map).

Water Stress

Annual Water Withdrawls as a Percentage of Available Supply

- Less than 10%
- 10–19.9%
- 20–39.9%
- 40–80%
- Greater than 80%
- Arid with low demand
- No data

Map Source: WRI

WATER USES

DOMESTIC. In many less developed regions, women, such as these in Central America, haul water for daily use.

AGRICULTURAL. Irrigation has made agriculture possible in dry areas such as the San Pedro Valley in Arizona, U.S.A., shown here.

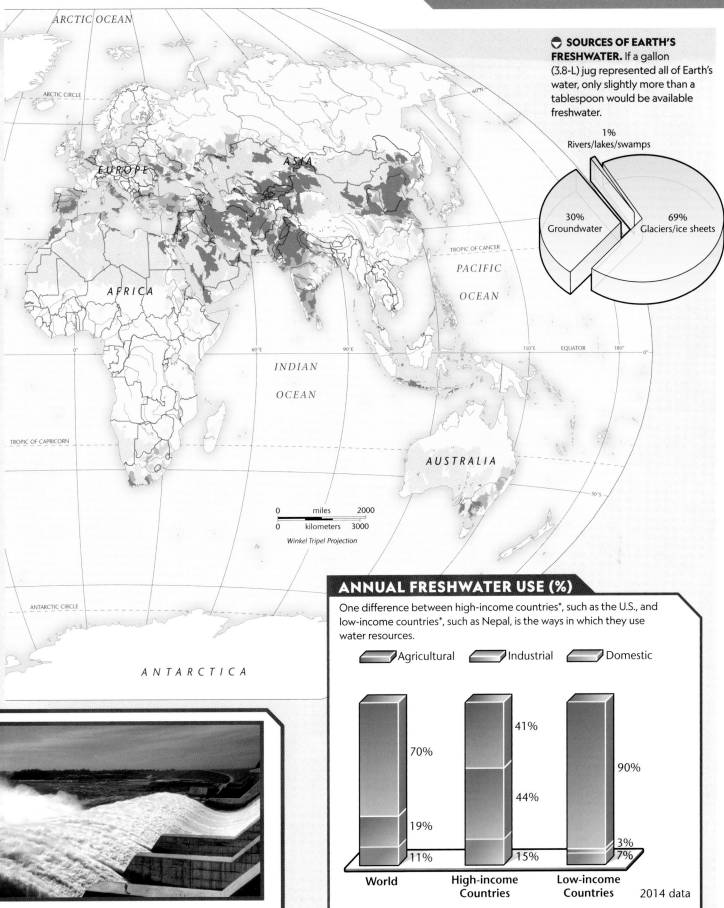

ARCTIC OCEAN

ARCTIC CIRCLE

EUROPE

ASIA

AFRICA

TROPIC OF CANCER

PACIFIC

OCEAN

INDIAN

OCEAN

TROPIC OF CAPRICORN

AUSTRALIA

ANTARCTIC CIRCLE

ANTARCTICA

EQUATOR

0   miles   2000
0   kilometers   3000
Winkel Tripel Projection

SOURCES OF EARTH'S FRESHWATER. If a gallon (3.8-L) jug represented all of Earth's water, only slightly more than a tablespoon would be available freshwater.

1%
Rivers/lakes/swamps

30%
Groundwater

69%
Glaciers/ice sheets

ANNUAL FRESHWATER USE (%)

One difference between high-income countries*, such as the U.S., and low-income countries*, such as Nepal, is the ways in which they use water resources.

Agricultural   Industrial   Domestic

World
70%
19%
11%

High-income Countries
41%
44%
15%

Low-income Countries
90%
3%
7%

2014 data

*According to the World Bank, high-income countries have gross national incomes per capita of more than $12,235 (US$), and low-income countries have GNI/capita incomes of $1,005 (US$) or less.

INDUSTRIAL. Hydroelectric dams, such as this one in Tucuruí, Brazil, generate electricity to power industry.

Environmental Hot Spots

As Earth's human population increases, pressures on the natural environment also increase. In industrialized countries, landfills overflow with the volume of trash produced. Industries generate waste and pollution that foul the air and water. Farmers use chemical fertilizers and pesticides that run off into streams and groundwater. Cars release exhaust fumes that pollute the air, contributing to global climate change.

In less developed countries, forests are cut and not replanted, making the land vulnerable to erosion. Fragile grasslands turn into deserts when farmers and herders move onto marginal land as they try to make a living. And cities struggle with issues such as water safety, sanitation, and basic services that accompany the explosive urban growth that characterizes many less developed countries.

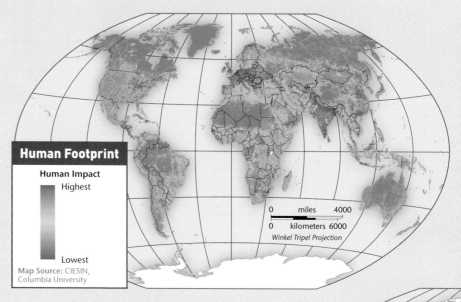

Human Footprint

Human Impact

Highest

Lowest

Map Source: CIESIN, Columbia University

0   miles   4000
0   kilometers 6000
Winkel Tripel Projection

HUMAN ACTIVITY has altered nearly 75 percent of Earth's habitable surface. Referred to as the "human footprint," this disturbance is greatest in areas of high population.

FORESTS play a critical role in Earth's natural systems. They regulate water flow, release oxygen and retain carbon, cycle nutrients, and build soils. But humans have cut, burned, altered, and removed half of all forests that stood 8,000 years ago.

Fragile Forests

Current frontier forest (large, relatively undisturbed forest)

Current non-frontier forest (degraded, regrown, replanted, plantation, or other forest areas)

Estimated extent of frontier forest 8,000 years ago

Map Source: WRI

DESERT SANDS, moved by high winds, cover large areas of Mauritania. The shifting sands threaten to cover an important transportation route (upper right), which must be cleared daily. A grid of branches has been laid over the sand to try to slow the advancing desert, which has been expanding since the mid-1960s.

DEFORESTATION in Haiti (left side of photograph above) clearly defines its border with the Dominican Republic. Haiti was once 30 percent forested, but loss of trees for timber and subsistence agriculture has reduced forest cover to less than 2 percent.

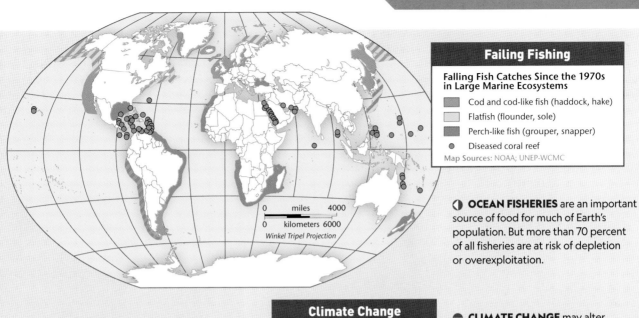

Failing Fishing

Falling Fish Catches Since the 1970s in Large Marine Ecosystems

- Cod and cod-like fish (haddock, hake)
- Flatfish (flounder, sole)
- Perch-like fish (grouper, snapper)
- Diseased coral reef

Map Sources: NOAA; UNEP-WCMC

0 miles 4000
0 kilometers 6000
Winkel Tripel Projection

◑ **OCEAN FISHERIES** are an important source of food for much of Earth's population. But more than 70 percent of all fisheries are at risk of depletion or overexploitation.

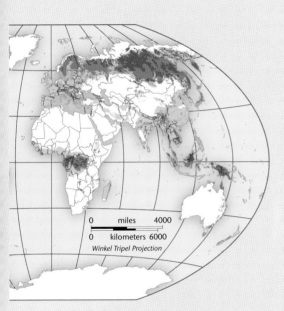

◐ **CLIMATE CHANGE** may alter Earth's ability to support many forms of life. Rising temperatures may lead to loss of habitat, glacial melting, and flooding of coastal population centers.

Climate Change

Habitat Loss Due to Climate Change
(risk over next 100 years)

- Critical
- High
- Low

- City vulnerable to sea-level rise
- △ Melting glaciers

Map Source: WWF

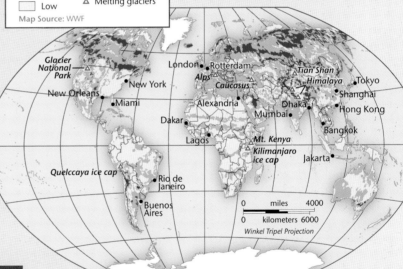

Glacier National Park
London Rotterdam
New York
Alps Caucasus Tian Shan Himalaya Tokyo
New Orleans Shanghai
Miami Alexandria Dhaka Hong Kong
Dakar Mumbai
Lagos Bangkok
Mt. Kenya
Kilimanjaro ice cap Jakarta
Quelccaya ice cap
Rio de Janeiro
Buenos Aires

0 miles 4000
0 kilometers 6000
Winkel Tripel Projection

AN OIL SPILL along the coast of Wales, in the United Kingdom, left this beach and the wildlife living there covered with potentially toxic crude oil.

SMOG hangs over Los Angeles, California, U.S.A. This type of air pollution is formed by a combination of vehicle emissions, terrain that traps pollution, and a warm, sunny climate.

The Political World

A map with the names and boundaries of countries shows the political world. Boundaries—some arrived at peacefully, others after years of conflict and war—carve up the land into 195 independent units, or countries. Boundaries are dynamic, meaning they change over time as political power shifts. For example, in 1990, West and East Germany became one country, removing a boundary that had separated them since 1949. In 2011, a boundary was established to separate the new country of South Sudan from Sudan.

Countries vary greatly in size. Russia, the largest, stretches across northern Asia into Europe. Other countries are small enough to fit inside another country. For instance, the country of Lesotho lies entirely within the country of South Africa, and tiny Vatican City lies within the city of Rome, Italy.

◗ **THE SCALE OF THIS MAP** makes it impossible to name all 195 independent countries and their capital cities. For a complete listing, refer to pages 126–133 or use the place-name index and the political maps in each continent section.

◗ **VIEW FROM THE NORTH POLE.** Ocean, not land, surrounds the area of the North Pole, so there are no political boundaries there. The Arctic Ocean, icebound much of the year, is part of the coastal waters of Earth's northernmost countries.

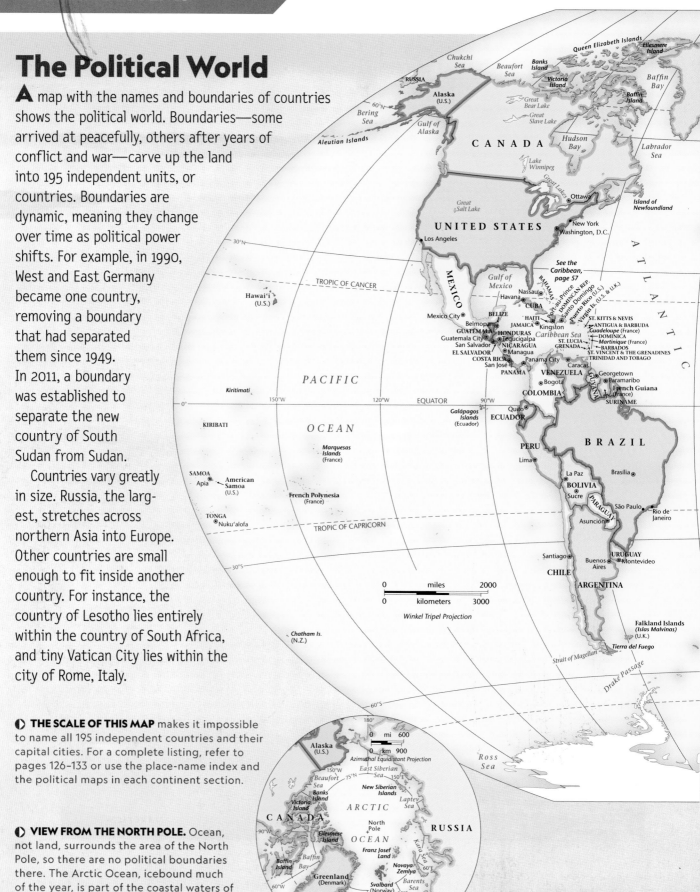

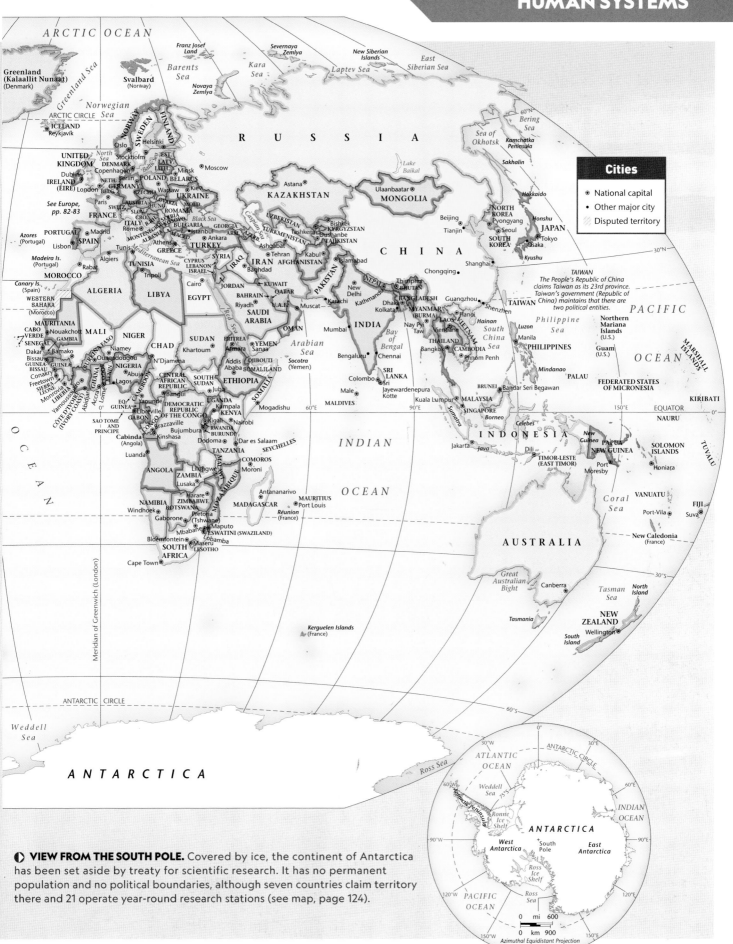

ARCTIC OCEAN

Greenland (Kalaallit Nunaat) (Denmark)

Franz Josef Land

Severnaya Zemlya

New Siberian Islands

East Siberian Sea

Svalbard (Norway)

Barents Sea

Novaya Zemlya

Kara Sea

Laptev Sea

Greenland Sea

Greenland Sea

Norwegian Sea

ARCTIC CIRCLE

ICELAND Reykjavík

NORWAY SWEDEN FINLAND

Oslo Helsinki Stockholm

R U S S I A

60°N Bering Sea

Sea of Okhotsk

Kamchatka Peninsula

UNITED KINGDOM North Sea DENMARK

IRELAND (ÉIRE) London

Dublin

Copenhagen

Moscow

Sakhalin

Hokkaido

Cities

Minsk EST. LATV. LITH.

● National capital

See Europe, pp. 82-83

FRANCE Paris

NETH. BELG. GERMANY

Berlin

POLAND BELARUS

Warsaw Kiev

KAZAKHSTAN

Astana

Ulaanbaatar

MONGOLIA

Beijing

NORTH KOREA Pyongyang

Honshu JAPAN

Tokyo

● Other major city

▨ Disputed territory

SWITZ. CZECHIA AUSTRIA HUNG.

Azores (Portugal)

PORTUGAL SPAIN

Lisbon Madrid

ITALY Rome

SLOVA. SLOV. CRO. B&H SERBIA MONTENEGRO ROMANIA BULGARIA

MOLD. UKRAINE

Black Sea

GEORGIA ARM. AZERB.

UZBEKISTAN

Tashkent

Bishkek KYRGYZSTAN

TURKMENISTAN Dushanbe

TAJIKISTAN

C H I N A

Tianjin

Shanghai

SOUTH KOREA Seoul

Osaka

Kyushu

30°N

TAIWAN

Chongqing

The People's Republic of China claims Taiwan as its 23rd province. Taiwan's government (Republic of China) maintains that there are two political entities.

PACIFIC

Madeira Is. (Portugal)

ALBANIA MACED.

GREECE TURKEY

Istanbul Ankara

Caspian Sea Ashgabat

Kabul

Islamabad

Guangzhou

Shenzhen

Canary Is. (Spain)

MOROCCO

Rabat

TUNISIA

Tunis Algiers

Athens

CYPRUS LEBANON ISRAEL

Mediterranean Sea

SYRIA IRAQ

Baghdad

IRAN AFGHANISTAN

Tehran

PAKISTAN

NEPAL Kathmandu

New Delhi

Thimphu BHUTAN

Dhaka BANGLADESH

Hanoi

Kolkata

Hainan

South China Sea

Luzon

Philippine Sea

Northern Mariana Islands (U.S.)

OCEAN

WESTERN SAHARA (Morocco)

ALGERIA

LIBYA

Tripoli

Cairo

EGYPT

JORDAN

Riyadh

KUWAIT

BAHRAIN QATAR U.A.E.

Red Sea

Muscat

OMAN

Karachi

INDIA

Mumbai

MYANMAR (BURMA)

Nay Pyi Taw

LAOS Vientiane

THAILAND

Bangkok

CAMBODIA

VIETNAM

Manila

PHILIPPINES

Guam (U.S.)

MARSHALL ISLANDS

MAURITANIA

CABO VERDE

Nouakchott

MALI

NIGER

CHAD

Khartoum

SUDAN

SAUDI ARABIA

ERITREA Asmara

Sanaa YEMEN

Arabian Sea

Socotra (Yemen)

Bengaluru

Chennai

Phnom Penh

PALAU

Mindanao

FEDERATED STATES OF MICRONESIA

GAMBIA SENEGAL

Dakar Bissau

Bamako BURKINA FASO Niamey Ouagadougou

N'Djamena

CENTRAL AFRICAN

DJIBOUTI

SOUTH

Addis Ababa

SOMALILAND

Colombo

SRI LANKA Sri Jayewardenepura Kotte

BRUNEI Bandar Seri Begawan

KIRIBATI

GUINEA-BISSAU GUINEA

Conakry Freetown

SIERRA LEONE

GHANA Accra

NIGERIA

Abuja

REPUBLIC

Bangui

SUDAN

Juba

ETHIOPIA

UGANDA

Male

MALDIVES

Kuala Lumpur

MALAYSIA

SINGAPORE

Borneo

EQUATOR

NAURU

LIBERIA Monrovia Yamoussoukro

CÔTE D'IVOIRE (IVORY COAST)

BENIN

Lomé TOGO Lagos

CAMEROON Yaoundé

EQ. GUINEA

Libreville

GABON

DEMOCRATIC REPUBLIC OF THE CONGO

CONGO Brazzaville

Kampala

Kigali RWANDA BURUNDI

KENYA Nairobi

Mogadishu

SOMALIA

60°E

90°E

Celebes

I N D O N E S I A

Jakarta Java

Sumatra

Dili TIMOR-LESTE (EAST TIMOR)

New Guinea

PAPUA NEW GUINEA

Port Moresby

SOLOMON ISLANDS

Honiara

TUVALU

SAO TOME AND PRINCIPE

Cabinda (Angola)

Kinshasa

Bujumbura

Dodoma

Dar es Salaam

TANZANIA

SEYCHELLES

INDIAN

Luanda

ANGOLA

ZAMBIA

Lusaka

MALAWI Lilongwe

COMOROS Moroni

OCEAN

Coral Sea

VANUATU

Port-Vila

FIJI Suva

NAMIBIA Windhoek

BOTSWANA

ZIMBABWE Harare

MOZAMBIQUE

MADAGASCAR

Antananarivo

MAURITIUS Port Louis

Réunion (France)

New Caledonia (France)

Gaborone

Pretoria (Tshwane)

Mbabane

Maputo

ESWATINI (SWAZILAND)

A U S T R A L I A

30°S

Bloemfontein Maseru Obamba LESOTHO

SOUTH AFRICA

Great Australian Bight

Canberra

Tasman Sea

North Island

O C E A N

Cape Town

Tasmania

NEW ZEALAND

Meridian of Greenwich (London)

Kerguelen Islands (France)

Wellington

South Island

ANTARCTIC CIRCLE

60°S

Weddell Sea

A N T A R C T I C A

Ross Sea

ATLANTIC OCEAN

ANTARCTIC CIRCLE

Weddell Sea

Antarctic Peninsula

Ronne Ice Shelf

West Antarctica

ANTARCTICA

South Pole

East Antarctica

INDIAN OCEAN

PACIFIC OCEAN

Ross Ice Shelf

Ross Sea

◖ **VIEW FROM THE SOUTH POLE.** Covered by ice, the continent of Antarctica has been set aside by treaty for scientific research. It has no permanent population and no political boundaries, although seven countries claim territory there and 21 operate year-round research stations (see map, page 124).

0 mi 600

0 km 900

Azimuthal Equidistant Projection

World Population

In 2017, the United Nations estimated Earth's population to be almost 7.6 billion. Although more than 83 million people are added each year, the rate, or annual percentage, at which the population is growing (1.1 percent) is gradually decreasing. Earth's population is unevenly distributed, with huge clusters in Asia and in Europe. Population density, the average number of people living in each square mile (or square kilometer), is high in these regions. For example, on average, there are more than 2,890 people per square mile (1,116 per sq km) in Bangladesh. Other areas, such as deserts and Arctic tundra, have fewer than two people per square mile (one person per sq km).

◗ **CROWDED STREETS,** like this one in Shanghai, China, may become commonplace as Earth's population continues to increase and as more people move to urban areas.

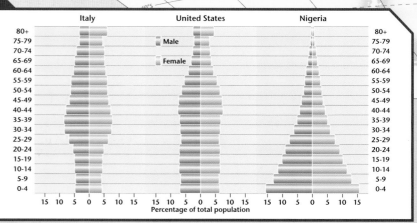

NORTH
AMERICA

New York

Los Angeles

30°N

TROPIC OF CANCER

Mexico City

PACIFIC
OCEAN

ATLANTIC
OCEAN

150°W   EQUATOR   120°W   90°W   30°W
0°

Lima

SOUTH
AMERICA

Rio de
Janeiro

São Paulo

Buenos Aires

60°S

THREE POPULATION PYRAMIDS

A population pyramid is a special type of bar graph that shows the distribution of a country's population by sex and age. Italy has a very narrow pyramid, which shows that most people are in middle age. Its population is said to be aging, meaning the median age is increasing. The United States also has a narrow pyramid, but one that shows some growth due to a median age of almost 38 years and a young immigrant population. By contrast, Nigeria's pyramid has a broad base, showing it has a young population. Almost half of its people are younger than 15 years.

Italy | United States | Nigeria

80+
75-79
70-74
65-69
60-64
55-59
50-54
45-49
40-44
35-39
30-34
25-29
20-24
15-19
10-14
5-9
0-4

■ Male

■ Female

15 10 5 0 5 10 15   15 10 5 0 5 10 15   15 10 5 0 5 10 15
Percentage of total population

C.E. 1 50 100 150 200 250 300 350 400 450 500 550 600 650 700 750 800 850
Year

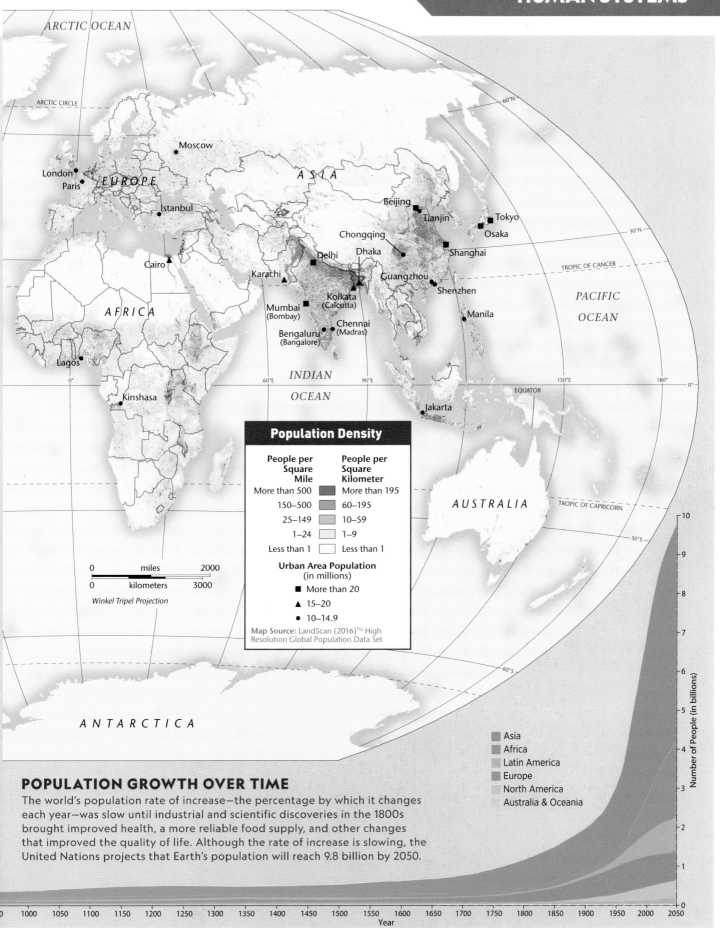

ARCTIC OCEAN

ARCTIC CIRCLE

Moscow

London
Paris

EUROPE

ASIA

Istanbul

Beijing

Tianjin

Tokyo

Osaka

Chongqing

Shanghai

Cairo

Delhi

Dhaka

Karachi

Guangzhou

AFRICA

Mumbai
(Bombay)

Kolkata
(Calcutta)

Shenzhen

Chennai
(Madras)

Manila

Bengaluru
(Bangalore)

INDIAN

OCEAN

PACIFIC

OCEAN

TROPIC OF CANCER

60°N

30°N

Lagos

0°

60°E

90°E

150°E

180°

0°

EQUATOR

Kinshasa

Jakarta

Population Density

People per Square Mile	People per Square Kilometer
More than 500	More than 195
150–500	60–195
25–149	10–59
1–24	1–9
Less than 1	Less than 1

Urban Area Population (in millions)
■ More than 20
▲ 15–20
● 10–14.9

Map Source: LandScan (2016)™ High Resolution Global Population Data Set

0   miles   2000
0   kilometers   3000

Winkel Tripel Projection

AUSTRALIA

TROPIC OF CAPRICORN

30°S

60°S

ANTARCTICA

Asia
Africa
Latin America
Europe
North America
Australia & Oceania

POPULATION GROWTH OVER TIME

The world's population rate of increase—the percentage by which it changes each year—was slow until industrial and scientific discoveries in the 1800s brought improved health, a more reliable food supply, and other changes that improved the quality of life. Although the rate of increase is slowing, the United Nations projects that Earth's population will reach 9.8 billion by 2050.

Number of People (in billions)

10
9
8
7
6
5
4
3
2
1
0

50 1000 1050 1100 1150 1200 1250 1300 1350 1400 1450 1500 1550 1600 1650 1700 1750 1800 1850 1900 1950 2000 2050

Year

World Refugees

Every day, people relocate. Most people move by choice, but some people, called refugees, move to escape war and persecution that make it impossible to remain where they are. Such forced movement creates severe hardship for families who must leave behind their possessions. They may find themselves in a place where they do not speak the local language, where customs are unfamiliar, and where basic necessities, such as food, shelter, and medical services, are in short supply.

The High Commissioner for Refugees (UNHCR), an agency of the United Nations, is responsible for the safety and well-being of refugees worldwide and for protecting their rights.

In 2016, the UNHCR estimated that there were more than 22.5 million refugees worldwide, and another 40.3 million internally displaced persons—people still living within their country, but forced to leave their homes.

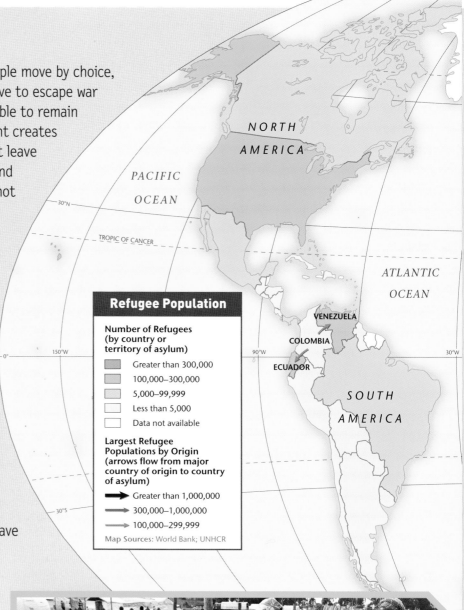

Refugee Population

**Number of Refugees
(by country or
territory of asylum)**

- Greater than 300,000
- 100,000–300,000
- 5,000–99,999
- Less than 5,000
- Data not available

**Largest Refugee
Populations by Origin
(arrows flow from major
country of origin to country
of asylum)**

- ➡ Greater than 1,000,000
- ➡ 300,000–1,000,000
- ➡ 100,000–299,999

Map Sources: World Bank; UNHCR

REFUGEE HOST COUNTRIES

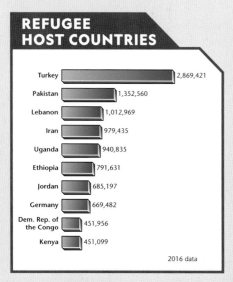

Turkey	2,869,421
Pakistan	1,352,560
Lebanon	1,012,969
Iran	979,435
Uganda	940,835
Ethiopia	791,631
Jordan	685,197
Germany	669,482
Dem. Rep. of the Congo	451,956
Kenya	451,099

2016 data

REFUGEES fleeing hostilities in the Democratic Republic of the Congo (DRC) receive food in a transit camp in Uganda. Almost four million people have been displaced—many within the DRC, others crossing into neighboring countries.

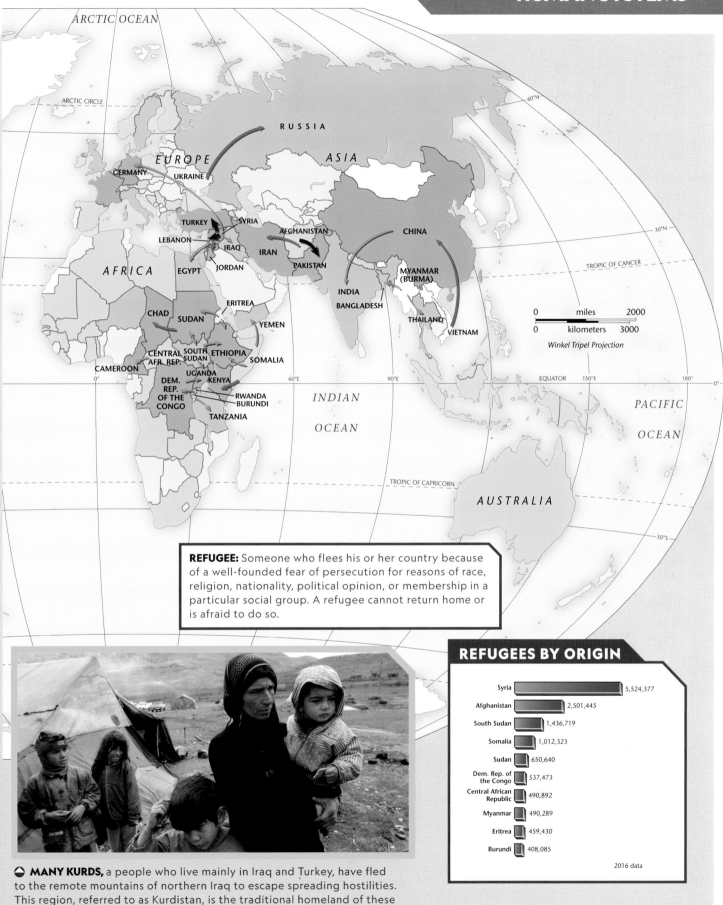

ARCTIC OCEAN

ARCTIC CIRCLE

60°N

RUSSIA

EUROPE

ASIA

GERMANY

UKRAINE

30°N

TURKEY   SYRIA

LEBANON   AFGHANISTAN   CHINA

IRAQ

JORDAN   IRAN   PAKISTAN

EGYPT

TROPIC OF CANCER

MYANMAR
(BURMA)

AFRICA

ERITREA

INDIA

CHAD   SUDAN   BANGLADESH

YEMEN   THAILAND

VIETNAM

CENTRAL   SOUTH   ETHIOPIA
AFR. REP.   SUDAN   SOMALIA

CAMEROON   UGANDA   KENYA   0°   60°E   90°E   EQUATOR   150°E   180°   0°

DEM.
REP.   RWANDA
OF THE   BURUNDI
CONGO   TANZANIA   INDIAN   PACIFIC

OCEAN   OCEAN

0   miles   2000
0   kilometers   3000

Winkel Tripel Projection

TROPIC OF CAPRICORN   AUSTRALIA

30°S

REFUGEE: Someone who flees his or her country because of a well-founded fear of persecution for reasons of race, religion, nationality, political opinion, or membership in a particular social group. A refugee cannot return home or is afraid to do so.

REFUGEES BY ORIGIN

Origin	Refugees
Syria	5,524,377
Afghanistan	2,501,445
South Sudan	1,436,719
Somalia	1,012,323
Sudan	650,640
Dem. Rep. of the Congo	537,473
Central African Republic	490,892
Myanmar	490,289
Eritrea	459,430
Burundi	408,085

2016 data

⬤ **MANY KURDS,** a people who live mainly in Iraq and Turkey, have fled to the remote mountains of northern Iraq to escape spreading hostilities. This region, referred to as Kurdistan, is the traditional homeland of these stateless people.

Quality of Life

The world's population is unevenly distributed (see map on pages 32–33), and not everyone experiences the same quality of life. The level of development in countries is often measured in economic terms, but beginning in 1990, the United Nations Development Program introduced a different and more complete way to evaluate the condition of life in the world's countries: the Human Development Index (HDI). The HDI combines both social and economic factors to rank the world's countries based on three indicators: health, education, and living standard (see map at right). Health is measured by life expectancy at birth (see map below). Education is measured by average years of schooling. And living standard is measured using gross national income (GNI) per capita—the total income earned in a country each year divided by the country's population (see graph).

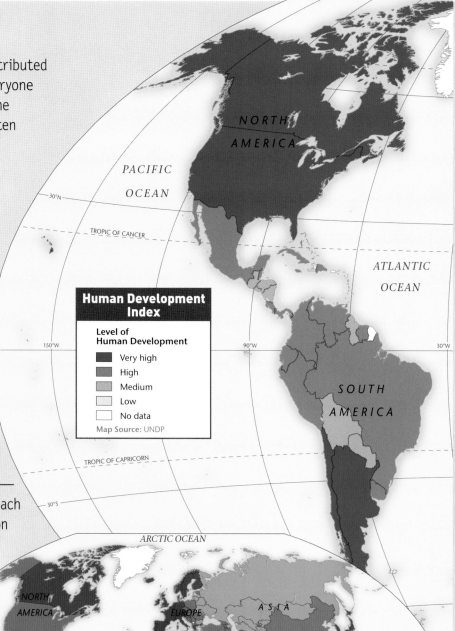

Human Development Index

Level of Human Development
- Very high
- High
- Medium
- Low
- No data

Map Source: UNDP

Life Expectancy at Birth

Life Expectancy in Years, Both Sexes
- 80 or older
- 75–79
- 65–74
- 55–64
- 54 or younger
- No data

Map Source: UNDP

0 — 2000 miles
0 — 3000 kilometers
Winkel Tripel Projection

◗ **LIFE EXPECTANCY** at birth is a strong indicator of people's access to food, safe water, and medical care, all of which are important to quality of life.

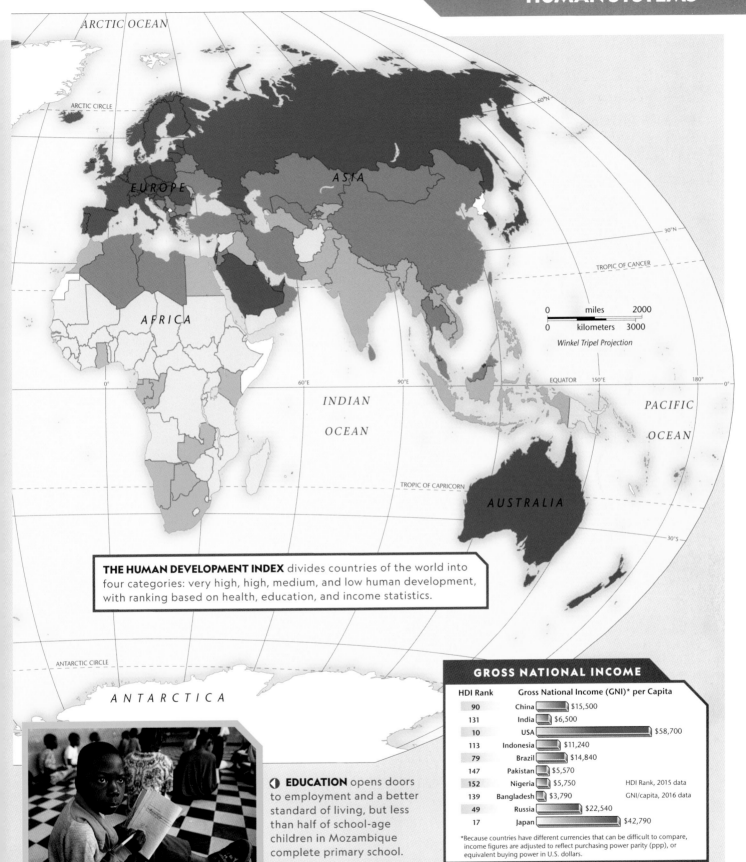

ARCTIC OCEAN

ARCTIC CIRCLE

60°N

EUROPE

ASIA

30°N

TROPIC OF CANCER

AFRICA

0   miles   2000
0   kilometers   3000

Winkel Tripel Projection

60°E   90°E   EQUATOR   150°E   180°

INDIAN

OCEAN

PACIFIC

OCEAN

TROPIC OF CAPRICORN

AUSTRALIA

30°S

THE HUMAN DEVELOPMENT INDEX divides countries of the world into four categories: very high, high, medium, and low human development, with ranking based on health, education, and income statistics.

ANTARCTIC CIRCLE

ANTARCTICA

GROSS NATIONAL INCOME

HDI Rank	Gross National Income (GNI)* per Capita	
90	China	$15,500
131	India	$6,500
10	USA	$58,700
113	Indonesia	$11,240
79	Brazil	$14,840
147	Pakistan	$5,570
152	Nigeria	$5,750
139	Bangladesh	$3,790
49	Russia	$22,540
17	Japan	$42,790

HDI Rank, 2015 data
GNI/capita, 2016 data

*Because countries have different currencies that can be difficult to compare, income figures are adjusted to reflect purchasing power parity (ppp), or equivalent buying power in U.S. dollars.

EDUCATION opens doors to employment and a better standard of living, but less than half of school-age children in Mozambique complete primary school.

QUALITY OF LIFE, as measured in terms of income per person, varies greatly among the world's 10 most populous countries.

World Cities

Throughout most of history, people have lived spread across the land, first as hunters and gatherers, later as farmers. But urban geographers—people who study cities—have determined that today more than half of Earth's population lives in urban areas. Urban areas include one or more cities and their surrounding suburbs. Large urban areas are sometimes called metropolitan areas. People living there are employed primarily in industry or service/technology-related jobs. In some countries, such as Belgium, almost everyone lives in cities. But throughout much of Africa and Asia, many people still live in rural areas. Even so, some of the world's fastest growing urban areas are towns and small cities in Africa and Asia.

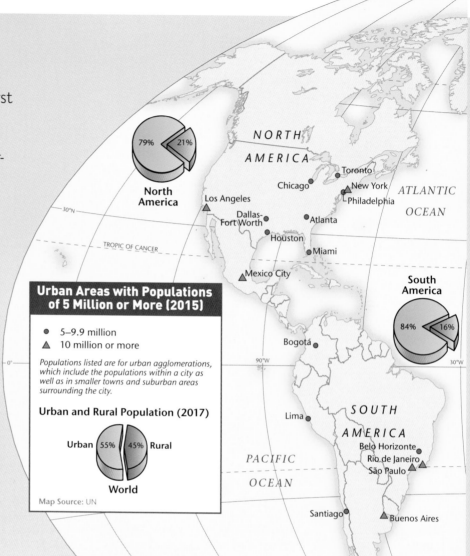

Urban Areas with Populations of 5 Million or More (2015)

- ● 5–9.9 million
- ▲ 10 million or more

Populations listed are for urban agglomerations, which include the populations within a city as well as in smaller towns and suburban areas surrounding the city.

Urban and Rural Population (2017)

Urban 55% / 45% Rural

World

Map Source: UN

MOST POPULOUS URBAN AREAS

In 1970, only Tokyo, New York, and Osaka, each with populations greater than 10 million, qualified as megacities. By 2015, there were 29 megacities. By 2030, the list is projected to include 43 cities, still led by Tokyo despite a projected decline in its population to 37 million people.

Urban areas with populations greater than 10 million for the years:

▱ 1970 ▱ 2000 ▱ 2015 ▱ 2030

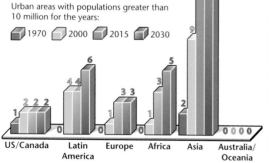

2015 data

◆ **CENTRAL TOKYO,** viewed from high above crowded city streets, contains a mix of modern high-rise and older low-rise buildings. With almost 38 million people, Tokyo is Japan's largest and most densely populated urban area and the world's largest urban agglomeration.

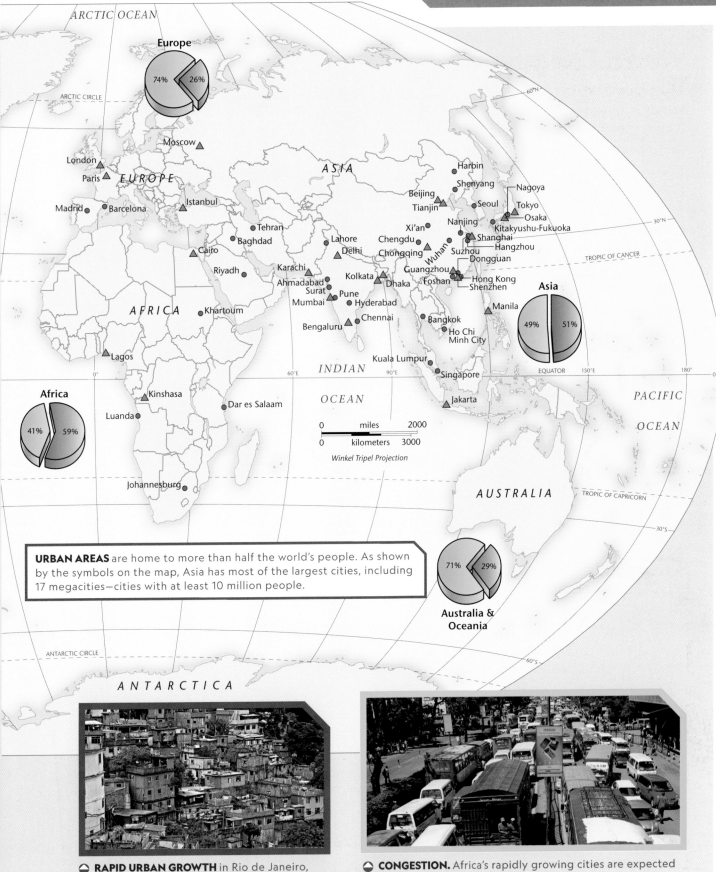

ARCTIC OCEAN

Europe
74% | 26%

ARCTIC CIRCLE

Moscow ▲

London ▲
Paris ▲ EUROPE

Madrid ● ● Barcelona ▲ Istanbul

● Tehran

● Baghdad

Cairo ●

Riyadh ●

Karachi ▲

AFRICA

Khartoum ●

Lahore ● Delhi ▲

ASIA

Harbin ▲

Shenyang ▲
Beijing ▲ Nagoya
Tianjin ▲ Seoul ▲ Tokyo
  Nanjing ▲ Osaka
Xi'an ▲ Kitakyushu-Fukuoka
Chengdu ● Shanghai ▲
Chongqing ● Wuhan ▲ Hangzhou
  Suzhou
  Dongguan
Guangzhou ▲
Foshan ▲ Hong Kong
  Shenzhen

60°N

30°N

TROPIC OF CANCER

Asia
49% | 51%

Ahmadabad ▲
Surat ●
Mumbai ▲ Pune ●
  Hyderabad ●

Kolkata ▲
Dhaka ▲

Bengaluru ▲ ● Chennai

Lagos ▲

Kinshasa ▲

Luanda ●

Dar es Salaam ●

INDIAN

OCEAN

Bangkok ●
Ho Chi
Minh City ●

Manila ▲

Kuala Lumpur ●

Singapore ●

Jakarta ▲

EQUATOR 150°E 180°

PACIFIC

OCEAN

Africa
41% | 59%

0 miles 2000
0 kilometers 3000

Winkel Tripel Projection

Johannesburg ●

AUSTRALIA

TROPIC OF CAPRICORN

30°S

URBAN AREAS are home to more than half the world's people. As shown by the symbols on the map, Asia has most of the largest cities, including 17 megacities—cities with at least 10 million people.

Australia & Oceania
71% | 29%

ANTARCTIC CIRCLE

60°S

ANTARCTICA

⬤ **RAPID URBAN GROWTH** in Rio de Janeiro, Brazil, has resulted in the spread of slums, called favelas, up the steep hillsides around the city.

⬤ **CONGESTION.** Africa's rapidly growing cities are expected to add almost 350 million residents by 2030, but the transportation infrastructure in cities like Nairobi, Kenya, cannot keep pace with such growth.

World Languages

Culture is all the shared traits that make different groups of people around the world unique. For example, customs, food and clothing preferences, housing styles, and music and art forms are all a part of each group's culture. Language is one of the most defining characteristics of culture.

Language reflects what people value and the way they understand the world. It also reveals how certain groups of people may have had common roots at some point in history. English and German, for example, are two very different languages, but both are part of the same Indo-European language family. This means that these two languages share certain characteristics that suggest they have evolved from a common ancestor language.

Patterns on the world language families map (right) offer clues to the diffusion, or movement, of groups of people. For example, the widespread use of English, extending from the United States to India and Australia, reflects the far-reaching effects of the British colonial empire. Today, English is the main language of the internet.

About 5,000 languages are spoken in the world today, but experts think many may become extinct as more people become involved in global trade, communications, and travel.

⬤ **THE GOLDEN ARCHES** icon helps you identify this restaurant in Moscow even if you don't know how to read the Cyrillic alphabet of the Russian language.

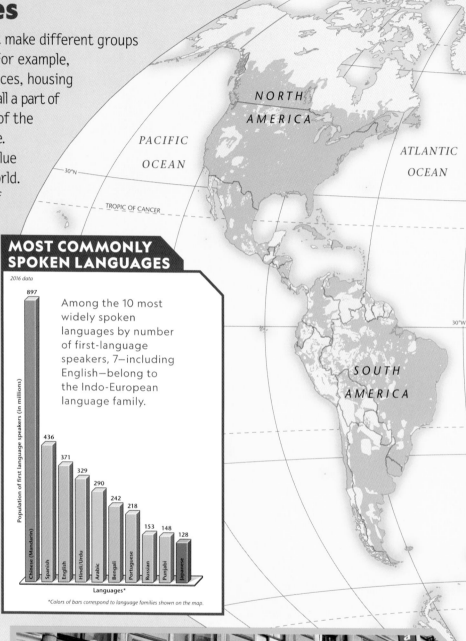

MOST COMMONLY SPOKEN LANGUAGES

2016 data

Among the 10 most widely spoken languages by number of first-language speakers, 7—including English—belong to the Indo-European language family.

Population of first language speakers (in millions)

Language	Speakers
Chinese (Mandarin)	897
Spanish	436
English	371
Hindi/Urdu	329
Arabic	290
Bengali	242
Portuguese	218
Russian	153
Punjabi	148
Japanese	128

Languages*

*Colors of bars correspond to language families shown on the map.

NORTH AMERICA

PACIFIC OCEAN

ATLANTIC OCEAN

30°N

TROPIC OF CANCER

30°W

SOUTH AMERICA

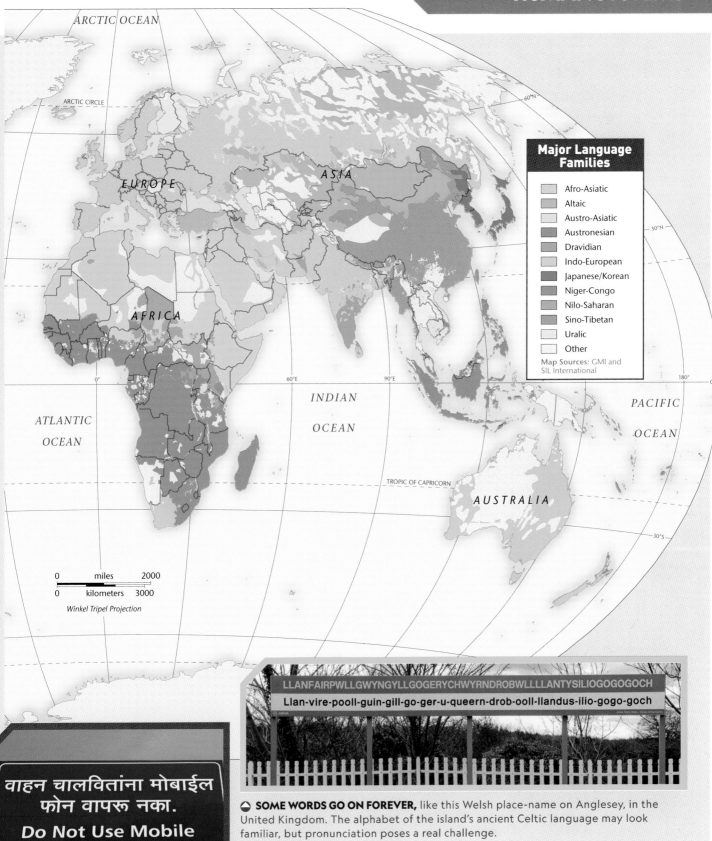

ARCTIC OCEAN

ARCTIC CIRCLE

EUROPE

ASIA

60°N

30°N

AFRICA

ATLANTIC
OCEAN

INDIAN

OCEAN

PACIFIC

OCEAN

TROPIC OF CAPRICORN

AUSTRALIA

30°S

0°   60°E   90°E   180°   0°

Major Language Families

	Afro-Asiatic
	Altaic
	Austro-Asiatic
	Austronesian
	Dravidian
	Indo-European
	Japanese/Korean
	Niger-Congo
	Nilo-Saharan
	Sino-Tibetan
	Uralic
	Other

Map Sources: GMI and SIL International

0   miles   2000
0   kilometers   3000

Winkel Tripel Projection

LLANFAIRPWLLGWYNGYLLGOGERYCHWYRNDROBWLLLLANTYSILIOGOGOGOCH
Llan-vire-pooll-guin-gill-go-ger-u-queern-drob-ooll-llandus-ilio-gogo-goch

वाहन चालविताना मोबाईल
फोन वापरू नका.
**Do Not Use Mobile
Phone While Driving.**

🔼 **SOME WORDS GO ON FOREVER,** like this Welsh place-name on Anglesey, in the United Kingdom. The alphabet of the island's ancient Celtic language may look familiar, but pronunciation poses a real challenge.

◖ **MARATHI,** an Indo-European language derived from ancient Sanskrit, appears on a highway sign in Pune, Maharashtra, India, warning drivers about a safety issue that is a worldwide problem.

World Religions

Religion is a central element of culture. Religious beliefs and practices help people deal with the unknown. But people in different places have developed a variety of belief systems.

Universalizing religions, such as Christianity, Islam, and Buddhism, seek converts. Carried by migration, colonization, and global trade, these religions have spread throughout the world from their places of origin in different parts of Asia. Ethnic religions, including Judaism, Hinduism, and Shinto, tend to be associated with particular groups of people and are generally concentrated in certain places. Some groups, especially indigenous, or native, people living in remote areas, believe that spirits inhabit all things in the natural world. These kinds of belief systems are known as animistic religions.

Places of worship are often a distinctive part of the cultural landscape. A cathedral, mosque, or temple can reveal much about the people who live in a particular place.

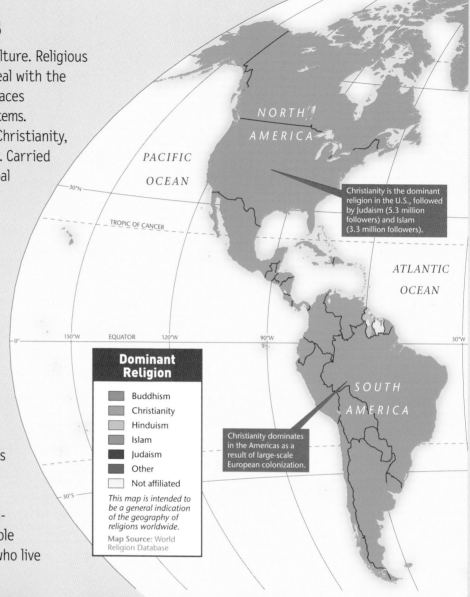

Christianity is the dominant religion in the U.S., followed by Judaism (5.3 million followers) and Islam (3.3 million followers).

Christianity dominates in the Americas as a result of large-scale European colonization.

Dominant Religion

- Buddhism
- Christianity
- Hinduism
- Islam
- Judaism
- Other
- Not affiliated

This map is intended to be a general indication of the geography of religions worldwide.

Map Source: World Religion Database

⬥ **MOST OF HINDUISM'S** one billion followers live in India and other South Asian countries. The goddess Durga (above) is regarded as Mother of the Universe and protector of the righteous.

⬥ **JERUSALEM IS HOLY** to Jews, Christians, and Muslims, a fact that has led to tension and conflict. Below, a Russian orthodox church (foreground) overlooks the Western Wall, sacred to Jews, while sunlight reflects off the Dome of the Rock, a Muslim shrine.

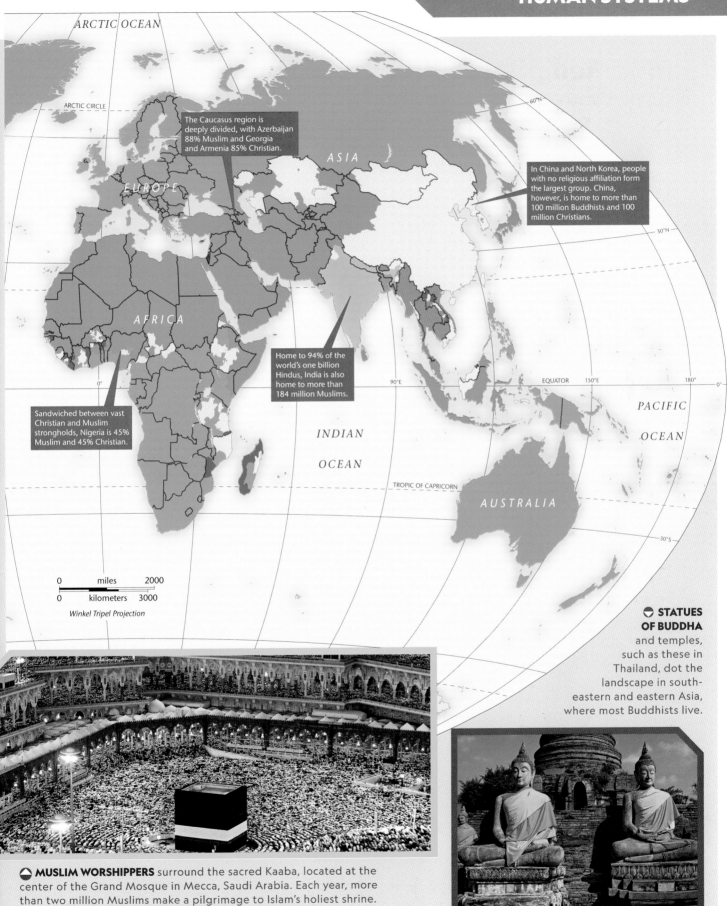

ARCTIC OCEAN

ARCTIC CIRCLE

ASIA

EUROPE

The Caucasus region is deeply divided, with Azerbaijan 88% Muslim and Georgia and Armenia 85% Christian.

In China and North Korea, people with no religious affiliation form the largest group. China, however, is home to more than 100 million Buddhists and 100 million Christians.

AFRICA

Home to 94% of the world's one billion Hindus, India is also home to more than 184 million Muslims.

Sandwiched between vast Christian and Muslim strongholds, Nigeria is 45% Muslim and 45% Christian.

INDIAN

OCEAN

PACIFIC

OCEAN

EQUATOR

TROPIC OF CAPRICORN

AUSTRALIA

| 0 | miles | 2000 |
| 0 | kilometers | 3000 |

Winkel Tripel Projection

◯ **STATUES OF BUDDHA** and temples, such as these in Thailand, dot the landscape in south-eastern and eastern Asia, where most Buddhists live.

◯ **MUSLIM WORSHIPPERS** surround the sacred Kaaba, located at the center of the Grand Mosque in Mecca, Saudi Arabia. Each year, more than two million Muslims make a pilgrimage to Islam's holiest shrine.

Predominant World Economies

People generate income to meet their needs and wants through a variety of activities that can be grouped into four categories, or sectors: primary (agriculture, fishing, and forestry); secondary (manufacturing and processing activities); tertiary (services ranging from retail sales to teaching, banking, and medicine); and quaternary (information creation and exchange and e-commerce—buying and selling over the internet). Services and industry generate higher incomes, and therefore account for a greater share of a country's GDP, although not necessarily a greater percentage of the workforce. In many less developed countries, a large part of the workforce is still engaged in agriculture, which generates low income and perpetuates poverty.

NORTH AMERICA

PACIFIC OCEAN

ATLANTIC OCEAN

TROPIC OF CANCER

SOUTH AMERICA

Dominant Economic Sector (as a percentage of GDP)

	Agriculture	Industry	Services
70%–100%			
50%–69.9%			
0%–49.9%			
No data			

Map Source: *The World Factbook*—CIA

◔ **SUBSISTENCE AGRICULTURE.** Many people in developing countries, such as these farmers in Bhutan, use traditional methods to grow crops for their daily food requirements rather than for commercial sale.

◔ **MANUFACTURING.** This mill in Slovakia processes raw materials such as coal and iron ore to make steel. Industries use steel to produce cars and other manufactured goods.

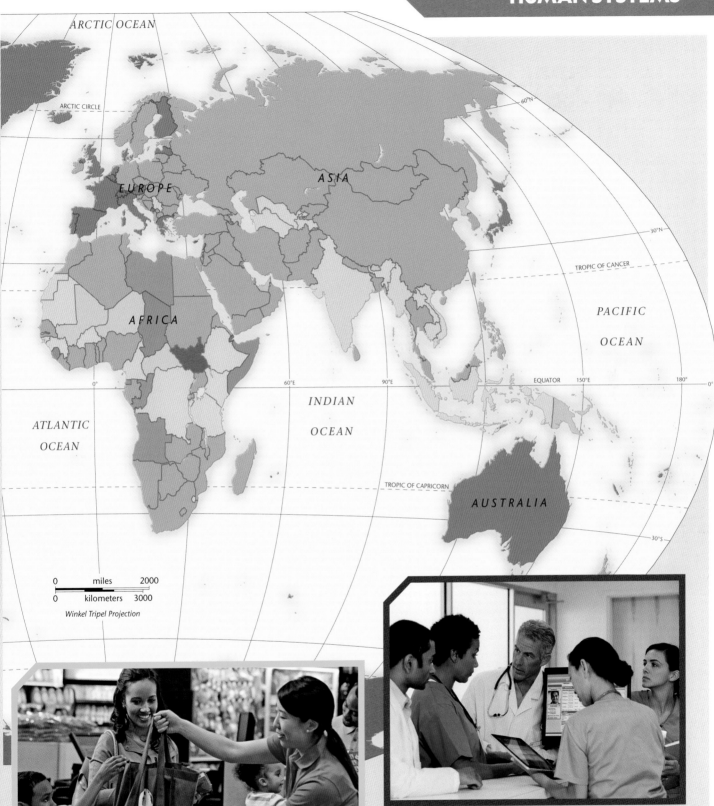

ARCTIC OCEAN

ARCTIC CIRCLE

EUROPE

ASIA

60°N

AFRICA

30°N

TROPIC OF CANCER

PACIFIC

OCEAN

0°

60°E

90°E

INDIAN

EQUATOR

150°E

180°E

0°

ATLANTIC

OCEAN

OCEAN

TROPIC OF CAPRICORN

AUSTRALIA

30°S

0   miles   2000
0   kilometers   3000

Winkel Tripel Projection

⬡ **SERVICES.** Ranging from banking to education to retail sales, service, or tertiary, jobs involve interacting with people, such as this grocery clerk handing over a family's purchases.

⬡ **COMMUNICATIONS AND TECHNOLOGY.** Medical professionals use computers as they consult about patient treatment. The internet and advanced technologies have introduced new ways of exchanging information in order to solve problems. Email and social media connect people near and far, while e-commerce makes possible buying and selling from home or office.

World Food

In 2017, the world's population reached 7.6 billion people—all needing to be fed. However, the productive potential of Earth's surface varies greatly from place to place. Some areas are good for growing crops; some are better for grazing animals; and others have little or no agricultural potential. Grains, such as rice, corn, and wheat, are main sources of food calories, while meat, poultry, and fish are sources of protein.

◖ **RICE** is an important staple food crop, especially in eastern and southern Asia. Although China produces more than 40 percent of the world's rice, it is also a major importer of rice to feed its population of more than a billion people.

Agricultural Land Use

Pasture   Cropland

☐ No data

Map Source: University of Minnesota

NORTH AMERICA

PACIFIC OCEAN

ATLANTIC OCEAN

SOUTH AMERICA

30°N

TROPIC OF CANCER

150°W   0°   90°W   30°W

TROPIC OF CAPRICORN

30°S

◖ **CORN,** which originated in the Americas, is an important food grain for people and livestock. Corn is also used to make ethanol, which is added to gasoline to make a cleaner fuel.

⬭ **WHEAT,** the world's leading export grain, is a main ingredient in bread and pasta and is grown on every inhabited continent. Each year, trade in this grain exceeds 175 million tons (159 million t).

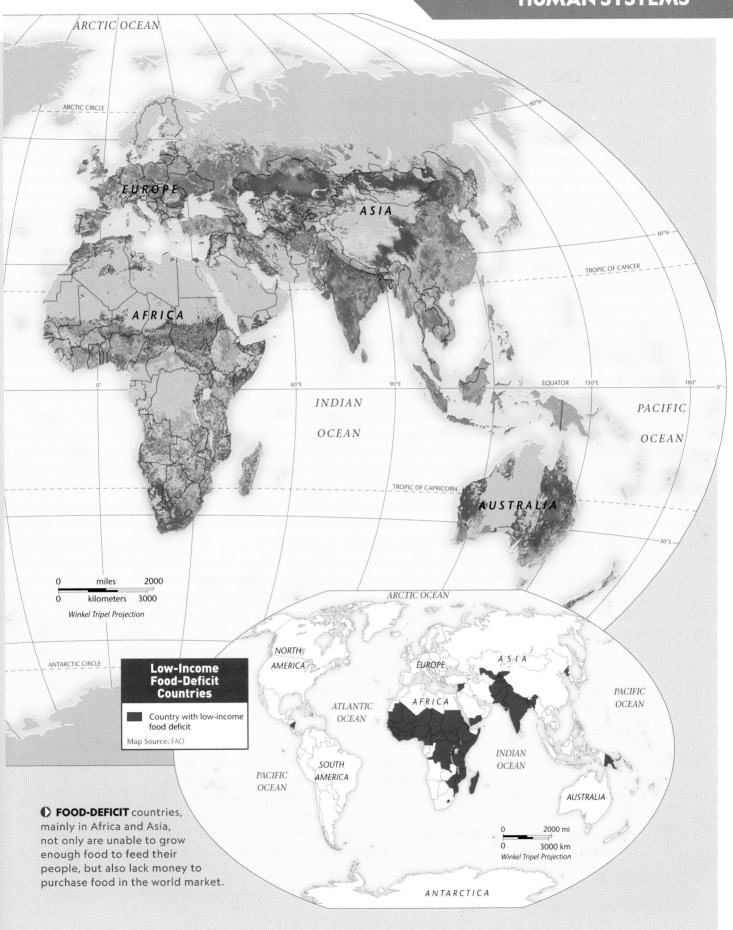

ARCTIC OCEAN

ARCTIC CIRCLE

60°N

EUROPE

ASIA

30°N

TROPIC OF CANCER

AFRICA

0°

60°E

90°E

EQUATOR

150°E

180°

0°

INDIAN

OCEAN

PACIFIC

OCEAN

TROPIC OF CAPRICORN

AUSTRALIA

30°S

0   miles   2000

0   kilometers   3000

Winkel Tripel Projection

ANTARCTIC CIRCLE

Low-Income Food-Deficit Countries

Country with low-income food deficit

Map Source: FAO

ARCTIC OCEAN

NORTH
AMERICA

EUROPE

ASIA

ATLANTIC
OCEAN

AFRICA

PACIFIC
OCEAN

INDIAN
OCEAN

PACIFIC
OCEAN

SOUTH
AMERICA

AUSTRALIA

0   2000 mi

0   3000 km

Winkel Tripel Projection

◖ **FOOD-DEFICIT** countries, mainly in Africa and Asia, not only are unable to grow enough food to feed their people, but also lack money to purchase food in the world market.

ANTARCTICA

World Energy & Mineral Resources

Beginning in the 19th century, as the industrial revolution spread across Europe and around the world, the demand for energy and non-fuel mineral resources skyrocketed. Fossil fuels—first coal, then oil and natural gas—have provided the energy that keeps the wheels of industry turning. Non-fuel minerals such as iron ore (essential for steel production) and copper (for electrical wiring) have become increasingly important.

Energy and non-fuel minerals, like all nonrenewable resources, are in limited supply and are unevenly distributed. Exporting countries with major deposits can influence both supply and prices of these resources, thus playing an important role in the global economy.

RENEWABLE ENERGY, including energy from the sun, wind, running water, and heat from within Earth, is an important alternative to fossil fuels. Some examples are shown below.

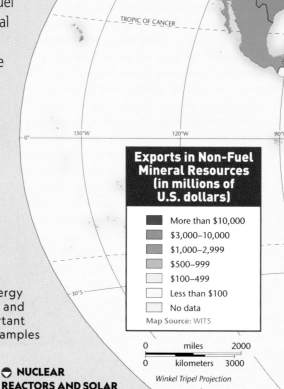

NORTH AMERICA

PACIFIC OCEAN

30°N

TROPIC OF CANCER

ATLANTIC OCEAN

150°W   120°W   90°W   30°W
0°

SOUTH AMERICA

30°S

60°S

Exports in Non-Fuel Mineral Resources (in millions of U.S. dollars)

- More than $10,000
- $3,000–10,000
- $1,000–2,999
- $500–999
- $100–499
- Less than $100
- No data

Map Source: WITS

```
0         miles      2000
0       kilometers    3000
```

Winkel Tripel Projection

◑ WINDMILLS rising above ancient temples near Jaisalmer, India, generate electricity by capturing the energy of winds blowing off the Indian Ocean.

◑ NUCLEAR REACTORS AND SOLAR PANELS near Sacramento, California, U.S.A., produce renewable energy to meet the state's power demand.

◐ A GEOTHERMAL POWER PLANT, fueled by heat from within Earth, produces energy to heat homes in Iceland. Runoff creates a warm pool for bathers.

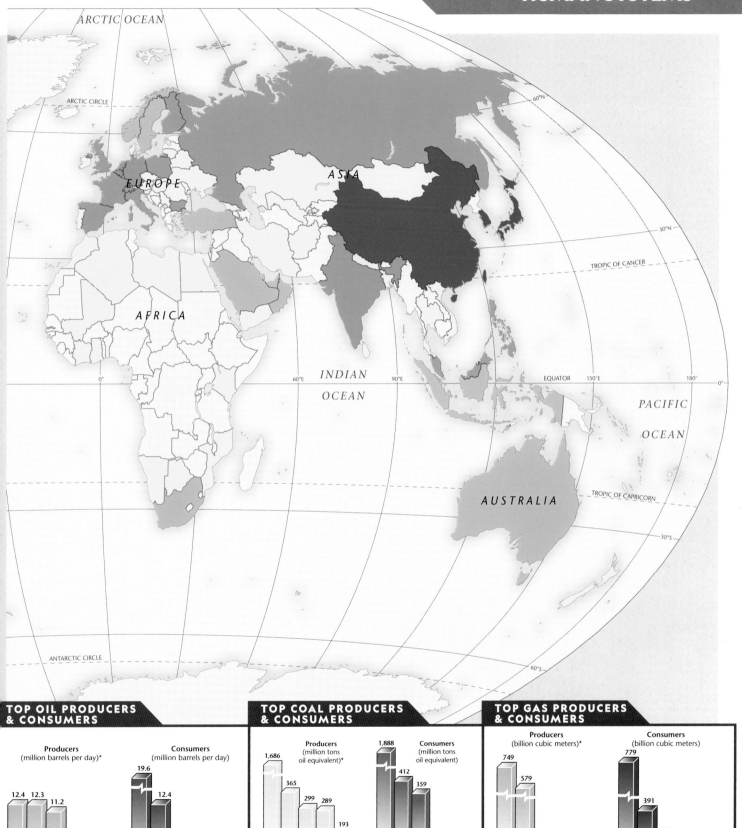

ARCTIC OCEAN

ARCTIC CIRCLE

60°N

EUROPE

ASIA

30°N

TROPIC OF CANCER

AFRICA

0°

60°E

INDIAN
OCEAN

90°E

EQUATOR

150°E

180°

0°

PACIFIC

OCEAN

AUSTRALIA

TROPIC OF CAPRICORN

30°S

ANTARCTIC CIRCLE

60°S

TOP OIL PRODUCERS & CONSUMERS

Producers
(million barrels per day)*

United States	12.4
Saudi Arabia	12.3
Russia	11.2
Iran	4.6
Iraq	4.5

Consumers
(million barrels per day)

United States	19.6
China	12.4
India	4.5
Japan	4.0
Saudi Arabia	3.9

*1 barrel = 42 gallons (159 L)   2016 data

TOP COAL PRODUCERS & CONSUMERS

Producers
(million tons
oil equivalent)*

China	1,686
United States	365
Australia	299
India	289
Russia	193

Consumers
(million tons
oil equivalent)

China	1,888
India	412
United States	359
Indonesia	120
Russia	87

*1 metric ton = energy equivalent to burning 7.4 barrels of oil   2016 data

TOP GAS PRODUCERS & CONSUMERS

Producers
(billion cubic meters)*

United States	749
Russia	579
Iran	202
Qatar	181
Canada	152

Consumers
(billion cubic meters)

United States	779
Russia	391
China	210
Iran	201
Japan	111

*1 cubic meter = 264 liquid gallons   2016 data

Globalization

The early years of the 21st century have seen a technology revolution that has changed the way people and countries relate to each other. This revolution in technology is part of a process known as globalization.

Globalization refers to the complex network of interconnections linking people, companies, and places without regard for national boundaries. Although it began when some countries became increasingly active in international trade, the process of globalization has gained momentum in recent years, expanding to include political and social interactions. But not all countries are major players in the global arena.

Improvements in communications and transportation have made it possible for companies to employ workers in distant countries. Some workers make clothing; some perform accounting tasks; and others work in call centers answering inquiries about products or services. Technology also allows banking transactions to take place faster and over greater distances than ever before. Companies that conduct business in multiple countries around the world are called transnational companies.

An important part of today's global communications system is the internet, a vast system of computer networks that allows people to access information around the world in seconds. Ideas and images now travel over the internet, introducing change and making places more and more alike.

◗ **MAQUILADORAS,** foreign-owned assembly plants located in Mexico, import parts and materials duty-free to produce finished goods for consumers in the U.S. and around the world. Maquiladoras, such as this one in Ciudad Juárez, employ a large workforce.

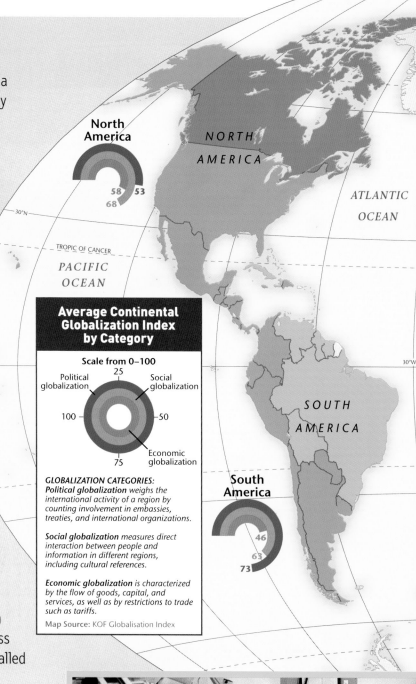

North America
58 53
68

South America
46
63
73

Average Continental Globalization Index by Category

Scale from 0–100

25
Political globalization — — Social globalization
100 — — 50
75
Economic globalization

GLOBALIZATION CATEGORIES:
Political globalization weighs the international activity of a region by counting involvement in embassies, treaties, and international organizations.

Social globalization measures direct interaction between people and information in different regions, including cultural references.

Economic globalization is characterized by the flow of goods, capital, and services, as well as by restrictions to trade such as tariffs.

Map Source: KOF Globalisation Index

NORTH AMERICA
ATLANTIC OCEAN
PACIFIC OCEAN
TROPIC OF CANCER
30°N
0°
30°W
SOUTH AMERICA

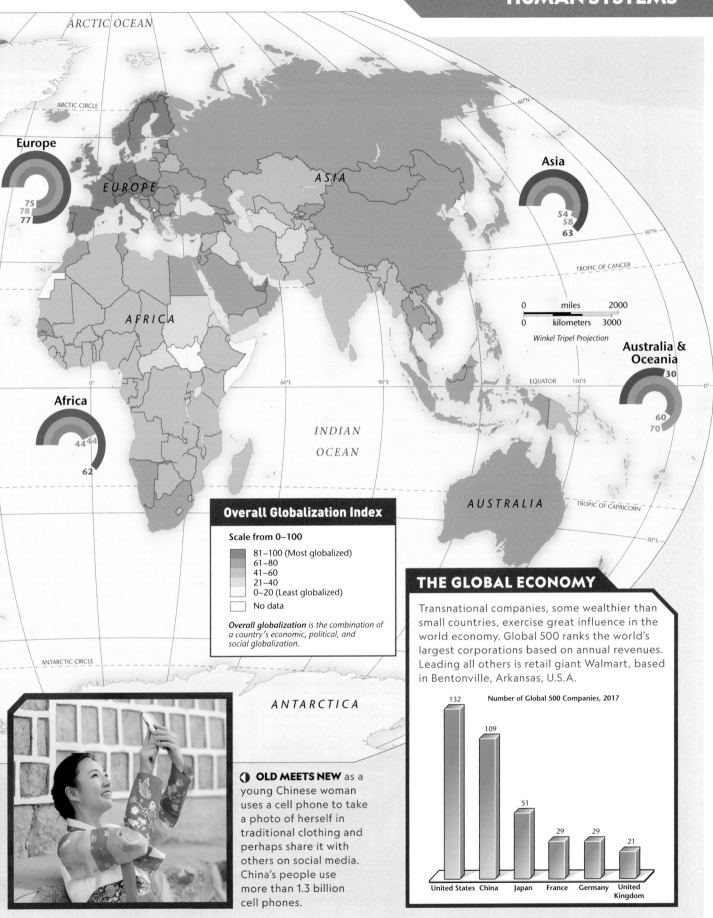

ARCTIC OCEAN

ARCTIC CIRCLE

60°N

Europe
75
78
77

EUROPE

ASIA

Asia
54
58
63

30°N

TROPIC OF CANCER

0 miles 2000
0 kilometers 3000

Winkel Tripel Projection

Australia & Oceania
30

Africa
44 44
62

AFRICA

0°

60°E

90°E

EQUATOR

150°E

60
70

0°

INDIAN
OCEAN

AUSTRALIA

TROPIC OF CAPRICORN

30°S

Overall Globalization Index

Scale from 0–100

- 81–100 (Most globalized)
- 61–80
- 41–60
- 21–40
- 0–20 (Least globalized)
- No data

Overall globalization is the combination of a country's economic, political, and social globalization.

ANTARCTIC CIRCLE

ANTARCTICA

THE GLOBAL ECONOMY

Transnational companies, some wealthier than small countries, exercise great influence in the world economy. Global 500 ranks the world's largest corporations based on annual revenues. Leading all others is retail giant Walmart, based in Bentonville, Arkansas, U.S.A.

Number of Global 500 Companies, 2017

United States	China	Japan	France	Germany	United Kingdom
132	109	51	29	29	21

◖ OLD MEETS NEW as a young Chinese woman uses a cell phone to take a photo of herself in traditional clothing and perhaps share it with others on social media. China's people use more than 1.3 billion cell phones.

Cultural Diffusion

In the past, when groups of people lived in relative isolation, cultures varied widely from place to place. Customs, styles, and preferences were handed down from one generation to the next.

Today, as a result of globalization, cultures all around the world are encountering and adopting new ideas. New customs, clothing and music trends, food habits, and life-styles are being introduced into cultures everywhere at almost the same time. Some people are concerned that this trend may result in a loss of cultural distinctiveness that makes places unique. For example, fast-food chains once found only in the United States can now be seen in major cities around the world. And denim jeans, once a distinctively American clothing style, are worn by young people everywhere in place of more traditional clothing.

An important key to the spread, or diffusion, of popular culture is the increasing contact between people and places around the world. Cellular phones, digital television, social media, and cybercafes have introduced styles and trends popular in local markets to people and places all around the world. And tourists, traveling to places once considered remote and isolated, carry with them ideas and fashions that are catalysts for two-way cultural exchange.

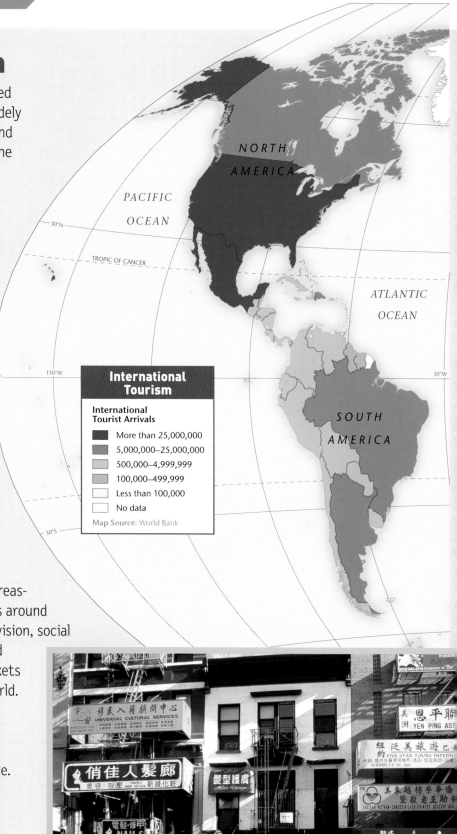

International Tourism

International Tourist Arrivals

- More than 25,000,000
- 5,000,000–25,000,000
- 500,000–4,999,999
- 100,000–499,999
- Less than 100,000
- No data

Map Source: World Bank

◗ **THE INFLUENCE OF IMMIGRANT CULTURES** on the American cultural landscape is evident in ethnic communities such as Chinatown in the heart of New York City, U.S.A.

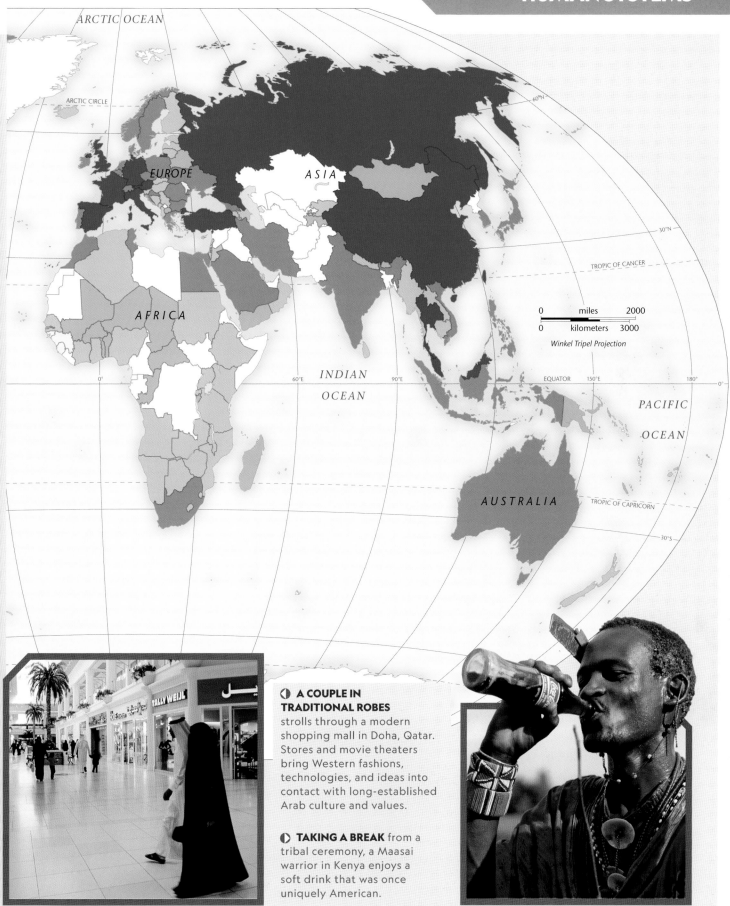

ARCTIC OCEAN

ARCTIC CIRCLE

EUROPE

ASIA

60°N

30°N

TROPIC OF CANCER

AFRICA

0° 60°E INDIAN 90°E
OCEAN

EQUATOR 150°E 180° 0°

PACIFIC

OCEAN

0 miles 2000
0 kilometers 3000
Winkel Tripel Projection

AUSTRALIA TROPIC OF CAPRICORN

30°S

◖ **A COUPLE IN TRADITIONAL ROBES** strolls through a modern shopping mall in Doha, Qatar. Stores and movie theaters bring Western fashions, technologies, and ideas into contact with long-established Arab culture and values.

◖ **TAKING A BREAK** from a tribal ceremony, a Maasai warrior in Kenya enjoys a soft drink that was once uniquely American.

North America:
A View From Space

Viewed from space, North America stretches from the frozen expanses of the Arctic Ocean and Greenland to the lush green of Panama's tropical forests. Hudson Bay and the Great Lakes, fingerprints of long-departed glaciers, dominate the continent's east, while the brown landscapes of the west and southwest tell of dry lands where water is scarce.

North America

PHYSICAL

Land area 9,449,000 sq mi (24,474,000 sq km)	**Lowest point** Death Valley, California, U.S.A. -282 ft (-86 m)	**Largest lake** Lake Superior, U.S.-Canada 31,700 sq mi (82,100 sq km)
Highest point Denali (Mt. McKinley), Alaska, U.S.A. 20,310 ft (6,190 m)	**Longest river** Mississippi-Missouri, United States 3,710 mi (5,970 km)	

POLITICAL

Population 569,914,000	**Largest country** Canada 3,855,101 sq mi (9,984,670 sq km)	**Most populous country** United States Pop. 326,626,000
Number of independent countries 23	**Smallest country** St. Kitts and Nevis 101 sq mi (261 sq km)	**Least populous country** St. Kitts and Nevis Pop. 53,000

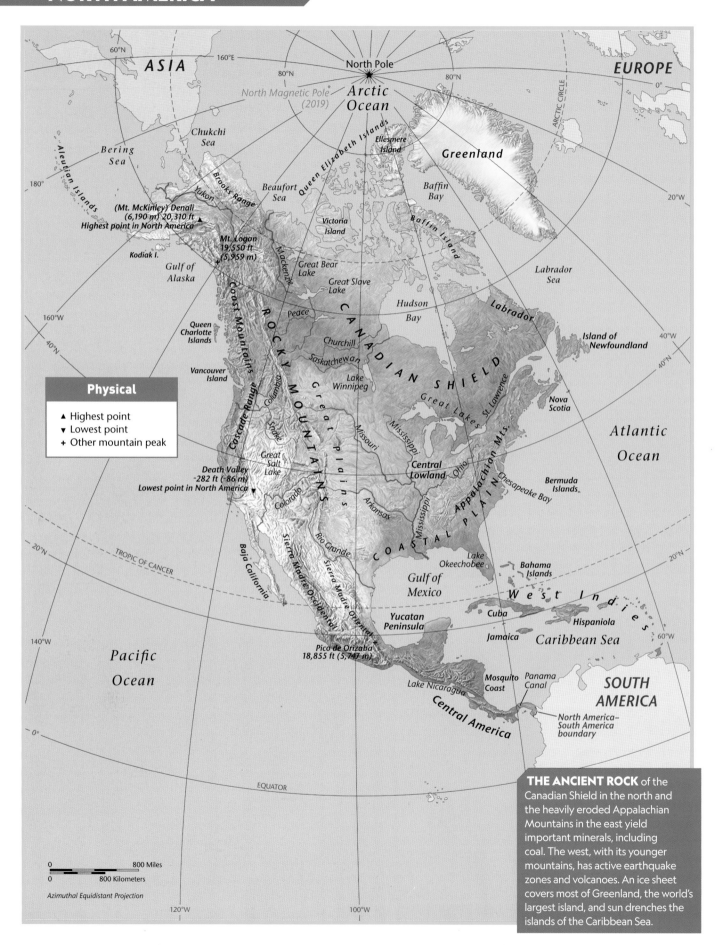

ASIA

160°E

North Pole

EUROPE

80°N

0°

Arctic
Ocean

North Magnetic Pole
(2019)

80°N

ARCTIC CIRCLE

Chukchi
Sea

Ellesmere
Island

Greenland

20°W

Bering
Sea

Beaufort
Sea

Queen Elizabeth Islands

Baffin
Bay

180°

Aleutian Islands

Brooks Range

Victoria
Island

Baffin Island

(Mt. McKinley) Denali
(6,190 m) 20,310 ft ▲
Highest point in North America

Yukon

Mackenzie

Great Bear
Lake

Labrador
Sea

Mt. Logan
19,550 ft
+ (5,959 m)

Great Slave
Lake

20°W

Kodiak I.

Gulf of
Alaska

Great Bear
Lake

Hudson
Bay

Labrador

Island of
Newfoundland

40°W

160°W

Peace

CANADIAN SHIELD

40°N

Queen
Charlotte
Islands

Coast Mountains

ROCKY MOUNTAINS

Churchill

Saskatchewan

40°N

Vancouver
Island

Great Plains

Lake
Winnipeg

Great Lakes

St. Lawrence

Nova
Scotia

Physical

▲ Highest point
▼ Lowest point
+ Other mountain peak

Cascade Range

Columbia

Snake

Mississippi

Ohio

Appalachian Mts.

Chesapeake Bay

Atlantic
Ocean

Death Valley
-282 ft (-86 m)
Lowest point in North America ▼

Great
Salt
Lake

Missouri

Central
Lowland

Bermuda
Islands

Colorado

Arkansas

Mississippi

COASTAL PLAIN

20°N

140°W

TROPIC OF CANCER

Baja California

Rio Grande

Sierra Madre Occidental

Lake
Okeechobee

Bahama
Islands

West Indies

20°N

60°W

Sierra Madre Oriental

Yucatan
Peninsula

Gulf of
Mexico

Cuba

Hispaniola

Pico de Orizaba
18,855 ft (5,747 m)

Jamaica

Caribbean Sea

Pacific
Ocean

Lake Nicaragua

Mosquito
Coast

Panama
Canal

SOUTH
AMERICA

North America–
South America
boundary

0°

Central America

EQUATOR

0

800 Miles

0

800 Kilometers

Azimuthal Equidistant Projection

120°W

100°W

THE ANCIENT ROCK of the
Canadian Shield in the north and
the heavily eroded Appalachian
Mountains in the east yield
important minerals, including
coal. The west, with its younger
mountains, has active earthquake
zones and volcanoes. An ice sheet
covers most of Greenland, the world's
largest island, and sun drenches the
islands of the Caribbean Sea.

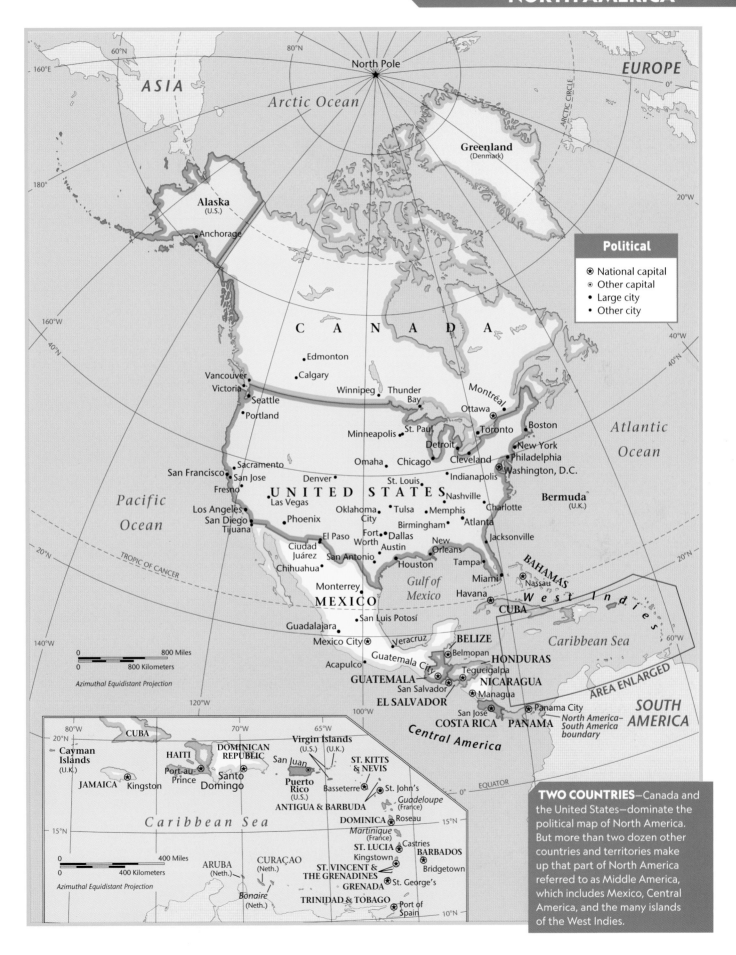

Political

⊗ National capital
⊙ Other capital
• Large city
• Other city

ASIA

Arctic Ocean

North Pole

EUROPE

Greenland
(Denmark)

ARCTIC CIRCLE

Alaska
(U.S.)

•Anchorage

C A N A D A

•Edmonton
•Calgary

Vancouver•
Victoria•
Seattle•
•Portland

Winnipeg• Thunder
Bay

Montréal
Ottawa⊙
Toronto• Boston

Atlantic
Ocean

Minneapolis•
St. Paul⊙
Detroit•
Cleveland•
New York
Philadelphia

Omaha• Chicago•
Indianapolis•
Washington, D.C.⊗

Sacramento⊙
San Francisco•
San Jose•
Fresno•

Denver•
U N I T E D   S T A T E S
St. Louis•
Nashville•
Charlotte•

Bermuda
(U.K.)

Pacific
Ocean

Las Vegas•
Los Angeles•
San Diego•
Tijuana•

Oklahoma
City•
Phoenix•

Tulsa• Memphis•
Birmingham•
Atlanta•

El Paso•
Fort
Worth•
Dallas•
Austin•

New
Orleans•
Jacksonville•

Ciudad
Juárez•
San Antonio•

TROPIC OF CANCER

Chihuahua•

Houston•
Tampa•
Miami•

BAHAMAS
•Nassau

West Indies

Monterrey•
Gulf of
Mexico
Havana⊗

M E X I C O
•San Luis Potosí
CUBA

Guadalajara•
Caribbean Sea

Mexico City⊗ Veracruz• BELIZE
Acapulco• Guatemala City Belmopan⊙ HONDURAS
GUATEMALA Tegucigalpa⊗ NICARAGUA
San Salvador⊗ Managua⊗
EL SALVADOR
San José⊗ Panama City⊗
COSTA RICA PANAMA
Central America
North America–
South America
boundary

SOUTH
AMERICA

AREA ENLARGED

0 800 Miles
0 800 Kilometers
Azimuthal Equidistant Projection

80°W
CUBA
Cayman
Islands
(U.K.)
HAITI
DOMINICAN
REPUBLIC
Virgin Islands
(U.S.) (U.K.)
ST. KITTS
& NEVIS
Port-au-
Prince⊙ Santo
Domingo⊗
San Juan⊙
Puerto
Rico
(U.S.)
Basseterre⊗
St. John's⊗
Guadeloupe
(France)

JAMAICA Kingston⊗
ANTIGUA & BARBUDA
DOMINICA •Roseau
Martinique
(France)
ST. LUCIA Castries⊗
BARBADOS
Caribbean Sea
Kingstown⊗
ST. VINCENT &
THE GRENADINES
⊗Bridgetown
ARUBA CURAÇAO
(Neth.) (Neth.)
GRENADA •St. George's
Bonaire
(Neth.)
TRINIDAD & TOBAGO
Port of
Spain⊗

0 400 Miles
0 400 Kilometers
Azimuthal Equidistant Projection

EQUATOR

TWO COUNTRIES—Canada and the United States—dominate the political map of North America. But more than two dozen other countries and territories make up that part of North America referred to as Middle America, which includes Mexico, Central America, and the many islands of the West Indies.

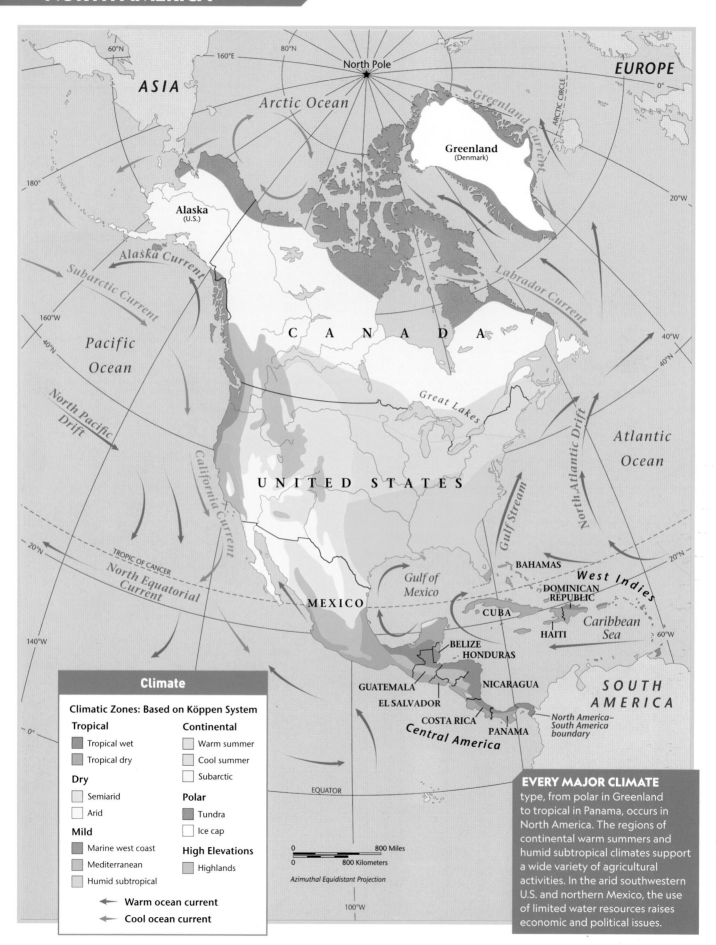

ASIA

Arctic Ocean

North Pole

EUROPE

Greenland
(Denmark)

ARCTIC CIRCLE

Greenland Current

Alaska
(U.S.)

Subarctic Current

Alaska Current

Labrador Current

Pacific
Ocean

North Pacific
Drift

C A N A D A

Great Lakes

Atlantic
Ocean

North Atlantic Drift

California Current

UNITED STATES

TROPIC OF CANCER

North Equatorial
Current

MEXICO

Gulf of
Mexico

CUBA

Gulf Stream

BAHAMAS

West Indies

DOMINICAN
REPUBLIC

HAITI

Caribbean
Sea

BELIZE
HONDURAS

GUATEMALA
EL SALVADOR

NICARAGUA

COSTA RICA

PANAMA

Central America

SOUTH
AMERICA

North America–
South America
boundary

EQUATOR

Climate

Climatic Zones: Based on Köppen System

Tropical
- Tropical wet
- Tropical dry

Dry
- Semiarid
- Arid

Mild
- Marine west coast
- Mediterranean
- Humid subtropical

Continental
- Warm summer
- Cool summer
- Subarctic

Polar
- Tundra
- Ice cap

High Elevations
- Highlands

← Warm ocean current
← Cool ocean current

0   800 Miles
0   800 Kilometers

Azimuthal Equidistant Projection

EVERY MAJOR CLIMATE
type, from polar in Greenland
to tropical in Panama, occurs in
North America. The regions of
continental warm summers and
humid subtropical climates support
a wide variety of agricultural
activities. In the arid southwestern
U.S. and northern Mexico, the use
of limited water resources raises
economic and political issues.

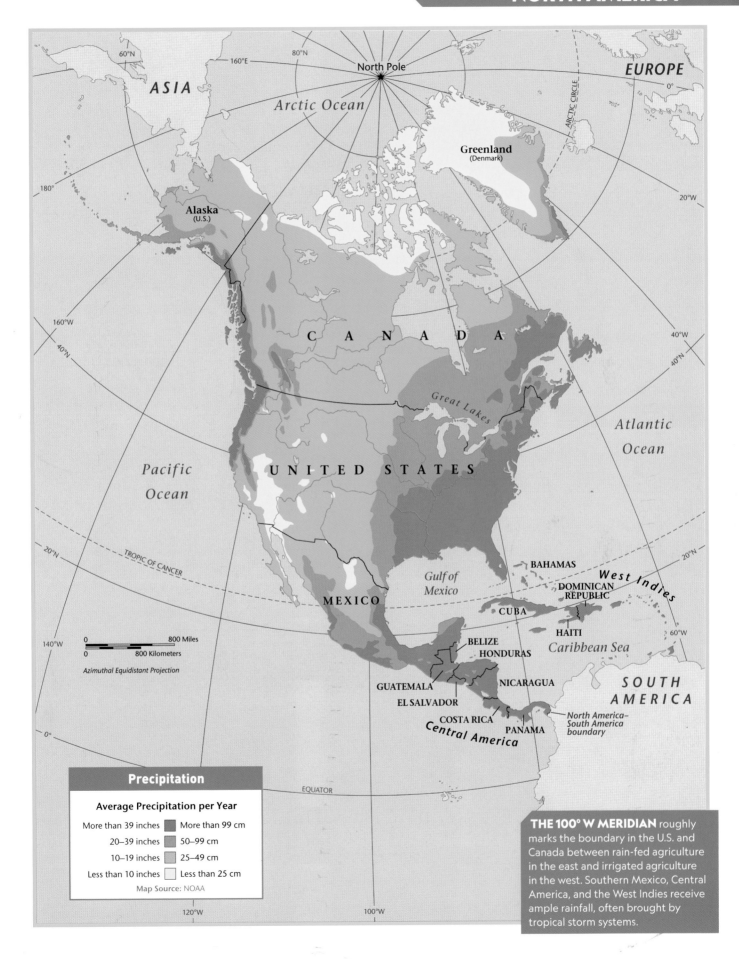

ASIA

60°N
160°E
80°N
North Pole
Arctic Ocean

EUROPE
0°
20°W

Greenland
(Denmark)

180°

ARCTIC CIRCLE

Alaska
(U.S.)

C A N A D A

40°W
40°N

160°W

40°N

Pacific
Ocean

Great Lakes

Atlantic
Ocean

U N I T E D   S T A T E S

20°N

TROPIC OF CANCER

BAHAMAS
West Indies

Gulf of
Mexico

DOMINICAN
REPUBLIC

20°N

140°W

MEXICO

CUBA

HAITI

60°W

0   800 Miles
0   800 Kilometers

BELIZE
HONDURAS

Caribbean Sea

Azimuthal Equidistant Projection

GUATEMALA

NICARAGUA

SOUTH
AMERICA

EL SALVADOR

0°

COSTA RICA

PANAMA

North America–
South America
boundary

Central America

EQUATOR

Precipitation

Average Precipitation per Year

More than 39 inches ▓ More than 99 cm
20–39 inches ▓ 50–99 cm
10–19 inches ▓ 25–49 cm
Less than 10 inches ▢ Less than 25 cm

Map Source: NOAA

120°W

100°W

THE 100° W MERIDIAN roughly
marks the boundary in the U.S. and
Canada between rain-fed agriculture
in the east and irrigated agriculture
in the west. Southern Mexico, Central
America, and the West Indies receive
ample rainfall, often brought by
tropical storm systems.

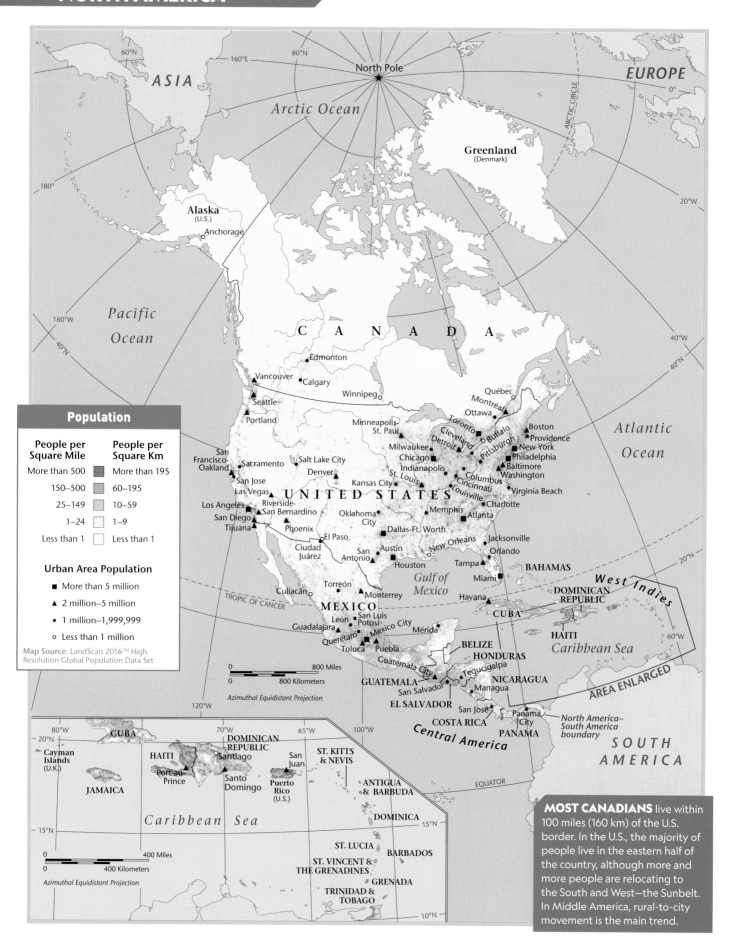

Population

People per Square Mile / **People per Square Km**

People per Square Mile	People per Square Km
More than 500	More than 195
150–500	60–195
25–149	10–59
1–24	1–9
Less than 1	Less than 1

Urban Area Population

- ■ More than 5 million
- ▲ 2 million–5 million
- ● 1 million–1,999,999
- ○ Less than 1 million

Map Source: LandScan 2016™ High Resolution Global Population Data Set

ASIA

EUROPE

North Pole

Arctic Ocean

Greenland
(Denmark)

Alaska
(U.S.)
Anchorage

Pacific Ocean

C A N A D A

Atlantic Ocean

Edmonton
Vancouver Calgary
Seattle Winnipeg
Portland

Québec
Montréal
Ottawa
Toronto
Minneapolis-St. Paul
Cleveland Buffalo Boston
Milwaukee Detroit Pittsburgh Providence
Chicago New York
Salt Lake City Indianapolis Columbus Philadelphia
Denver St. Louis Cincinnati Baltimore
Kansas City Louisville Washington
San Francisco-Oakland Sacramento
San Jose
Las Vegas U N I T E D   S T A T E S Virginia Beach
Los Angeles Riverside-San Bernardino Charlotte
San Diego Oklahoma City Memphis Atlanta
Tijuana Phoenix
El Paso Dallas-Ft. Worth New Orleans Jacksonville
Ciudad Juárez San Antonio Austin Orlando
Houston Tampa Miami BAHAMAS

Culiacán Torreón Monterrey Gulf of Mexico Havana DOMINICAN REPUBLIC

West Indies

TROPIC OF CANCER

MEXICO CUBA HAITI Caribbean Sea
León San Luis Potosí Mérida
Guadalajara Mexico City
Querétaro Puebla BELIZE
Toluca HONDURAS
Guatemala City Tegucigalpa NICARAGUA
GUATEMALA Managua
San Salvador
EL SALVADOR San José
COSTA RICA Panama City North America–South America boundary
PANAMA

AREA ENLARGED

Central America

SOUTH AMERICA

0   800 Miles
0   800 Kilometers
Azimuthal Equidistant Projection

Inset map (Caribbean):

CUBA
Cayman Islands (U.K.)
JAMAICA
HAITI DOMINICAN REPUBLIC Santiago
Port-au-Prince Santo Domingo San Juan Puerto Rico (U.S.)
ST. KITTS & NEVIS
ANTIGUA & BARBUDA
Caribbean Sea
DOMINICA
ST. LUCIA BARBADOS
ST. VINCENT & THE GRENADINES GRENADA
TRINIDAD & TOBAGO

0   400 Miles
0   400 Kilometers
Azimuthal Equidistant Projection

EQUATOR

MOST CANADIANS live within 100 miles (160 km) of the U.S. border. In the U.S., the majority of people live in the eastern half of the country, although more and more people are relocating to the South and West—the Sunbelt. In Middle America, rural-to-city movement is the main trend.

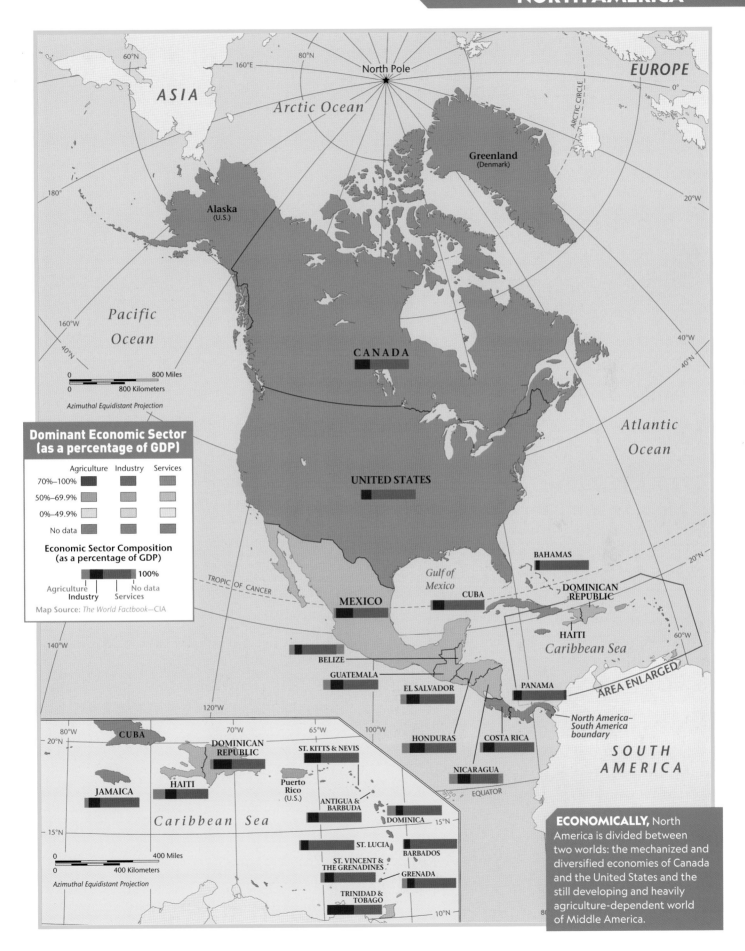

ASIA

Arctic Ocean

North Pole

EUROPE

ARCTIC CIRCLE

Greenland
(Denmark)

Alaska
(U.S.)

Pacific
Ocean

CANADA

0   800 Miles
0   800 Kilometers
Azimuthal Equidistant Projection

Atlantic
Ocean

**Dominant Economic Sector
(as a percentage of GDP)**

	Agriculture	Industry	Services
70%–100%			
50%–69.9%			
0%–49.9%			
No data			

**Economic Sector Composition
(as a percentage of GDP)**

100%

Agriculture   No data
Industry   Services

Map Source: *The World Factbook—CIA*

UNITED STATES

TROPIC OF CANCER

BAHAMAS

Gulf of
Mexico

CUBA

DOMINICAN
REPUBLIC

MEXICO

HAITI

Caribbean Sea

AREA ENLARGED

BELIZE

GUATEMALA

EL SALVADOR

PANAMA

North America–
South America
boundary

HONDURAS

COSTA RICA

SOUTH
AMERICA

NICARAGUA

EQUATOR

CUBA

DOMINICAN
REPUBLIC

ST. KITTS & NEVIS

JAMAICA

HAITI

Puerto
Rico
(U.S.)

ANTIGUA &
BARBUDA

Caribbean Sea

DOMINICA

0   400 Miles
0   400 Kilometers
Azimuthal Equidistant Projection

ST. LUCIA

BARBADOS

ST. VINCENT &
THE GRENADINES

GRENADA

TRINIDAD &
TOBAGO

ECONOMICALLY, North
America is divided between
two worlds: the mechanized and
diversified economies of Canada
and the United States and the
still developing and heavily
agriculture-dependent world
of Middle America.

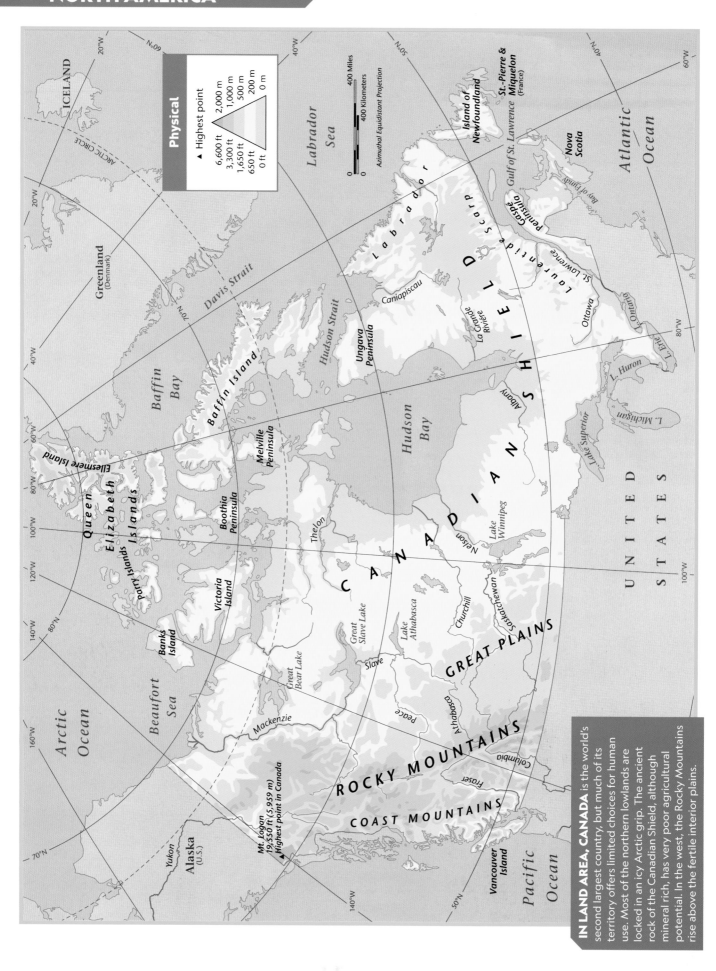

Physical

▲ Highest point

6,600 ft — 2,000 m
3,300 ft — 1,000 m
1,650 ft — 500 m
650 ft — 200 m
0 ft — 0 m

400 Miles
400 Kilometers

Azimuthal Equidistant Projection

ICELAND

ARCTIC CIRCLE

Greenland
(Denmark)

Davis Strait

Labrador
Sea

Island of
Newfoundland

St-Pierre &
Miquelon
(France)

Nova
Scotia

Atlantic
Ocean

Gulf of St. Lawrence

Bay of Fundy

Gaspé
Peninsula

Laurentide Escarpment

St. Lawrence

Labrador

Caniapiscau

La Grande
Rivière

Ottawa

L. Ontario

Baffin
Bay

Baffin Island

Hudson Strait

Ungava
Peninsula

C A N A D I A N   S H I E L D

L. Erie

L. Huron

L. Michigan

Lake Superior

Queen
Elizabeth
Islands

Ellesmere Island

Melville
Peninsula

Boothia
Peninsula

Thelon

Hudson
Bay

Albany

Nelson

Lake
Winnipeg

U N I T E D

S T A T E S

Parry Islands

Victoria
Island

Banks
Island

Great
Bear Lake

Great
Slave Lake

Slave

Lake
Athabasca

Churchill

Saskatchewan

G R E A T   P L A I N S

Beaufort
Sea

Mackenzie

Peace

Athabasca

Columbia

R O C K Y   M O U N T A I N S

Fraser

Arctic
Ocean

Mt. Logan
19,550 ft (5,959 m)
Highest point in Canada

Alaska
(U.S.)

Yukon

C O A S T   M O U N T A I N S

Vancouver
Island

Pacific
Ocean

IN LAND AREA, CANADA is the world's second largest country, but much of its territory offers limited choices for human use. Most of the northern lowlands are locked in an icy Arctic grip. The ancient rock of the Canadian Shield, although mineral rich, has very poor agricultural potential. In the west, the Rocky Mountains rise above the fertile interior plains.

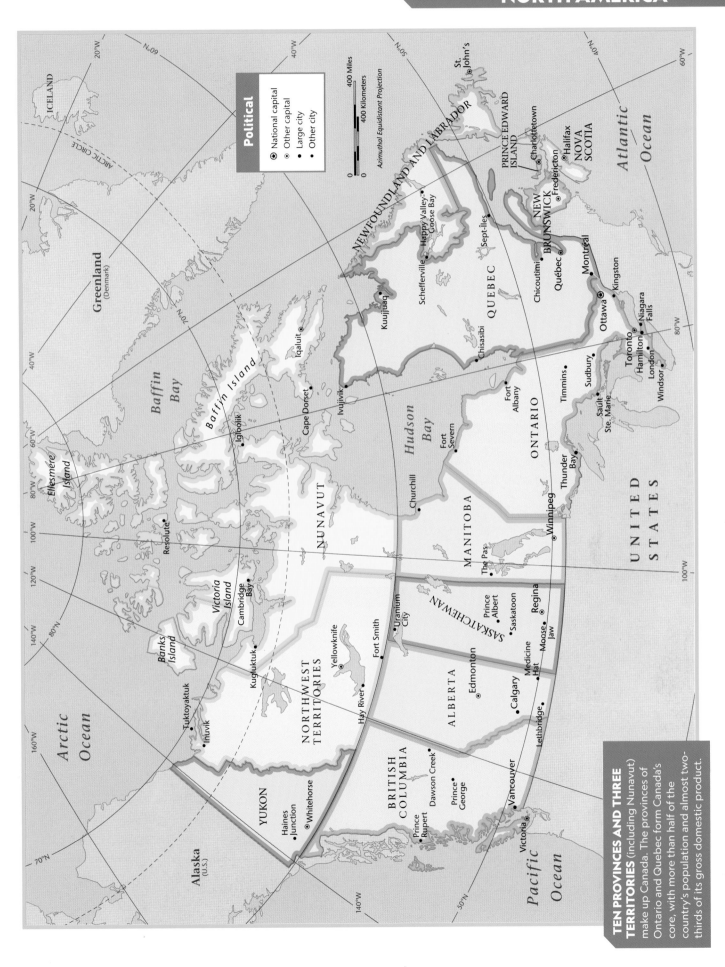

Political

⊛ National capital
◉ Other capital
• Large city
• Other city

400 Miles
400 Kilometers

Azimuthal Equidistant Projection

ICELAND

Greenland
(Denmark)

ARCTIC CIRCLE

Baffin
Bay

Ellesmere
Island

Baffin Island

Resolute

Igloolik

Cape Dorset

Iqaluit

Victoria
Island

Cambridge
Bay

Banks
Island

Kugluktuk

Tuktoyaktuk
Inuvik

Arctic
Ocean

Alaska
(U.S.)

YUKON

Haines
Junction
⊙ Whitehorse

BRITISH
COLUMBIA

Prince
Rupert
Dawson Creek
Prince
George

Victoria
Vancouver

Pacific
Ocean

NORTHWEST
TERRITORIES

Yellowknife ⊙

Hay River
Fort Smith

ALBERTA

Edmonton ◉

Calgary
Medicine
Hat
Lethbridge

NUNAVUT

Uranium
City

SASKATCHEWAN

Prince
Albert
Saskatoon
Regina ◉
Moose
Jaw

MANITOBA

The Pas

Winnipeg ◉

Churchill

Hudson
Bay

Fort
Severn

Fort
Albany

ONTARIO

Timmins

Sudbury

Thunder
Bay

Sault
Ste. Marie

Ivujivik

Kuujjuaq

NEWFOUNDLAND AND LABRADOR

Schefferville

Happy Valley-
Goose Bay

Sept-Îles

QUEBEC

Chisasibi

Chicoutimi

Québec ◉
Montréal

Ottawa ⊛

Kingston

Toronto
Hamilton
London
Windsor

Niagara
Falls

St.
John's

PRINCE EDWARD
ISLAND
Charlottetown

NEW
BRUNSWICK

Fredericton ◉

Halifax
NOVA
SCOTIA

Atlantic
Ocean

UNITED
STATES

**TEN PROVINCES AND THREE
TERRITORIES** (including Nunavut)
make up Canada. The provinces of
Ontario and Quebec form Canada's
core, with more than half of the
country's population and almost two-
thirds of its gross domestic product.

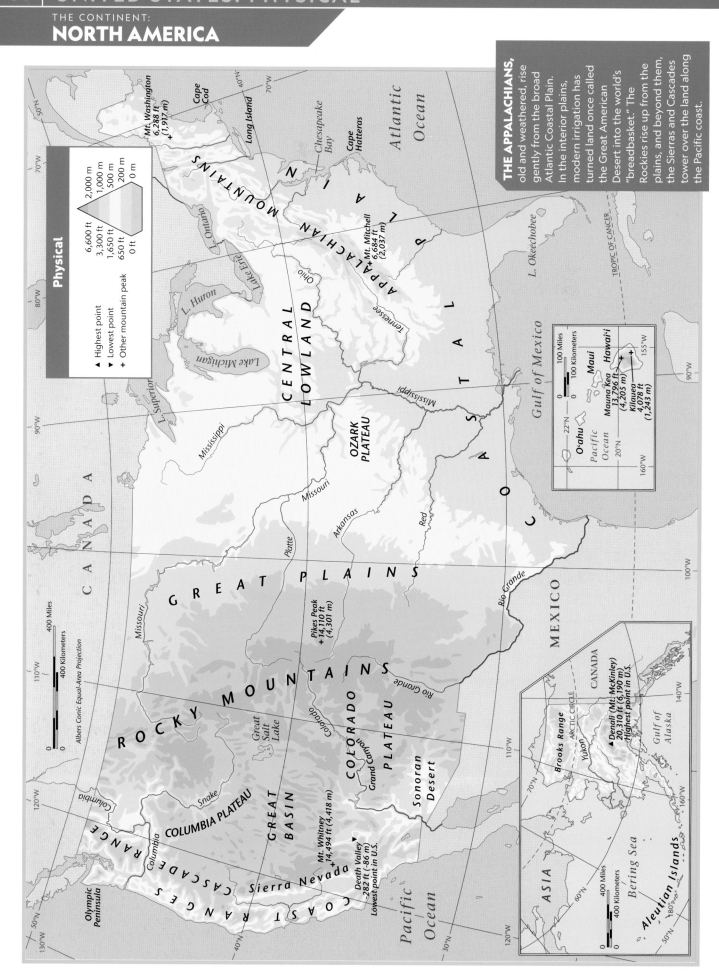

THE APPALACHIANS, old and weathered, rise gently from the broad Atlantic Coastal Plain. In the interior plains, modern irrigation has turned land once called the Great American Desert into the world's "breadbasket." The Rockies rise up from the plains, and beyond them, the Sierras and Cascades tower over the land along the Pacific coast.

Physical

2,000 m
1,000 m
500 m
200 m
0 m

6,600 ft
3,300 ft
1,650 ft
650 ft
0 ft

▲ Highest point
▼ Lowest point
+ Other mountain peak

Mt. Washington
6,288 ft
(1,917 m)
+

Cape Cod

Long Island

Chesapeake Bay

Cape Hatteras

Atlantic Ocean

CANADA

APPALACHIAN MOUNTAINS

L. Ontario

Lake Erie

L. Huron

Lake Michigan

L. Superior

CENTRAL LOWLAND

Ohio

Tennessee

Mt. Mitchell
+ 6,684 ft
(2,037 m)

COASTAL PLAIN

Mississippi

Mississippi

OZARK PLATEAU

Missouri

Arkansas

Red

L. Okeechobee

Gulf of Mexico

TROPIC OF CANCER

100 Miles
100 Kilometers

Maui

Hawai'i

O'ahu

Pacific Ocean

22°N

20°N

Mauna Kea
13,796 ft
(4,205 m)
+

Kilauea
4,078 ft
(1,243 m)
+

160°W

155°W

GREAT PLAINS

Pikes Peak
+ 14,110 ft
(4,301 m)

Platte

ROCKY MOUNTAINS

Great Salt Lake

Colorado

Colorado

COLORADO PLATEAU

Grand Canyon

Rio Grande

Rio Grande

MEXICO

Snake

GREAT BASIN

COLUMBIA PLATEAU

Mt. Whitney
+ 14,494 ft (4,418 m)

Death Valley
282 ft (-86 m)
Lowest point in U.S.
▼

Sonoran Desert

100°W

110°W

Columbia

Columbia

CASCADE RANGE

COAST RANGES

Sierra Nevada

Olympic Peninsula

Pacific Ocean

130°W

120°W

40°N

30°N

400 Miles
400 Kilometers

Albers Conic Equal-Area Projection

110°W

90°W

80°W

70°W

70°N

60°N

50°N

40°N

70°W

60°W

50°N

CANADA

ASIA

Brooks Range

ARCTIC CIRCLE

Yukon

▲ Denali (Mt. McKinley)
20,310 ft (6,190 m)
Highest point in U.S.

Gulf of Alaska

Bering Sea

Aleutian Islands

70°N

60°N

50°N

170°W

160°W

150°W

140°W

180°

400 Miles
400 Kilometers

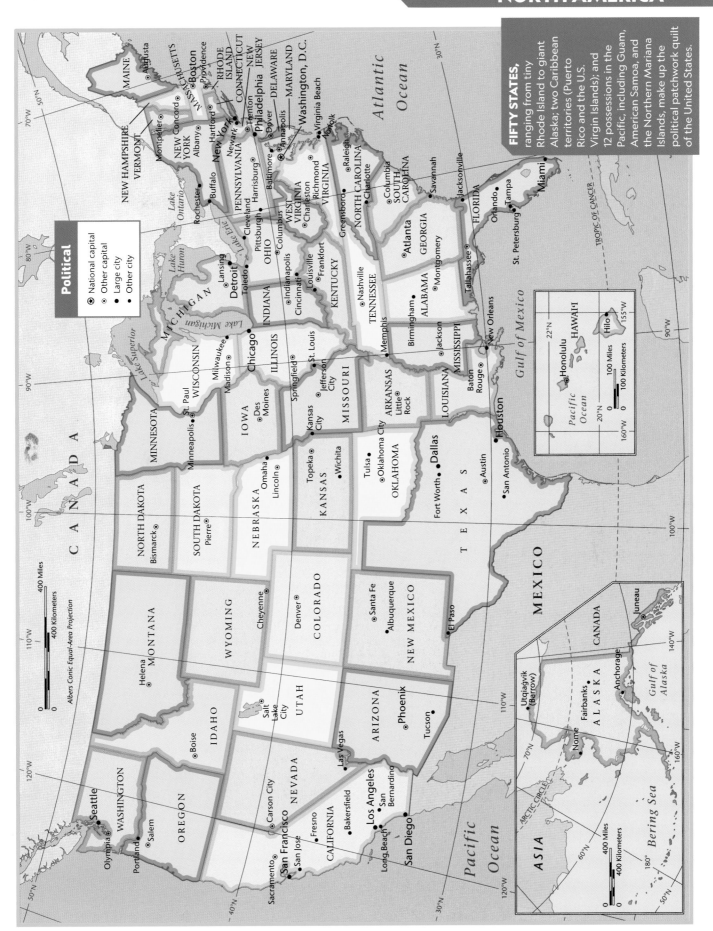

FIFTY STATES, ranging from tiny Rhode Island to giant Alaska; two Caribbean territories (Puerto Rico and the U.S. Virgin Islands); and 12 possessions in the Pacific, including Guam, American Samoa, and the Northern Mariana Islands, make up the political patchwork quilt of the United States.

Political
⊛ National capital
⊙ Other capital
● Large city
• Other city

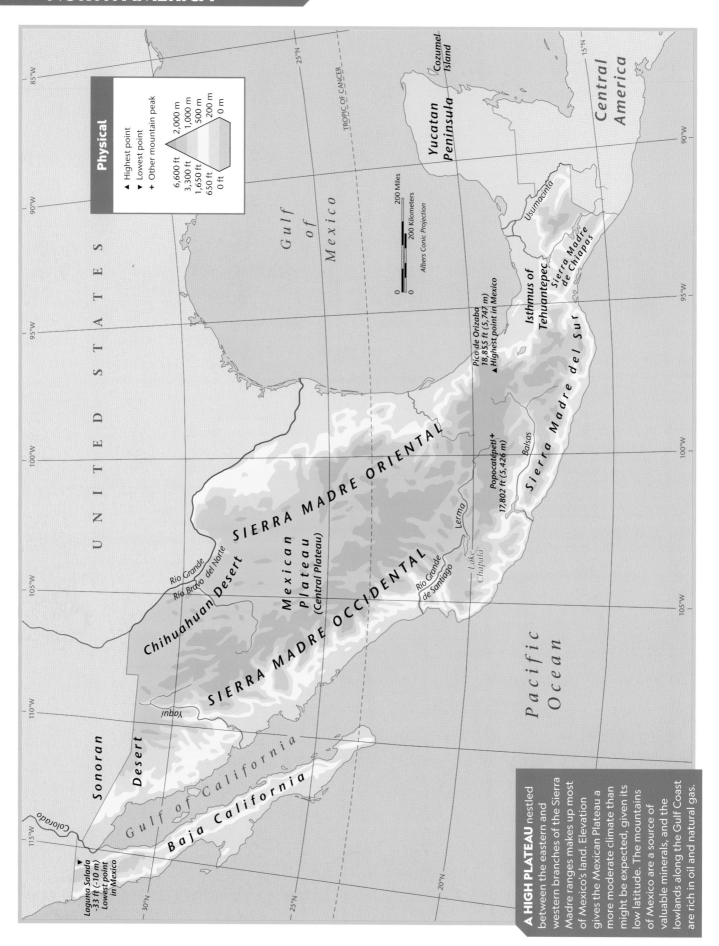

Physical

▲ Highest point
▼ Lowest point
+ Other mountain peak

6,600 ft — 2,000 m
3,300 ft — 1,000 m
1,650 ft — 500 m
650 ft — 200 m
0 ft — 0 m

UNITED STATES

Gulf of Mexico

TROPIC OF CANCER

Cozumel Island

Yucatan Peninsula

Central America

200 Miles
200 Kilometers
Albers Conic Projection

Usumacinta

Sierra Madre de Chiapas

Isthmus of Tehuantepec

Pico de Orizaba 18,855 ft (5,747 m) ▲ Highest point in Mexico

SIERRA MADRE ORIENTAL

Rio Grande
Rio Bravo del Norte

Chihuahuan Desert

Mexican Plateau (Central Plateau)

SIERRA MADRE OCCIDENTAL

Lerma

Rio Grande de Santiago

Lake Chapala

Popocatépetl + 17,802 ft (5,426 m)

Balsas

Sierra Madre del Sur

Pacific Ocean

Yaqui

Sonoran Desert

Gulf of California

Baja California

Colorado

▼ Laguna Salada -33 ft (-10 m) Lowest point in Mexico

A HIGH PLATEAU nestled between the eastern and western branches of the Sierra Madre ranges makes up most of Mexico's land. Elevation gives the Mexican Plateau a more moderate climate than might be expected, given its low latitude. The mountains of Mexico are a source of valuable minerals, and the lowlands along the Gulf Coast are rich in oil and natural gas.

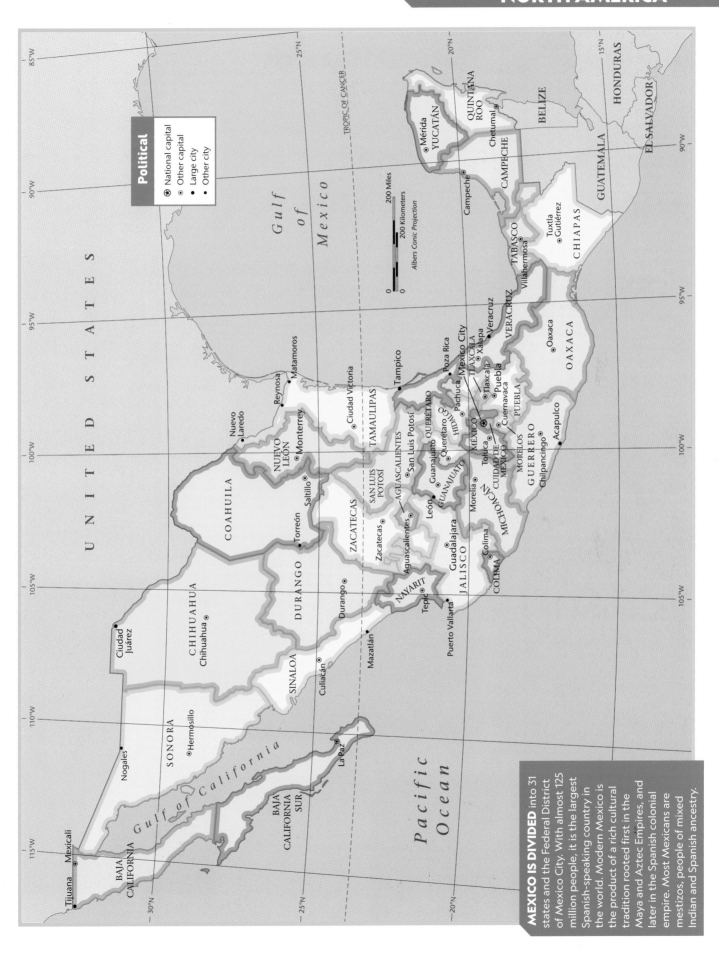

Political

- ⊛ National capital
- ⊙ Other capital
- ● Large city
- ○ Other city

200 Miles

200 Kilometers

Albers Conic Projection

UNITED STATES

Gulf of Mexico

Pacific Ocean

Gulf of California

TROPIC OF CANCER

BAJA CALIFORNIA

BAJA CALIFORNIA SUR

SONORA

CHIHUAHUA

COAHUILA

DURANGO

SINALOA

NAYARIT

ZACATECAS

SAN LUIS POTOSÍ

AGUASCALIENTES

JALISCO

COLIMA

MICHOACÁN

GUANAJUATO

QUERÉTARO

HIDALGO

MÉXICO

CUIDAD DE MÉXICO

MORELOS

TLAXCALA

PUEBLA

GUERRERO

OAXACA

VERACRUZ

TAMAULIPAS

NUEVO LEÓN

TABASCO

CHIAPAS

CAMPECHE

YUCATÁN

QUINTANA ROO

GUATEMALA

BELIZE

HONDURAS

EL SALVADOR

Tijuana
Mexicali
Nogales
Ciudad Juárez
Hermosillo
Chihuahua
La Paz
Culiacán
Mazatlán
Torreón
Saltillo
Durango
Zacatecas
Aguascalientes
Tepic
Puerto Vallarta
Guadalajara
Colima
León
Guanajuato
Morelia
San Luis Potosí
Querétaro
Toluca
Pachuca
Cuernavaca
Chilpancingo
Acapulco
MÉXICO
Tlaxcala
Puebla
Xalapa
Veracruz
Poza Rica
Oaxaca
Tampico
Ciudad Victoria
Matamoros
Reynosa
Monterrey
Nuevo Laredo
Mexico City
Tuxtla Gutiérrez
Villahermosa
Campeche
Mérida
Chetumal

MEXICO IS DIVIDED into 31 states and the Federal District of Mexico City. With almost 125 million people, it is the largest Spanish-speaking country in the world. Modern Mexico is the product of a rich cultural tradition rooted first in the Maya and Aztec Empires, and later in the Spanish colonial empire. Most Mexicans are mestizos, people of mixed Indian and Spanish ancestry.

NATURAL HAZARDS: SELECTED STATISTICS

HURRICANES
This list names North America's eight most intense hurricanes (based on barometric pressure at landfall) since 1960. Average sea-level pressure is 1,013.25 millibars (mbr), or 29.92 inches.

Year	Name	Pressure
1969	Camille	909 mbr/26.84 in
2017	Irma	914 mbr/26.99 in
2017	Maria	917 mbr/27.08 in
2018	Michael	919 mbr/27.14 in
2005	Katrina	920 mbr/27.17 in
1992	Andrew	922 mbr/27.23 in
1960	Donna	930 mbr/27.46 in
1961	Carla	930 mbr/27.46 in

TORNADOES
The following states had the highest average annual number of tornadoes from 1991 to 2015.

Texas: 147	Illinois: 54
Kansas: 92	Colorado: 50
Oklahoma: 65	Iowa: 49
Florida: 55	Alabama: 47
Nebraska: 55	Missouri: 47

EARTHQUAKES
This list shows the number of earthquakes in North America since 1900 that had a magnitude of 8.0 or greater on the Richter scale.

Alaska (U.S.): 6	
Mexico: 4	
British Columbia (Canada): 1	
Dominican Republic: 1 (see inset map p. 57)	

VOLCANOES
This list shows major volcanic eruptions in North America since 1980.

Mount St. Helens (WA): 1980–ongoing	
El Chichon (Mexico): 1982	
Augustine (AK): 1986	
Redoubt (AK): 1989–1990	
Spurr (AK): 1992	
Okmok (AK): 2008	
Kasatochi (AK): 2008	

Natural Hazards

The forces of nature inspire awe. They can also bring damage and destruction, especially when people locate homes and businesses in places that are at risk of experiencing violent storms, earthquakes, volcanoes, floods, wildfires, or other natural hazards. Tornadoes—violent, swirling storms with winds that can exceed 200 miles an hour (320 km/h)—strike the U.S. on average more than 1,000 times each year. Hurricanes, massive low-pressure storms that form over warm ocean waters, bring destructive winds and rain primarily to the Gulf of Mexico and the southeastern mainland. Melting spring snows and heavy rains trigger flooding; periods of drought make other regions vulnerable to wildfires. When natural hazards take human lives and destroy property, they become natural disasters.

◐ VOLCANOES. From deep inside Earth, molten rock, called magma, rises and breaks through the surface, sometimes quietly, but more often violently, shooting billowing ash clouds, as shown here at Mount St. Helens, in Washington State.

◐ WILDFIRES. Putting lives and property at great risk, wildfires destroy millions of acres (ha) of forest each year. At the same time, fires help renew ecosystems by removing debris and encouraging seedling growth.

◐ FLOODS. In August, 2017, Hurricane Harvey brought torrential rains to southeast Texas, resulting in widespread flooding in Houston and surrounding communities. Some people had to resort to boats to escape the floodwaters.

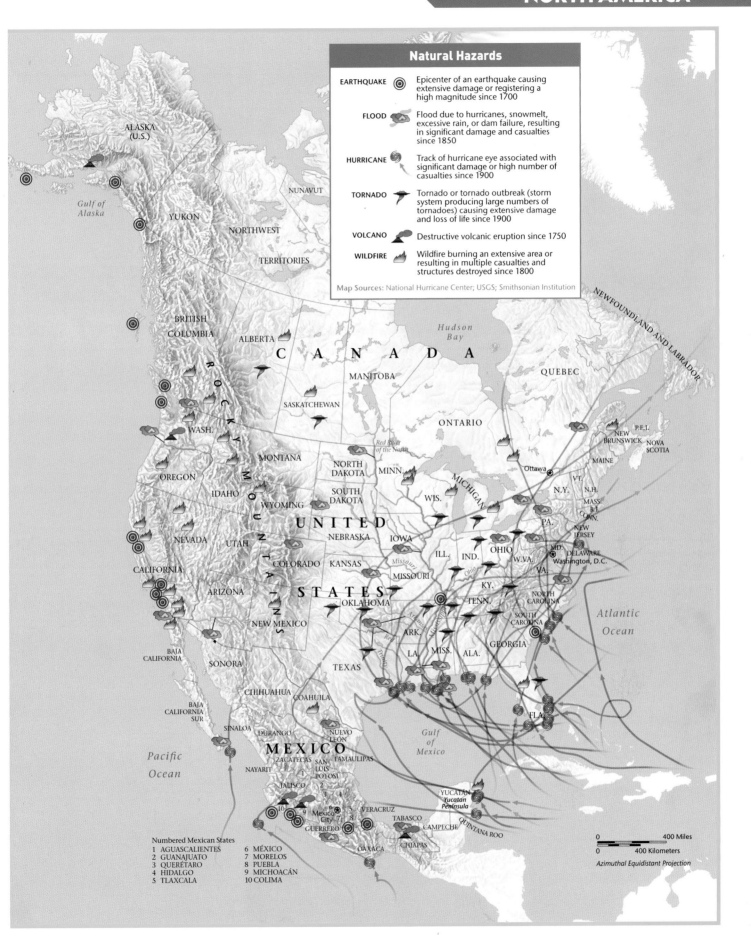

Natural Hazards

EARTHQUAKE — Epicenter of an earthquake causing extensive damage or registering a high magnitude since 1700

FLOOD — Flood due to hurricanes, snowmelt, excessive rain, or dam failure, resulting in significant damage and casualties since 1850

HURRICANE — Track of hurricane eye associated with significant damage or high number of casualties since 1900

TORNADO — Tornado or tornado outbreak (storm system producing large numbers of tornadoes) causing extensive damage and loss of life since 1900

VOLCANO — Destructive volcanic eruption since 1750

WILDFIRE — Wildfire burning an extensive area or resulting in multiple casualties and structures destroyed since 1800

Map Sources: National Hurricane Center; USGS; Smithsonian Institution

ALASKA (U.S.)

Gulf of Alaska

YUKON

NORTHWEST

TERRITORIES

NUNAVUT

BRITISH COLUMBIA

ALBERTA

CANADA

MANITOBA

SASKATCHEWAN

Hudson Bay

QUEBEC

NEWFOUNDLAND AND LABRADOR

WASH.

ROCKY MOUNTAINS

MONTANA

NORTH DAKOTA

MINN.

ONTARIO

Red River of the North

Ottawa

P.E.I.

NEW BRUNSWICK

NOVA SCOTIA

MAINE

OREGON

IDAHO

WYOMING

SOUTH DAKOTA

WIS.

MICHIGAN

VT.

N.H.

MASS.

R.I.

CONN.

N.Y.

PA.

NEW JERSEY

NEVADA

UTAH

NEBRASKA

IOWA

ILL.

IND.

OHIO

Ohio

W.VA.

MD.

DELAWARE

Washington, D.C.

CALIFORNIA

COLORADO

KANSAS

MISSOURI

Missouri

KY.

VA.

UNITED STATES

ARIZONA

NEW MEXICO

OKLAHOMA

TENN.

NORTH CAROLINA

SOUTH CAROLINA

Atlantic Ocean

BAJA CALIFORNIA

SONORA

TEXAS

Red

Arkansas

Mississippi

ARK.

LA.

MISS.

ALA.

GEORGIA

BAJA CALIFORNIA SUR

CHIHUAHUA

COAHUILA

Trinity

FLA.

Pacific Ocean

SINALOA

DURANGO

NUEVO LEÓN

TAMAULIPAS

Gulf of Mexico

ZACATECAS

NAYARIT

SAN LUIS POTOSÍ

1

MEXICO

JALISCO

2

3

4

5

YUCATÁN

Yucatán Peninsula

10

9

6

Mexico City

VERACRUZ

7

8

TABASCO

CAMPECHE

QUINTANA ROO

GUERRERO

OAXACA

CHIAPAS

Numbered Mexican States
1 AGUASCALIENTES
2 GUANAJUATO
3 QUERÉTARO
4 HIDALGO
5 TLAXCALA

6 MÉXICO
7 MORELOS
8 PUEBLA
9 MICHOACÁN
10 COLIMA

0   400 Miles
0   400 Kilometers

Azimuthal Equidistant Projection

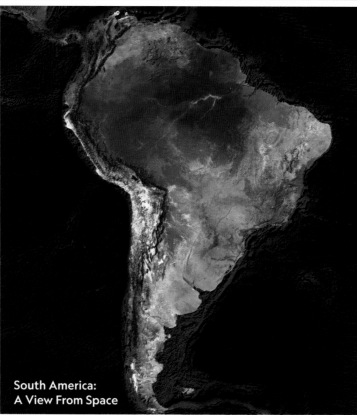

South America:
A View From Space

From the towering, snowcapped Andes in the west to the steamy rain forest of the Amazon Basin in the north, and from the fertile grasslands of the Pampas to the arid Atacama Desert along the Pacific coast, South America is a continent of extremes. North to south, the continent extends from the tropical waters of the Caribbean Sea to the wind-swept islands of Tierra del Fuego. Its longest river, the Amazon, carries more water than any other river in the world.

Snow- and ice-covered Mount Fitzroy rises above Los Glaciares National Park in Patagonia, Argentina.

South America

PHYSICAL

Land area
6,880,000 sq mi
(17,819,000 sq km)

Highest point
Cerro Aconcagua,
Argentina
22,831 ft (6,959 m)

Lowest point
Laguna del Carbón,
Argentina
-344 ft (-105 m)

Longest river
Amazon
4,150 mi (6,679 km)

Largest lake
Lake Titicaca,
Bolivia-Peru
3,200 sq mi
(8,288 sq km)

POLITICAL

Population
423,750,000

**Number of
independent
countries**
12

Largest country
Brazil
3,287,956 sq mi (8,515,770 sq km)

Smallest country
Suriname
63,251 sq mi (163,820 sq km)

Most populous country
Brazil
Pop. 207,353,000

Least populous country
Suriname
Pop. 592,000

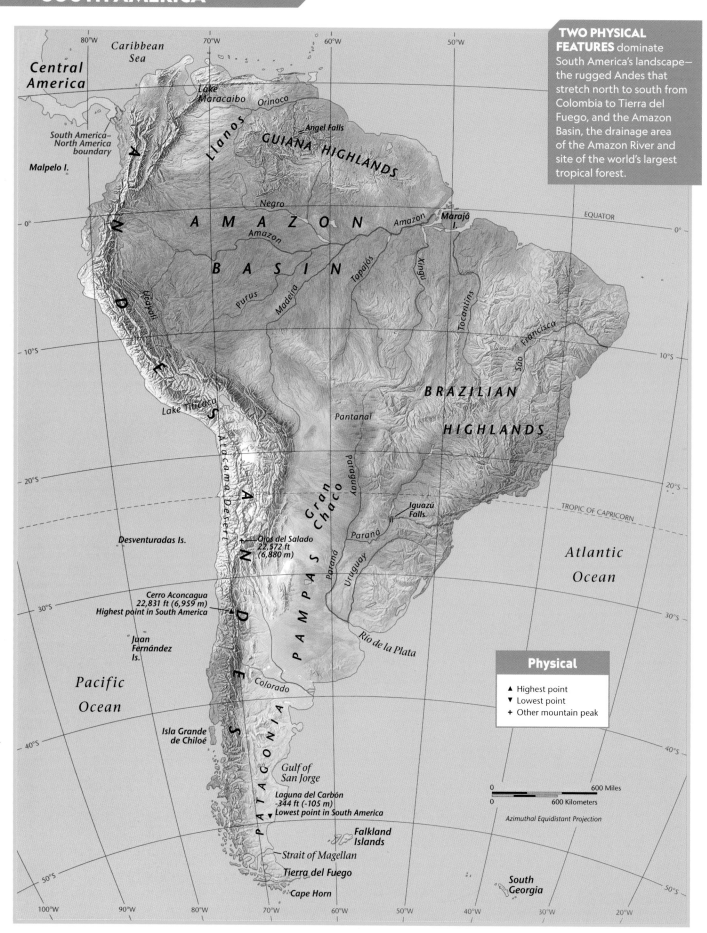

80°W   70°W   60°W   50°W

Caribbean
Sea

Central
America

Lake
Maracaibo   Orinoco

South America–
North America
boundary

Malpelo I.

Llanos

GUIANA HIGHLANDS

Angel Falls

Negro   Amazon   Marajó I.   EQUATOR

0°   A M A Z O N   Amazon   0°

Amazon

B A S I N

Ucayali   Purus   Madeira   Topajós   Xingu   Tocantins

São Francisco

10°S   BRAZILIAN   10°S

Lake Titicaca

Pantanal   HIGHLANDS

Atacama Desert

20°S   Gran Chaco   Paraguay   20°S

TROPIC OF CAPRICORN

Desventuradas Is.

Iguazú
Falls

Ojos del Salado
22,572 ft
(6,880 m)   Paraná

Atlantic
Ocean

PAMPAS

Cerro Aconcagua
22,831 ft (6,959 m)
Highest point in South America   Uruguay

30°S   Río de la Plata   30°S

Juan
Fernández
Is.

Pacific
Ocean   Colorado

Physical

▲ Highest point
▼ Lowest point
+ Other mountain peak

Isla Grande
de Chiloé

40°S   40°S

Gulf of
San Jorge

Laguna del Carbón
-344 ft (-105 m)
Lowest point in South America

0   600 Miles

0   600 Kilometers

Azimuthal Equidistant Projection

Falkland
Islands

Strait of Magellan

Tierra del Fuego   South
Georgia

50°S   Cape Horn   50°S

100°W   90°W   80°W   70°W   60°W   50°W   40°W   30°W   20°W

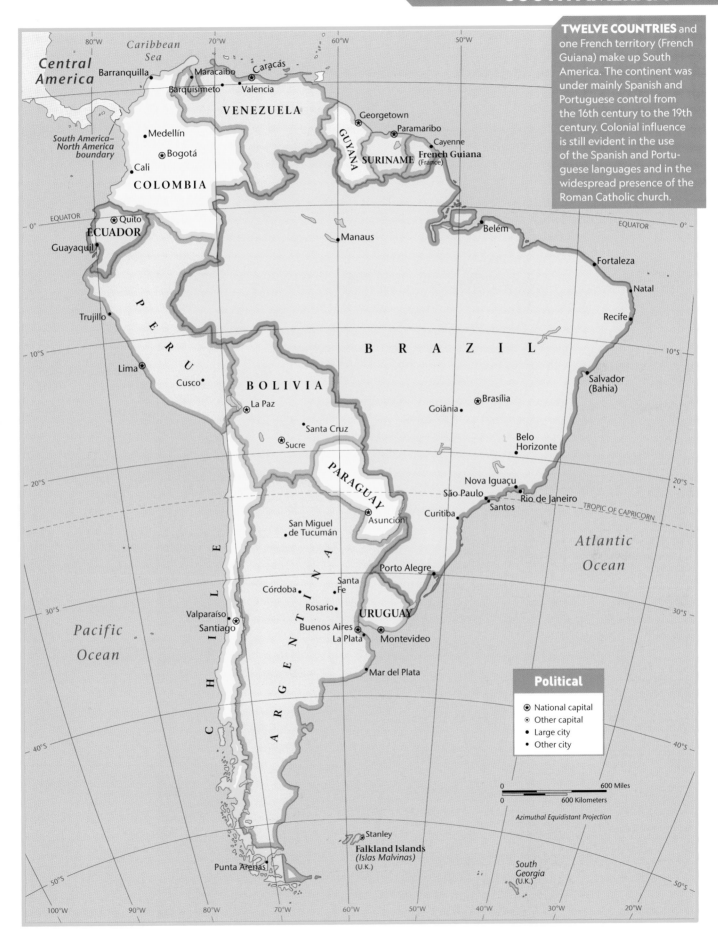

TWELVE COUNTRIES and one French territory (French Guiana) make up South America. The continent was under mainly Spanish and Portuguese control from the 16th century to the 19th century. Colonial influence is still evident in the use of the Spanish and Portuguese languages and in the widespread presence of the Roman Catholic church.

Caribbean Sea

Central America

Barranquilla

Maracaibo
Caracás
Valencia
Barquisimeto

VENEZUELA

Medellín

South America–North America boundary

Bogotá

Cali

COLOMBIA

Georgetown
Paramaribo
Cayenne

GUYANA
SURINAME
French Guiana
(France)

EQUATOR   0°

Quito

ECUADOR

Guayaquil

Manaus

Belém

EQUATOR   0°

Fortaleza

Natal

P E R U

Trujillo

Recife

B R A Z I L

10°S

Lima

Cusco

BOLIVIA

Salvador
(Bahia)

La Paz

Goiânia
Brasília

Santa Cruz

Sucre

Belo Horizonte

PARAGUAY

Nova Iguaçu
São Paulo
Rio de Janeiro
Santos

20°S

Asunción

Curitiba

TROPIC OF CAPRICORN

San Miguel de Tucumán

Atlantic Ocean

Porto Alegre

Pacific Ocean

Córdoba

Santa Fe

Rosario

A R G E N T I N A

URUGUAY

C H I L E

Valparaíso
Santiago

Buenos Aires
La Plata
Montevideo

30°S

Mar del Plata

Political

⊛ National capital
◉ Other capital
• Large city
• Other city

Stanley
Falkland Islands
(Islas Malvinas)
(U.K.)

South Georgia
(U.K.)

Punta Arenas

0   600 Miles
0   600 Kilometers

Azimuthal Equidistant Projection

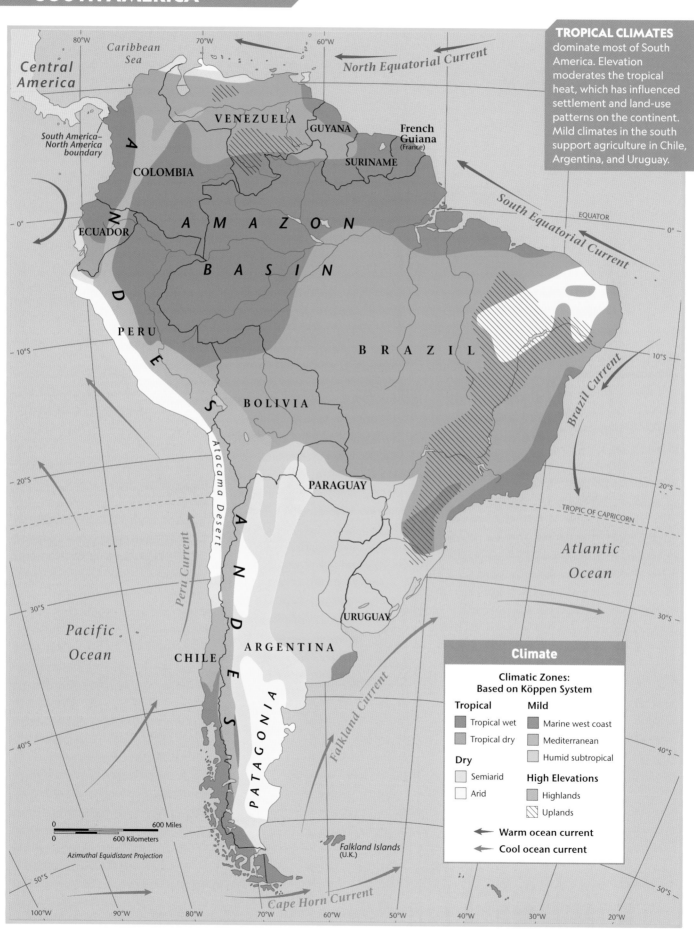

TROPICAL CLIMATES dominate most of South America. Elevation moderates the tropical heat, which has influenced settlement and land-use patterns on the continent. Mild climates in the south support agriculture in Chile, Argentina, and Uruguay.

Caribbean Sea

Central America

North Equatorial Current

VENEZUELA

GUYANA

French Guiana (France)

South America–North America boundary

COLOMBIA

SURINAME

South Equatorial Current

EQUATOR

ECUADOR

A M A Z O N

B A S I N

A N D E S

PERU

BRAZIL

Brazil Current

BOLIVIA

PARAGUAY

TROPIC OF CAPRICORN

Atlantic Ocean

Atacama Desert

Peru Current

Pacific Ocean

URUGUAY

ARGENTINA

CHILE

Falkland Current

P A T A G O N I A

0   600 Miles
0   600 Kilometers

Azimuthal Equidistant Projection

Falkland Islands (U.K.)

Cape Horn Current

Climate

**Climatic Zones:
Based on Köppen System**

Tropical
- Tropical wet
- Tropical dry

Dry
- Semiarid
- Arid

Mild
- Marine west coast
- Mediterranean
- Humid subtropical

High Elevations
- Highlands
- Uplands

← Warm ocean current
← Cool ocean current

WARM AIR RISING rapidly over the Equator triggers daily rainfall, which supports the rain forest vegetation of the Amazon Basin. In contrast, the combined effects of rain shadow and cold ocean currents along the western coast create the Atacama Desert, parts of which have never recorded rainfall.

Central America

Caribbean Sea

VENEZUELA

South America–North America boundary

GUYANA

French Guiana (France)

SURINAME

COLOMBIA

A N D E S

EQUATOR

ECUADOR

A M A Z O N

B A S I N

PERU

BRAZIL

BOLIVIA

Arica, Chile Driest place in the world

Atacama Desert

PARAGUAY

TROPIC OF CAPRICORN

CHILE

Atlantic Ocean

A N D E S

URUGUAY

Pacific Ocean

ARGENTINA

PATAGONIA

0   600 Miles
0   600 Kilometers

Azimuthal Equidistant Projection

Falkland Islands (U.K.)

Precipitation

Average Precipitation per Year

More than 39 inches	■	More than 99 cm	
20–39 inches	■	50–99 cm	
10–19 inches	■	25–49 cm	
Less than 10 inches	□	Less than 25 cm	

Map Source: NOAA

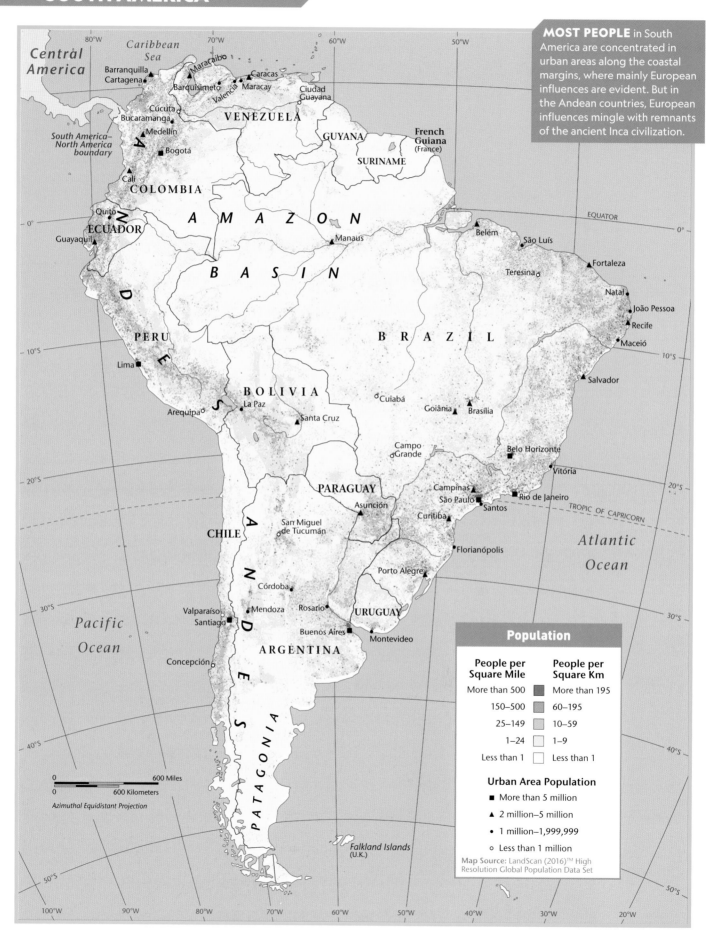

MOST PEOPLE in South America are concentrated in urban areas along the coastal margins, where mainly European influences are evident. But in the Andean countries, European influences mingle with remnants of the ancient Inca civilization.

Central America

Caribbean Sea

Barranquilla
Cartagena
Maracaibo
Caracas
Barquisimeto
Valencia
Maracay
Ciudad Guayana
Cúcuta
Bucaramanga
VENEZUELA
GUYANA
French Guiana (France)
SURINAME
Medellín
South America–North America boundary
Bogotá
Cali
COLOMBIA
EQUATOR
Quito
ECUADOR
Guayaquil
A M A Z O N
Belém
São Luís
Fortaleza
Teresina
Manaus
B A S I N
Natal
João Pessoa
Recife
PERU
B R A Z I L
Maceió
Lima
Salvador
BOLIVIA
Cuiabá
La Paz
Goiânia
Brasília
Arequipa
Santa Cruz
Campo Grande
Belo Horizonte
Vitória
PARAGUAY
Campinas
São Paulo
Rio de Janeiro
Asunción
Santos
Curitiba
San Miguel de Tucumán
CHILE
Florianópolis
Porto Alegre
Atlantic Ocean
Córdoba
Valparaíso
Mendoza
Rosario
URUGUAY
Santiago
Buenos Aires
Montevideo
Pacific Ocean
ARGENTINA
Concepción
A N D E S
P A T A G O N I A

0   600 Miles
0   600 Kilometers
Azimuthal Equidistant Projection

Falkland Islands (U.K.)

Population

People per Square Mile
More than 500
150–500
25–149
1–24
Less than 1

People per Square Km
More than 195
60–195
10–59
1–9
Less than 1

Urban Area Population
■ More than 5 million
▲ 2 million–5 million
• 1 million–1,999,999
○ Less than 1 million

Map Source: LandScan (2016)™ High Resolution Global Population Data Set

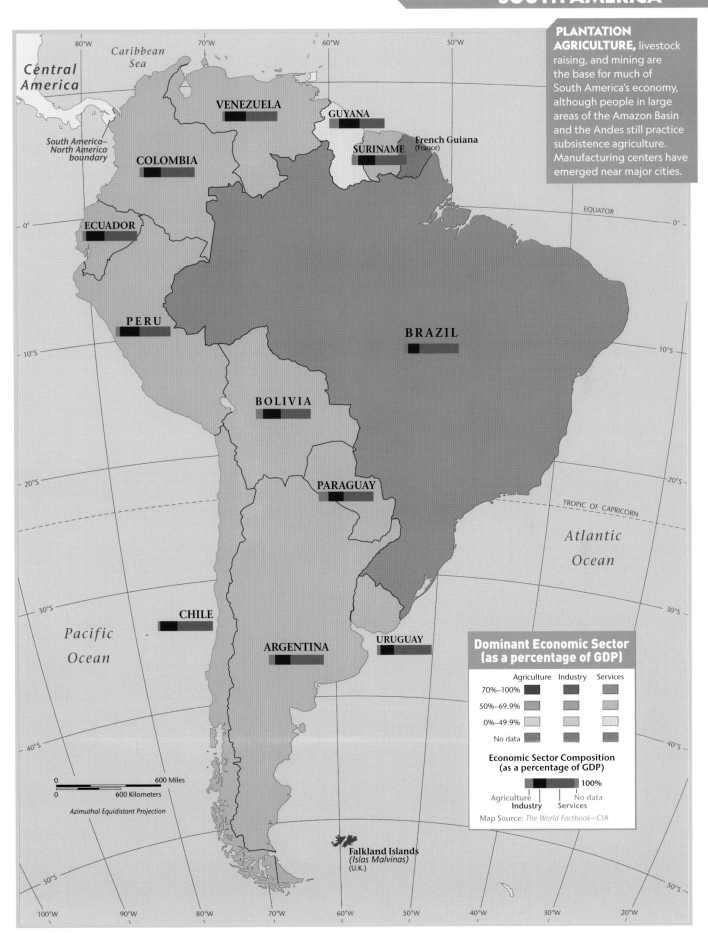

PLANTATION AGRICULTURE, livestock raising, and mining are the base for much of South America's economy, although people in large areas of the Amazon Basin and the Andes still practice subsistence agriculture. Manufacturing centers have emerged near major cities.

Caribbean Sea

Central America

Central America

South America–North America boundary

VENEZUELA

GUYANA

SURINAME

French Guiana (France)

COLOMBIA

EQUATOR

ECUADOR

PERU

BRAZIL

BOLIVIA

PARAGUAY

TROPIC OF CAPRICORN

Atlantic Ocean

CHILE

URUGUAY

Pacific Ocean

ARGENTINA

0   600 Miles
0   600 Kilometers

Azimuthal Equidistant Projection

Falkland Islands
(Islas Malvinas)
(U.K.)

**Dominant Economic Sector
(as a percentage of GDP)**

	Agriculture	Industry	Services
70%–100%			
50%–69.9%			
0%–49.9%			
No data			

**Economic Sector Composition
(as a percentage of GDP)**

100%

Agriculture   No data
Industry   Services

Map Source: *The World Factbook*—CIA

Amazon Rain Forest

The Amazon rain forest, which covers approximately 2.7 million square miles (7 million sq km), is the world's largest tropical forest. Located mainly in Brazil, the Amazon rain forest accounts for more than one-third of all the world's tropical forests. Known in Brazil as the selva, the rain forest is a vast storehouse of biological diversity, filled with plants and animals both familiar and exotic. According to estimates, at least half of all terrestrial species are found in tropical forests, but many of these species have not yet been identified.

Tropical forests contain many valuable resources, including cacao (chocolate), nuts, spices, rare hardwoods, and plant extracts used to make medicines. Some drugs used in treating cancer and heart disease come from plants found only in tropical forests. But human intervention—logging, mining, and clearing land for crops and grazing—has put tropical forests at great risk. In Brazil, roads cut into the rain forest have opened the way for settlers, who clear away the forest only to discover soil too poor in nutrients to sustain agriculture for more than a few years. Land usually is cleared by a method called slash-and-burn, which contributes to global warming by releasing great amounts of carbon dioxide into the atmosphere.

◍ **SLOW-MOVING,** this three-toed sloth spends most of its life in the treetops. It is one of the many unusual species of animals that make their home in the forests of the Amazon Basin.

◍ **THE DENSE CANOPY OF THE RAIN FOREST** stands in sharp contrast to the silt-laden waters of one of the Amazon's many tributaries. Although seemingly endless, the forest in Brazil is decreasing in size due to mining, farming, ranching, and logging.

◍ **SLASH-AND-BURN** is a method used in the tropics for clearing land for farms. But the soil is poor in nutrients, and good yields are short-lived.

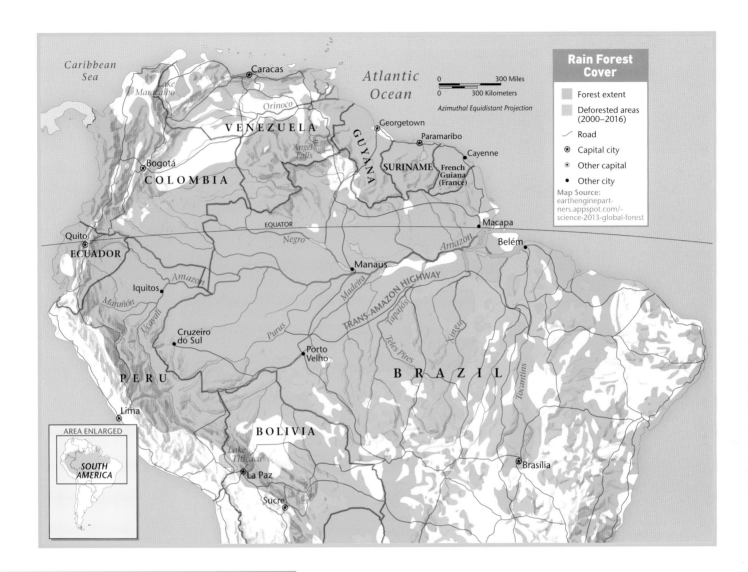

Rain Forest Cover

- Forest extent
- Deforested areas (2000–2016)
- Road
- ⊗ Capital city
- ⊙ Other capital
- • Other city

Map Source:
earthenginepartners.appspot.com/-science-2013-global-forest

0   300 Miles
0   300 Kilometers
Azimuthal Equidistant Projection

Caribbean Sea
Atlantic Ocean
Lake Maracaibo
Caracas
Orinoco
VENEZUELA
Georgetown
GUYANA
Paramaribo
Cayenne
SURINAME
French Guiana (France)
Angel Falls
Bogotá
COLOMBIA
EQUATOR
Macapa
Negro
Amazon
Belém
Quito
ECUADOR
Manaus
Amazon
Iquitos
Marañón
Madeira
TRANS-AMAZON HIGHWAY
Ucayali
Purus
Tapajós
Xingu
Cruzeiro do Sul
Teles Pires
Porto Velho
PERU
B R A Z I L
Tocantins
Lima
AREA ENLARGED
SOUTH AMERICA
BOLIVIA
Lake Titicaca
Brasília
La Paz
Sucre

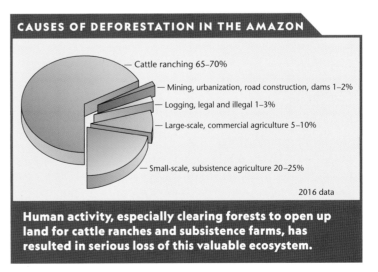

🌑 **MINING OPERATIONS,** such as this tin mine, remove forests to gain access to mineral deposits.

CAUSES OF DEFORESTATION IN THE AMAZON

- Cattle ranching 65–70%
- Mining, urbanization, road construction, dams 1–2%
- Logging, legal and illegal 1–3%
- Large-scale, commercial agriculture 5–10%
- Small-scale, subsistence agriculture 20–25%

2016 data

Human activity, especially clearing forests to open up land for cattle ranches and subsistence farms, has resulted in serious loss of this valuable ecosystem.

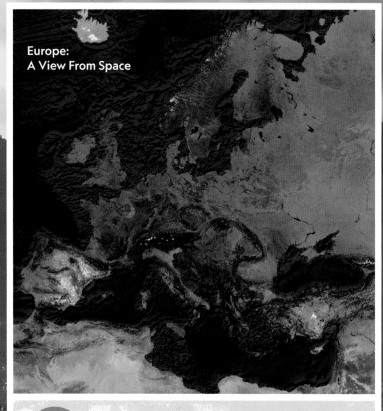

Europe:
A View From Space

Smaller than every other continent except Australia, Europe is a mosaic of islands and peninsulas. In fact, Europe itself is one big peninsula, jutting westward from the huge landmass of Asia and nearly touching Africa to the south. Europe's ragged coastline measures more than one and a half times the length of Earth's Equator and provides 32 of the continent's 46 countries direct access to the sea.

The Cathedral of Santa Maria del Fiore dominates the skyline of Florence, Italy.

Europe

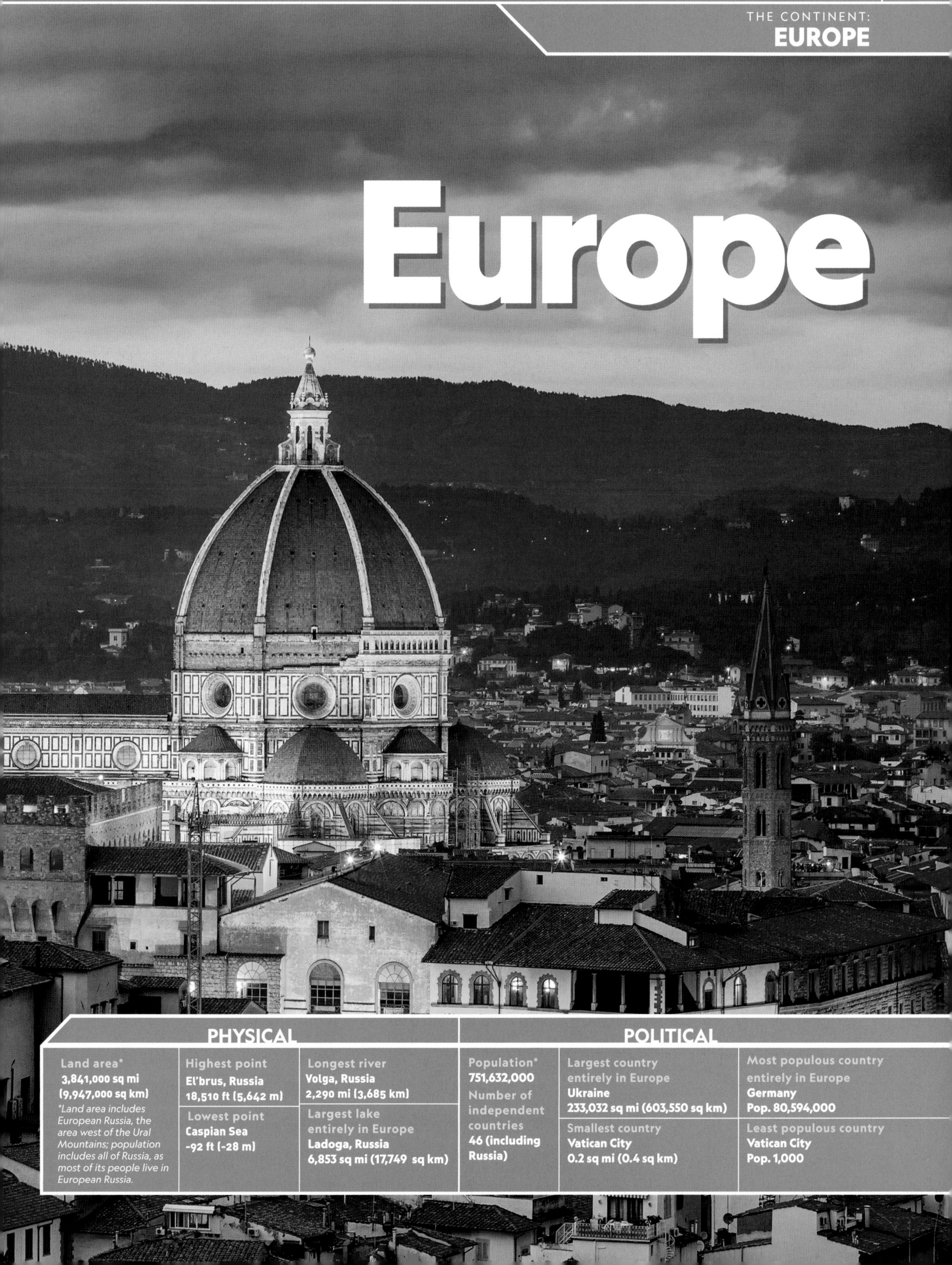

PHYSICAL

Land area*
3,841,000 sq mi
(9,947,000 sq km)

*Land area includes
European Russia, the
area west of the Ural
Mountains; population
includes all of Russia, as
most of its people live in
European Russia.

Highest point
El'brus, Russia
18,510 ft (5,642 m)

Lowest point
Caspian Sea
-92 ft (-28 m)

Longest river
Volga, Russia
2,290 mi (3,685 km)

**Largest lake
entirely in Europe**
Ladoga, Russia
6,853 sq mi (17,749 sq km)

POLITICAL

Population*
751,632,000

**Number of
independent
countries**
46 (including
Russia)

**Largest country
entirely in Europe**
Ukraine
233,032 sq mi (603,550 sq km)

Smallest country
Vatican City
0.2 sq mi (0.4 sq km)

**Most populous country
entirely in Europe**
Germany
Pop. 80,594,000

Least populous country
Vatican City
Pop. 1,000

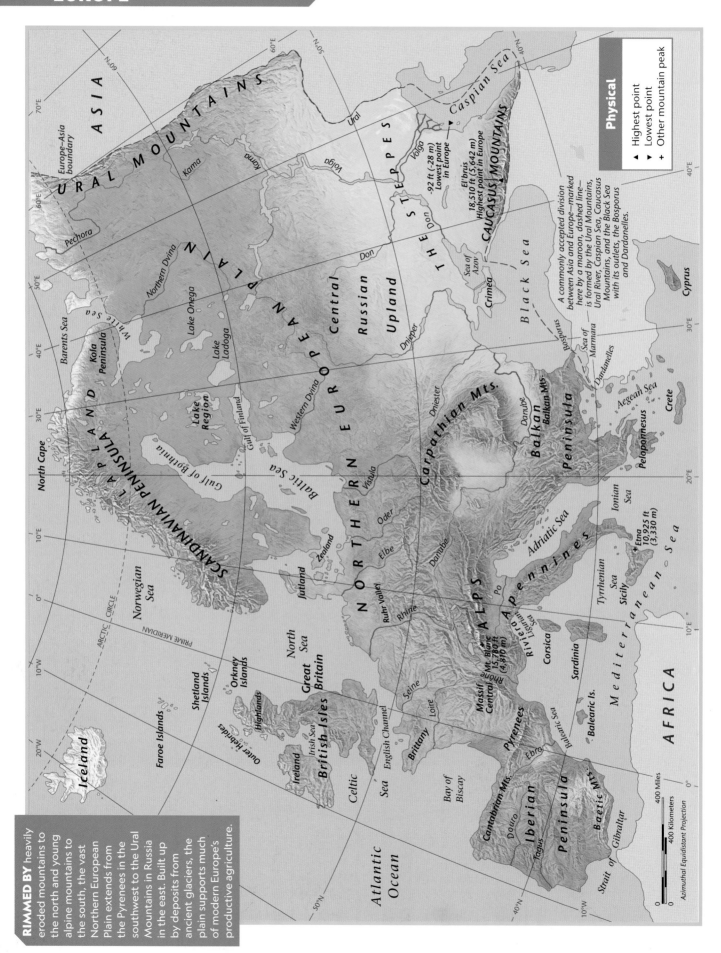

Physical

▲ Highest point
▼ Lowest point
+ Other mountain peak

ASIA

URAL MOUNTAINS

Europe-Asia boundary

Pechora

Kama

Kama

Ural

Volga

Volga

Caspian Sea

-92 ft (-28 m)
Lowest point in Europe

El'brus
18,510 ft (5,642 m)
Highest point in Europe

CAUCASUS MOUNTAINS

Don

Don

Sea of Azov

Crimea

Black Sea

Bosporus

Sea of Marmara

Dardanelles

A commonly accepted division between Asia and Europe—marked here by a maroon, dashed line—is formed by the Ural Mountains, Ural River, Caspian Sea, Caucasus Mountains, and the Black Sea with its outlets, the Bosporus and Dardanelles.

Cyprus

Barents Sea

Northern Dvina

Lake Onega

Lake Ladoga

Kola Peninsula

White Sea

Lake Region

Gulf of Finland

Western Dvina

NORTHERN EUROPEAN PLAIN

Central Russian Upland

THE STEPPES

Dnieper

Dniester

Danube

Carpathian Mts.

Balkan Mts.

Balkan Peninsula

Aegean Sea

Crete

Peloponnesus

SCANDINAVIAN PENINSULA

LAPLAND

North Cape

Gulf of Bothnia

Baltic Sea

Vistula

Oder

Elbe

Zealand

Jutland

Danube

Adriatic Sea

Ionian Sea

Etna
10,925 ft
(3,330 m)

Norwegian Sea

ARCTIC CIRCLE

PRIME MERIDIAN

North Sea

Ruhr Valley

Rhine

ALPS

Po

Apennines

Tyrrhenian Sea

Sicily

Mediterranean Sea

Faroe Islands

Shetland Islands

Orkney Islands

Highlands

Great Britain

British Isles

Outer Hebrides

Iceland

Ireland

Irish Sea

Celtic Sea

English Channel

Brittany

Seine

Loire

Bay of Biscay

Massif Central

Mt. Blanc
15,780 ft
(4,810 m)

Rhône

Riviera

Ligurian Sea

Corsica

Sardinia

Balearic Is.

Balearic Sea

AFRICA

Atlantic Ocean

Cantabrian Mts.

Douro

Tagus

Iberian Peninsula

Ebro

Pyrenees

Baetic Mts.

Strait of Gibraltar

400 Miles
400 Kilometers

Azimuthal Equidistant Projection

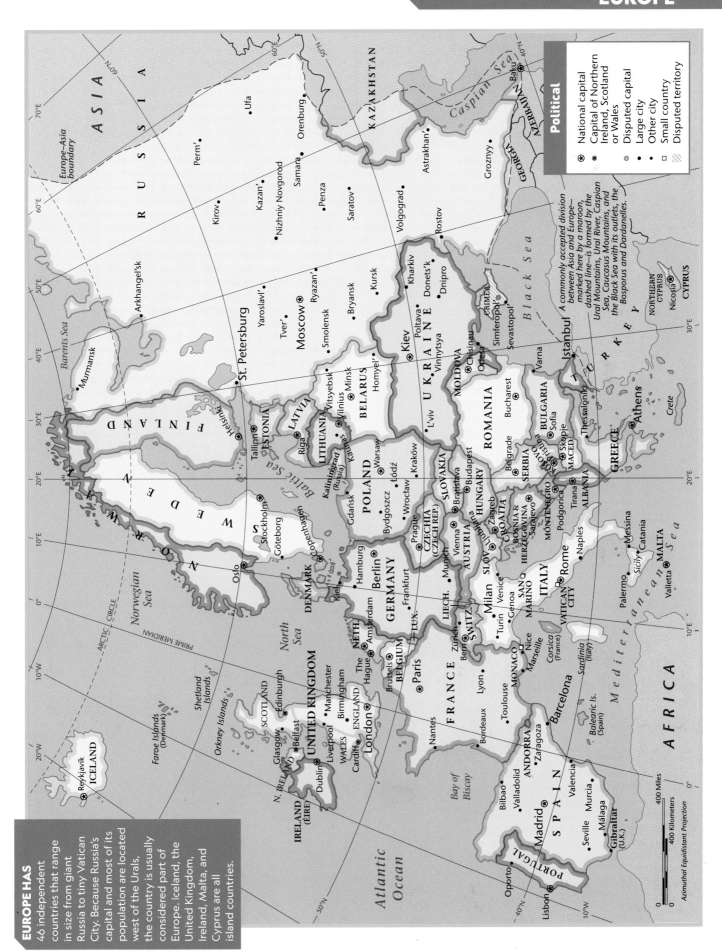

Political

⊛	National capital
⊛	Capital of Northern Ireland, Scotland or Wales
◎	Disputed capital
●	Large city
•	Other city
□	Small country
▨	Disputed territory

A commonly accepted division between Asia and Europe—marked here by a maroon, dashed line—is formed by the Ural Mountains, Ural River, Caspian Sea, Caucasus Mountains, and the Black Sea with its outlets, the Bosporus and Dardanelles.

EUROPE HAS
46 independent countries that range in size from giant Russia to tiny Vatican City. Because Russia's capital and most of its population are located west of the Urals, the country is usually considered part of Europe. Iceland, the United Kingdom, Ireland, Malta, and Cyprus are all island countries.

Azimuthal Equidistant Projection

400 Miles
400 Kilometers

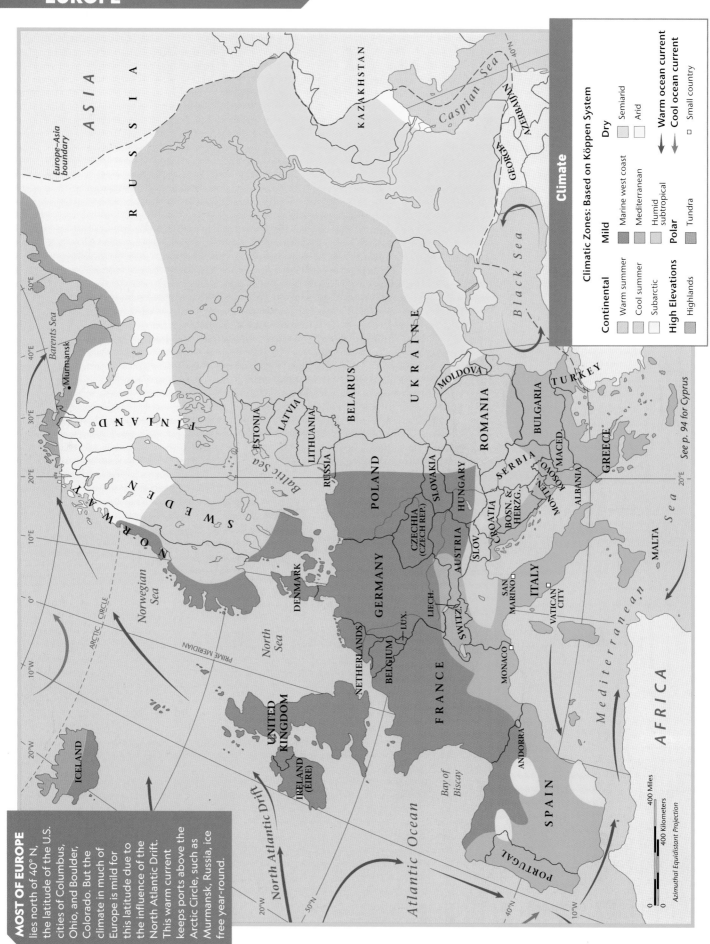

MOST OF EUROPE lies north of 40° N, the latitude of the U.S. cities of Columbus, Ohio, and Boulder, Colorado. But the climate in much of Europe is mild for this latitude due to the influence of the North Atlantic Drift. This warm current keeps ports above the Arctic Circle, such as Murmansk, Russia, ice free year-round.

Climate

Climatic Zones: Based on Köppen System

Continental
- Warm summer
- Cool summer
- Subarctic

Mild
- Marine west coast
- Mediterranean
- Humid subtropical

Dry
- Semiarid
- Arid

Polar
- Tundra

→ Warm ocean current
→ Cool ocean current

High Elevations
- Highlands

□ Small country

See p. 94 for Cyprus

Azimuthal Equidistant Projection

0 ⊢ 400 Miles
0 ⊢ 400 Kilometers

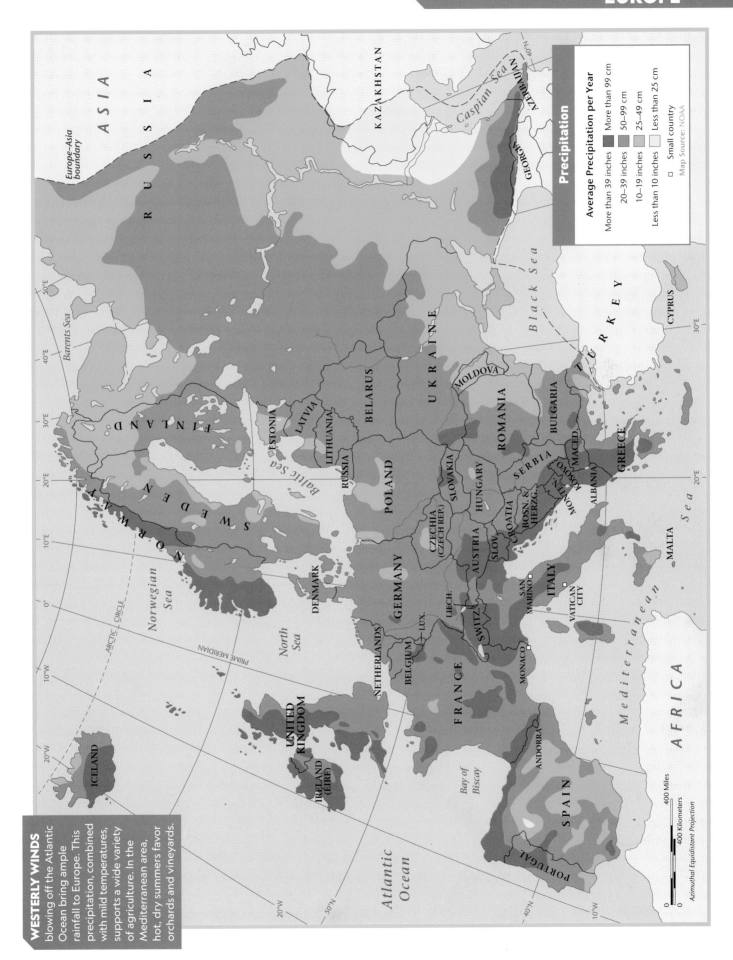

Precipitation

Average Precipitation per Year

More than 39 inches — More than 99 cm
20–39 inches — 50–99 cm
10–19 inches — 25–49 cm
Less than 10 inches — Less than 25 cm

□ Small country

Map Source: NOAA

WESTERLY WINDS blowing off the Atlantic Ocean bring ample rainfall to Europe. This precipitation, combined with mild temperatures, supports a wide variety of agriculture. In the Mediterranean area, hot, dry summers favor orchards and vineyards.

400 Miles

400 Kilometers

Azimuthal Equidistant Projection

THE CONTINENT:
EUROPE

THE THIRD MOST DENSELY populated continent after Asia and Africa, Europe has 74 percent of its population living in urban areas near the coasts and in river valleys. The Netherlands averages 1,301 people per square mile (502 per sq km); but Norway, rugged and more remote, averages only 37 people per square mile (14 per sq km).

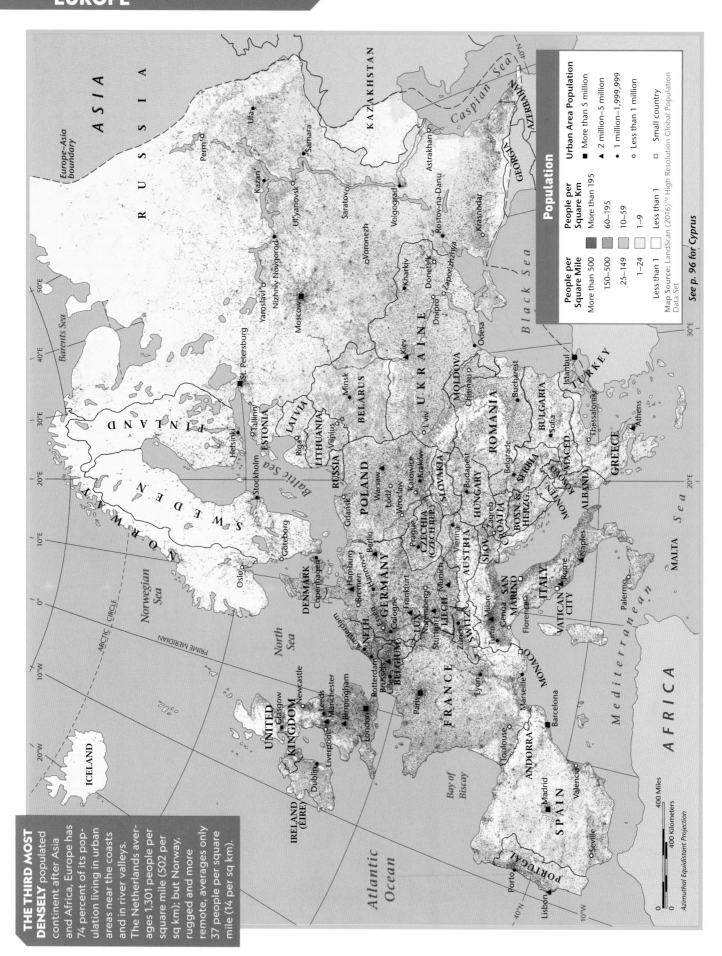

Population

People per Square Mile	People per Square Km
More than 500	More than 195
150–500	60–195
25–149	10–59
1–24	1–9
Less than 1	Less than 1

Urban Area Population
- ■ More than 5 million
- ▲ 2 million–5 million
- ● 1 million–1,999,999
- ○ Less than 1 million
- □ Small country

Map Source: LandScan (2016)™ High Resolution Global Population Data Set

See p. 96 for Cyprus

Azimuthal Equidistant Projection

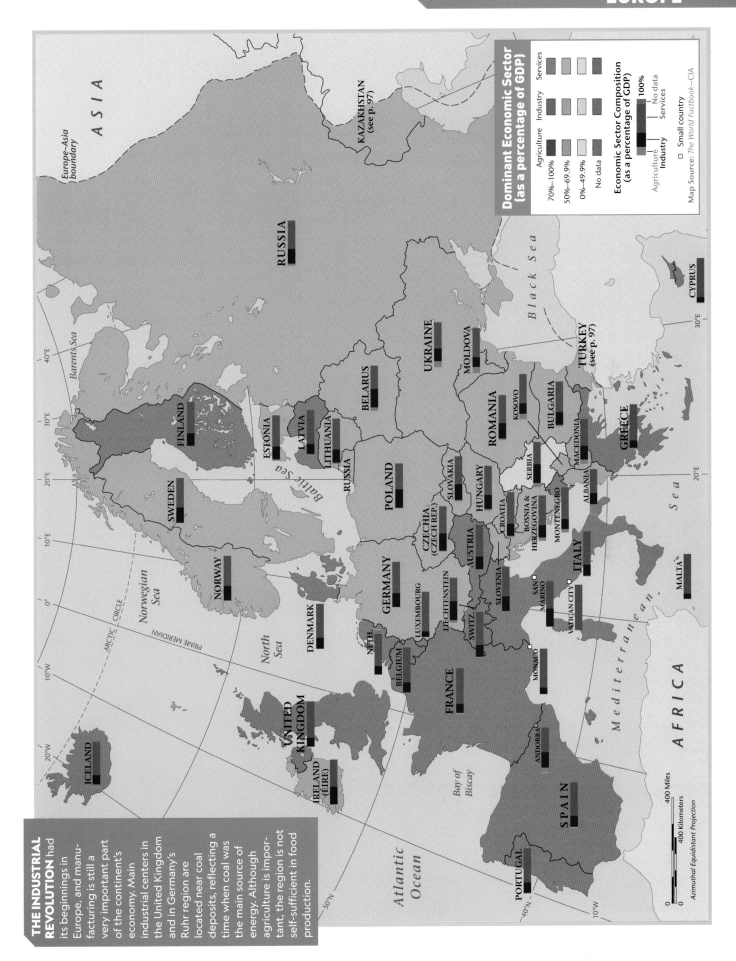

Dominant Economic Sector (as a percentage of GDP)

Agriculture | Industry | Services

70%–100%
50%–69.9%
0%–49.9%
No data

Economic Sector Composition (as a percentage of GDP)

100%
No data
Services
Industry
Agriculture

□ Small country

Map Source: *The World Factbook*—CIA

THE INDUSTRIAL REVOLUTION had its beginnings in Europe, and manufacturing is still a very important part of the continent's economy. Main industrial centers in the United Kingdom and in Germany's Ruhr region are located near coal deposits, reflecting a time when coal was the main source of energy. Although agriculture is important, the region is not self-sufficient in food production.

ASIA

Europe–Asia boundary

KAZAKHSTAN (see p. 97)

RUSSIA

Barents Sea

FINLAND

ESTONIA

LATVIA

LITHUANIA

RUSSIA

BELARUS

UKRAINE

MOLDOVA

Black Sea

TURKEY (see p. 97)

CYPRUS

SWEDEN

KOSOVO

ROMANIA

BULGARIA

MACEDONIA

GREECE

SERBIA

ALBANIA

NORWAY

Norwegian Sea

ARCTIC CIRCLE

POLAND

CZECHIA (CZECH REP.)

SLOVAKIA

HUNGARY

AUSTRIA

SLOVENIA

CROATIA

BOSNIA & HERZEGOVINA

MONTENEGRO

ITALY

Sea

GERMANY

DENMARK

NETH.

BELGIUM

LUXEMBOURG

LIECHTENSTEIN

SWITZ.

SAN MARINO

VATICAN CITY

MALTA

Mediterranean

AFRICA

North Sea

PRIME MERIDIAN

ICELAND

UNITED KINGDOM

IRELAND (EIRE)

FRANCE

MONACO

ANDORRA

SPAIN

PORTUGAL

Bay of Biscay

Atlantic Ocean

Baltic Sea

400 Miles
400 Kilometers
Azimuthal Equidistant Projection

EUROPEAN WATERWAYS

FACTS & FIGURES

○ More than 25,000 miles (40,000 km) of inland waterways link cities of Europe to a network of trade, both within the continent and around the world.

○ The Rhine and Danube Rivers have been important to trade and commerce since the time of the Roman Empire.

○ The Rhine and Danube Rivers were linked by a canal in 1992, opening up 2,175 miles (3,500 km) of water travel from the North Sea to the Black Sea.

○ The Upper Middle Rhine Valley in Germany has been named a UNESCO World Heritage site for its natural beauty and its many historic castles.

○ The Danube is the second longest river in Europe (after the Volga), draining 10 percent of the entire continent.

○ Using 18 locks, river vessels are able to descend more than 2,000 feet (610 m) along the Danube between Regensburg, Germany, and Bucharest, Romania.

○ The Rhine River empties into the North Sea at Rotterdam in the Netherlands. Expansion of the port's deep-water facilities has opened the port to the world's largest container ships, which can carry more than 21,000 TEUs of cargo (see page 98).

European Waterways

The physical landscape of Europe is crossed by many rivers that link the countries, people, and economies to the seas that border the continent. Fourteen of Europe's countries are landlocked (have no direct access to open waters), but the rivers and canals that make up Europe's network of waterways give even these countries access to global shipping routes.

Among these many waterways, the Rhine-Main-Danube system supports commercial and recreational traffic all the way from Rotterdam on the North Sea to Constanța on the Black Sea. Rotterdam, Europe's largest port as well as a major world port, handles 467 million tons (424 million t) of goods each year. And Constanța is the largest port on the Black Sea.

The Rhine-Main-Danube waterway boasts a rich historical and cultural tradition. During Roman times, the rivers were used to transport supplies to armies along the northern border of the empire. Cities, such as Cologne, Vienna, and Budapest, emerged as cultural centers, with churches, cathedrals, opera houses, and palaces that today attract tourists from around the world. And the Middle Rhine in Germany is famous for castles perched high above the banks of the river, where traders once were required to pay tolls to travel on the waterways.

⊙ **HEIDELBURG CASTLE** stands above the Rhine River in Germany, attracting millions of tourists each year.

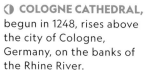

◖ **COLOGNE CATHEDRAL,** begun in 1248, rises above the city of Cologne, Germany, on the banks of the Rhine River.

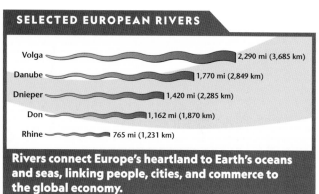

SELECTED EUROPEAN RIVERS

Volga — 2,290 mi (3,685 km)
Danube — 1,770 mi (2,849 km)
Dnieper — 1,420 mi (2,285 km)
Don — 1,162 mi (1,870 km)
Rhine — 765 mi (1,231 km)

Rivers connect Europe's heartland to Earth's oceans and seas, linking people, cities, and commerce to the global economy.

⊙ **IRON GATES.** The face of Decebalus, the last king of Dacia (modern Romania), is carved into the rocks above the Iron Gates gorges on the Danube River between Romania and Serbia.

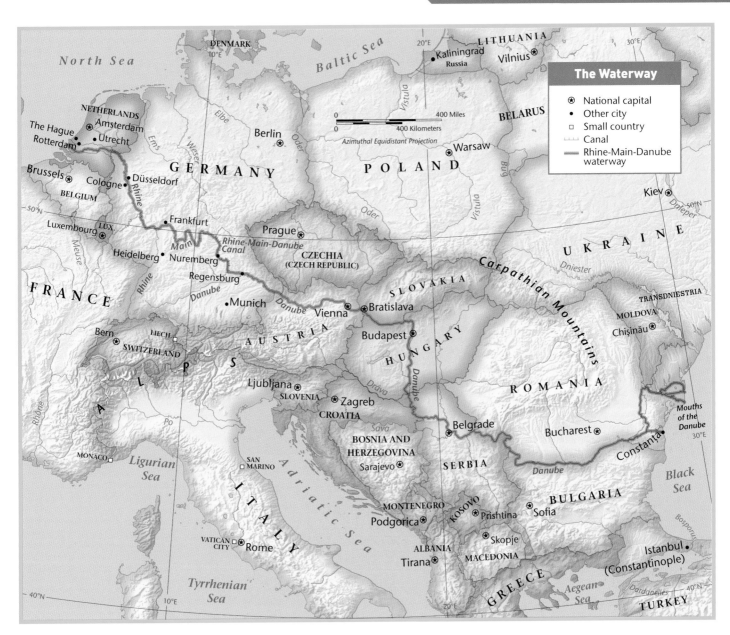

THE RHINE-MAIN-DANUBE CANAL, completed in 1992, connects the Rhine, Main, and Danube Rivers to create a continuous waterway from the North Sea to the Black Sea, which gives access to Turkey's Dardanelles and ports beyond. The canal is 106 miles (171 km) long and makes navigation by large barges and riverboats possible for the full length of the waterway.

A CITY DIVIDED, Budapest, Hungary, lies on both sides of the Danube River. Once two separate towns, Buda and Pest were united in 1872. The country's Parliament Building, an important city landmark, stretches 880 feet (268 m) along the Pest side of the river.

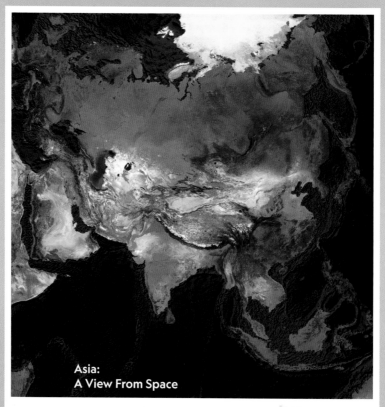

Asia:
A View From Space

From the frozen shores of the Arctic Ocean to the equatorial islands of Indonesia, Asia stretches across 90 degrees of latitude. From the Ural Mountains to the Pacific Ocean, it covers more than 150 degrees of longitude. Here, three of history's great culture hearths emerged in the valleys of the Tigris and Euphrates, the Indus, and the Yellow (Huang) Rivers. Today, Asia is home to 60 percent of Earth's people and some of the world's fastest growing economies.

The Taj Mahal in Agra, India

Asia

PHYSICAL

Land area*
**17,208,000 sq mi
(44,570,000 sq km)**
*Land area includes Asian
Russia, the area east of the
Ural Mountains; population
excludes Russia as its population is included in Europe,
where most of its people
live (see page 81).*

**Highest point
Mount Everest,
China-Nepal
29,035 ft (8,850 m)**

**Lowest point
Dead Sea, Israel-Jordan
-1,401 ft (-427 m)**

**Longest river
Yangtze (Chang), China
3,880 mi (6,244 km)**

**Largest lake entirely
in Asia
Lake Baikal
12,200 sq mi
(31,500 sq km)**

POLITICAL

Population*
4,402,007,000
**Number of
independent
countries
46 (excluding
Russia)**

**Largest country
entirely in Asia
China
3,705,405 sq mi (9,596,960 sq km)**

**Smallest country
Maldives
115 sq mi (298 sq km)**

**Most populous country
China
Pop. 1,379,303,000**

**Least populous country
Maldives
Pop. 393,000**

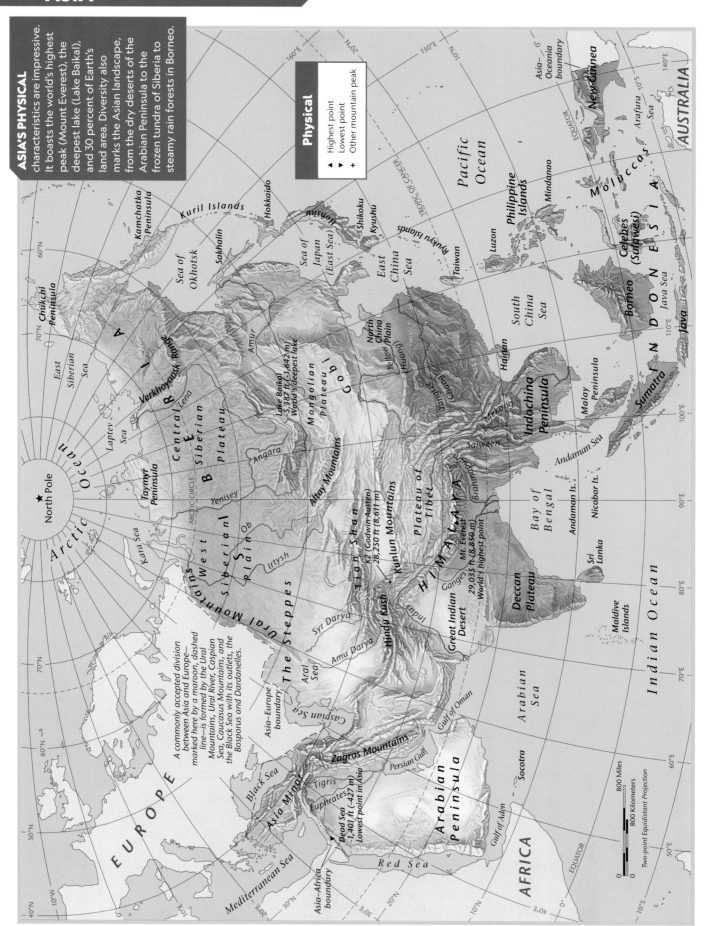

ASIA'S PHYSICAL characteristics are impressive. It boasts the world's highest peak (Mount Everest), the deepest lake (Lake Baikal), and 30 percent of Earth's land area. Diversity also marks the Asian landscape, from the dry deserts of the Arabian Peninsula to the frozen tundra of Siberia to steamy rain forests in Borneo.

Physical

◄ Highest point
► Lowest point
+ Other mountain peak

A commonly accepted division between Asia and Europe—marked here by a maroon, dashed line—is formed by the Ural Mountains, Ural River, Caspian Sea, Caucasus Mountains, and the Black Sea with its outlets, the Bosporus and Dardanelles.

North Pole

Arctic Ocean

Chukchi Peninsula
Kamchatka Peninsula
Kuril Islands
Hokkaido
Sakhalin
Sea of Okhotsk
Honshu
Shikoku
Kyushu
Sea of Japan (East Sea)
Ryukyu Islands
Taiwan
East China Sea
Pacific Ocean

East Siberian Sea
Laptev Sea
Kara Sea
Taymyr Peninsula
Verkhoyansk Range
Lena
Amur

Central Siberian Plateau
West Siberian Plain
Yenisey
Ob
Irtysh
Angara

Ural Mountains
The Steppes
Aral Sea
Caspian Sea
Asia–Europe boundary

Altay Mountains
Mongolian Plateau
Gobi
Lake Baikal -5,387 ft (-1,642 m) World's deepest lake

North China Plain
Yellow Plain
Huang
Yangtze (Chang)

Tian Shan
Kunlun Mountains
K2 (Godwin Austen) +28,250 ft (8,611 m)
Plateau of Tibet
Hindu Kush
Indus
Mt. Everest 29,035 ft (8,850 m) World's highest point

HIMALAYA
Ganges
Brahmaputra
Salween
Mekong
Irrawaddy

Hainan
South China Sea
Luzon
Mindanao
Philippine Islands

Syr Darya
Amu Darya

Great Indian Desert
Deccan Plateau
Sri Lanka
Bay of Bengal
Andaman Is.
Nicobar Is.
Andaman Sea

Indochina Peninsula
Malay Peninsula
Sumatra
Java
Java Sea
Borneo
Celebes (Sulawesi)
Moluccas
New Guinea
INDONESIA

Maldive Islands
Indian Ocean

Zagros Mountains
Persian Gulf
Tigris
Euphrates
Dead Sea -1,401 ft (-427 m) Lowest point in Asia
Asia Minor
Black Sea
Mediterranean Sea
EUROPE

Gulf of Oman
Arabian Sea
Arabian Peninsula
Socotra
Gulf of Aden
Red Sea
AFRICA
Asia–Africa boundary

Arafura Sea
AUSTRALIA
Asia–Oceania boundary

EQUATOR
TROPIC OF CANCER
ARCTIC CIRCLE

800 Miles
800 Kilometers
Two-point Equidistant Projection

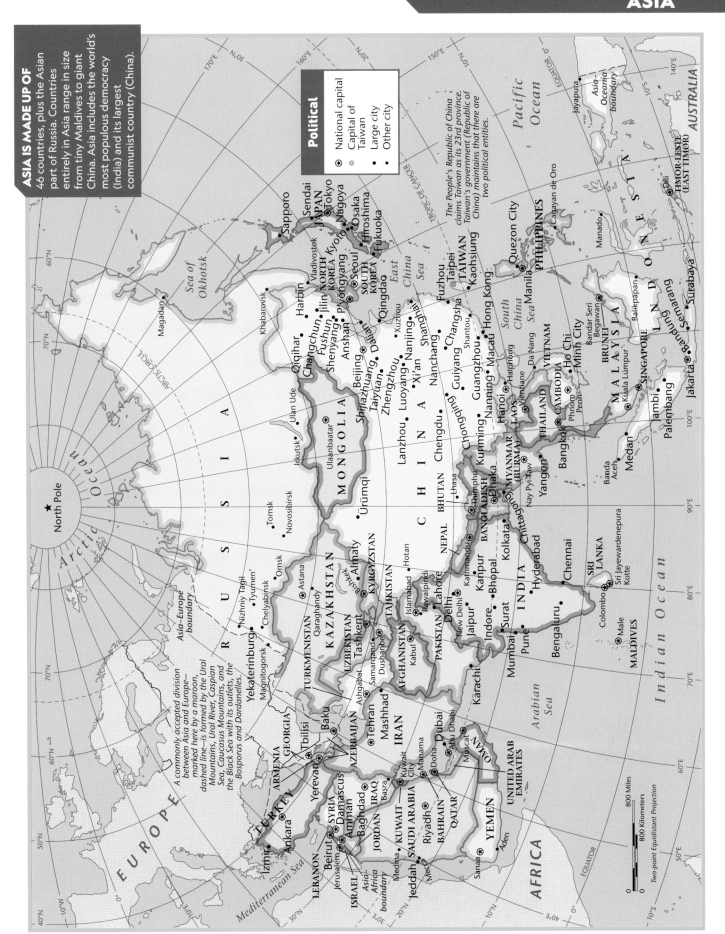

ASIA IS MADE UP OF
46 countries, plus the Asian part of Russia. Countries entirely in Asia range in size from tiny Maldives to giant China. Asia includes the world's most populous democracy (India) and its largest communist country (China).

Political

⊛ National capital
◎ Capital of Taiwan
● Large city
· Other city

The People's Republic of China claims Taiwan as its 23rd province. Taiwan's government (Republic of China) maintains that there are two political entities.

A commonly accepted division between Asia and Europe—marked here by a maroon, dashed line—is formed by the Ural Mountains, Ural River, Caspian Sea, Caucasus Mountains, and the Black Sea with its outlets, the Bosporus and Dardanelles.

Asia–Europe boundary

North Pole ★

Arctic Ocean

Sea of Okhotsk

Magadan

Khabarovsk

Sapporo

Sendai
JAPAN
Tokyo
Nagoya
Osaka
Kyoto
Hiroshima
Fukuoka

Vladivostok

Harbin
Jilin
Qiqihar
Changchun
Fushun
Shenyang
Anshan

NORTH KOREA
Pyongyang
Seoul
SOUTH KOREA

Dalian
Qingdao

East China Sea

Fuzhou
Taipei ◎
TAIWAN
Kaohsiung

Pacific Ocean

Quezon City
Manila ⊛
PHILIPPINES
Cagayan de Oro

Manado

Jayapura

Asia– Oceania boundary

AUSTRALIA

Ulan Ude

Irkutsk

Ulaanbaatar ⊛

MONGOLIA

Ürümqi

Beijing ⊛
Shijiazhuang
Taiyuan
Zhengzhou

Luoyang
Xi'an
Nanjing
Shanghai
Xuzhou

Nanchang
Changsha
Guiyang

CHINA

Lanzhou

Chengdu
Chongqing
Kunming

Guangzhou
Nanning
Macau
Hong Kong

Shantou

South China Sea

Da Nang

VIETNAM
Haiphong
Hanoi ⊛
LAOS
Vientiane
THAILAND
Bangkok ⊛

Ho Chi Minh City

CAMBODIA
Phnom Penh ⊛

BRUNEI
Bandar Seri Begawan ⊛

MALAYSIA
Kuala Lumpur ⊛
SINGAPORE ⊛

Balikpapan

Surabaya
Semarang
Bandung
Jakarta ⊛
Palembang
Jambi
Medan
Aceh
Banda Aceh

I N D O N E S I A

TIMOR-LESTE (EAST TIMOR)
Dili ⊛

Tomsk
Novosibirsk

Omsk

Astana ⊛
Qaraghandy

KAZAKHSTAN

Bishkek ⊛
Almaty
KYRGYZSTAN

Hotan

NEPAL
Kathmandu ⊛

BHUTAN
Thimphu ⊛
Lhasa

MYANMAR (BURMA)
Nay Pyi Taw ⊛
Yangon

BANGLADESH
Dhaka ⊛
Chittagong

Kanpur
Bhopal

Kolkata

Hyderabad
Chennai

SRI LANKA
Colombo
Sri Jayewardenepura Kotte ⊛

MALDIVES
Male ⊛

Nizhniy Tagil
Tyumen'
Yekaterinburg
Chelyabinsk
Magnitogorsk

R U S S I A

TURKMENISTAN
Ashgabat ⊛

UZBEKISTAN
Tashkent ⊛
Samarqand
Dushanbe ⊛
TAJIKISTAN

AFGHANISTAN
Kabul ⊛

Islamabad ⊛
Rawalpindi
Lahore
PAKISTAN

New Delhi ⊛
Delhi
Jaipur

Indore
Surat

Mumbai
Pune

Bengaluru

I N D I A

Indian Ocean

Arabian Sea

EUROPE

İzmir
Ankara ⊛
TURKEY

Tbilisi ⊛
GEORGIA
ARMENIA
Yerevan ⊛
AZERBAIJAN
Baku ⊛

Tehran ⊛
Mashhad
IRAN

Karachi

Beirut ⊛
LEBANON
Jerusalem ⊛
ISRAEL
Damascus ⊛
SYRIA
Amman ⊛
JORDAN
Baghdad ⊛
IRAQ
Basra

Medina
Jeddah
Mecca
SAUDI ARABIA
Riyadh ⊛

KUWAIT
Kuwait City ⊛
BAHRAIN
Manama ⊛
QATAR
Doha ⊛
Dubai
Abu Dhabi ⊛
UNITED ARAB EMIRATES
OMAN
Muscat ⊛

YEMEN
Sanaa ⊛
Aden

Asia–Africa boundary

Mediterranean Sea

AFRICA

EQUATOR

TROPIC OF CANCER

ARCTIC CIRCLE

0   800 Miles
0   800 Kilometers
Two-point Equidistant Projection

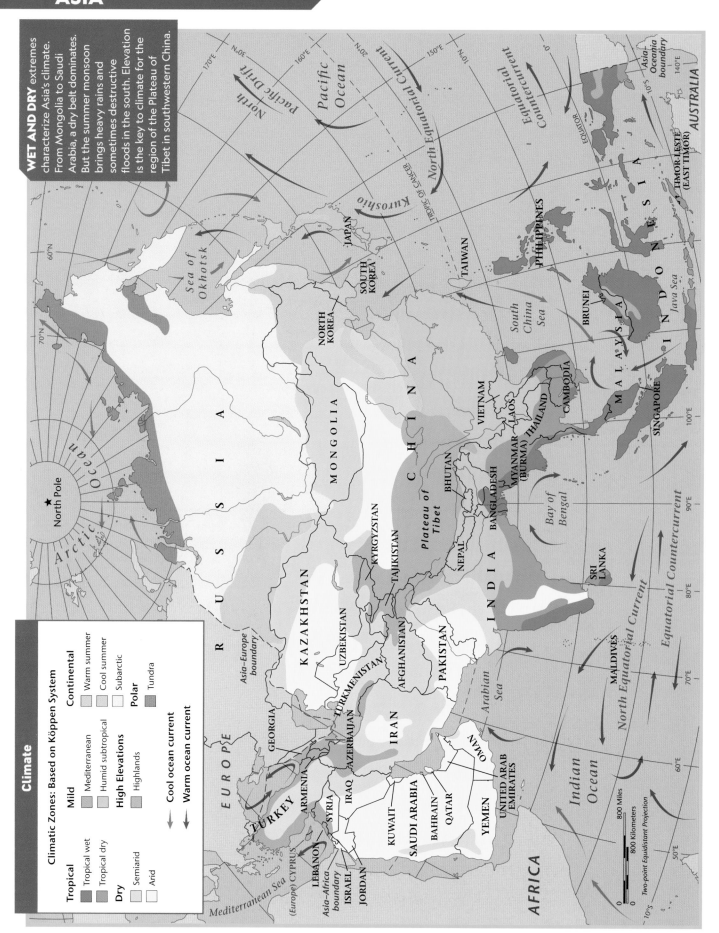

Climate

Climatic Zones: Based on Köppen System

Tropical
- Tropical wet
- Tropical dry

Dry
- Semiarid
- Arid

Mild
- Mediterranean
- Humid subtropical

High Elevations
- Highlands

Continental
- Warm summer
- Cool summer
- Subarctic

Polar
- Tundra

→ Cool ocean current
→ Warm ocean current

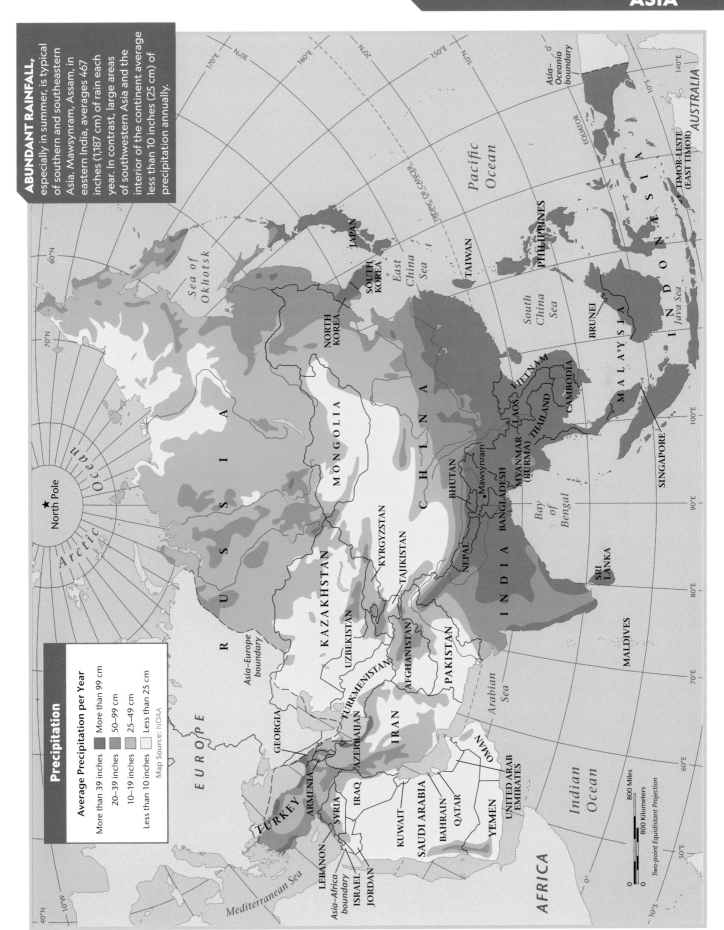

ABUNDANT RAINFALL, especially in summer, is typical of southern and southeastern Asia. Mawsynram, Assam, in eastern India, averages 467 inches (1,187 cm) of rain each year. In contrast, large areas of southwestern Asia and the interior of the continent average less than 10 inches (25 cm) of precipitation annually.

Precipitation

Average Precipitation per Year

More than 39 inches — More than 99 cm
20–39 inches — 50–99 cm
10–19 inches — 25–49 cm
Less than 10 inches — Less than 25 cm

Map Source: NOAA

North Pole

800 Miles
800 Kilometers
Two-point Equidistant Projection

THE CONTINENT:
ASIA

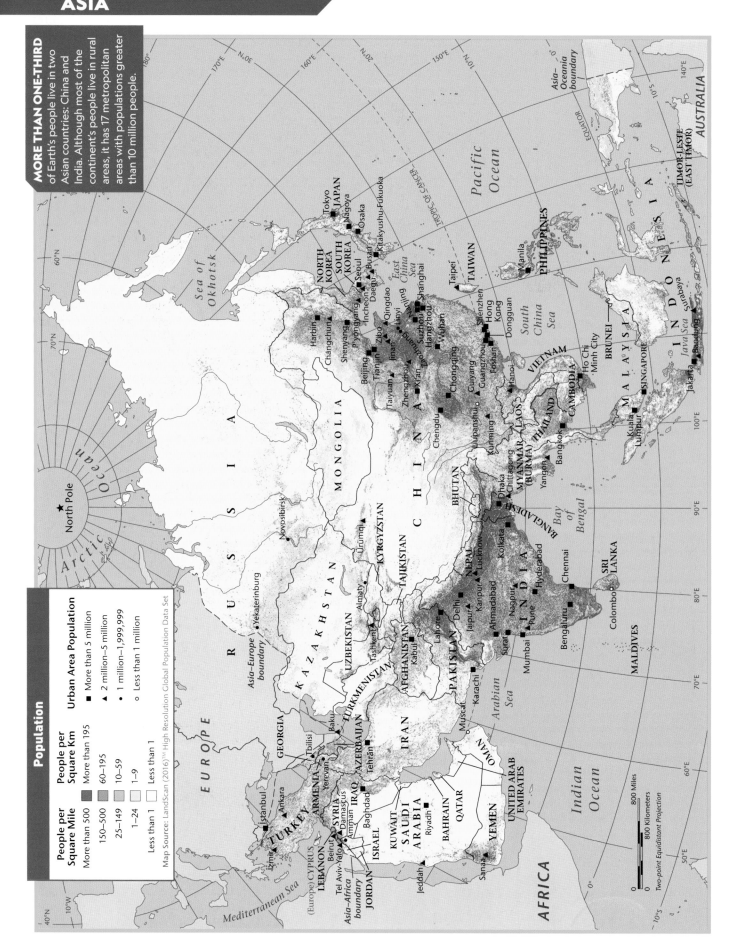

MORE THAN ONE-THIRD of Earth's people live in two Asian countries: China and India. Although most of the continent's people live in rural areas, it has 17 metropolitan areas with populations greater than 10 million people.

Population

People per Square Mile

More than 500	
150–500	
25–149	
1–24	
Less than 1	

People per Square Km

More than 195	
60–195	
10–59	
1–9	
Less than 1	

Urban Area Population

- ■ More than 5 million
- ▲ 2 million–5 million
- ● 1 million–1,999,999
- ○ Less than 1 million

Map Source: LandScan (2016)™ High Resolution Global Population Data Set

Two-point Equidistant Projection

800 Miles
800 Kilometers

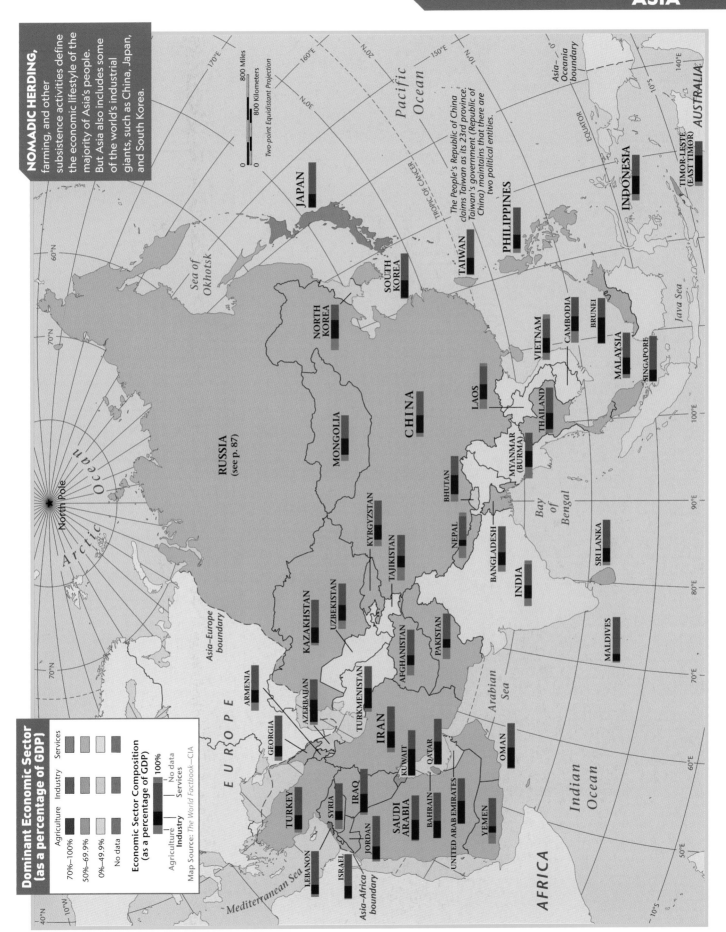

NOMADIC HERDING, farming, and other subsistence activities define the economic lifestyle of the majority of Asia's people. But Asia also includes some of the world's industrial giants, such as China, Japan, and South Korea.

Dominant Economic Sector (as a percentage of GDP)

	Agriculture	Industry	Services
70%–100%			
50%–69.9%			
0%–49.9%			
No data			

Economic Sector Composition (as a percentage of GDP)

100%

No data
Services
Industry
Agriculture
Map Source: *The World Factbook*—CIA

The People's Republic of China claims Taiwan as its 23rd province. Taiwan's government (Republic of China) maintains that there are two political entities.

Pacific Ocean

TROPIC OF CANCER

Asia–Oceania boundary

EQUATOR

AUSTRALIA

JAPAN

Sea of Okhotsk

SOUTH KOREA

NORTH KOREA

TAIWAN

PHILIPPINES

INDONESIA

TIMOR-LESTE (EAST TIMOR)

RUSSIA (see p. 87)

MONGOLIA

CHINA

LAOS

VIETNAM

CAMBODIA

BRUNEI

MALAYSIA

SINGAPORE

THAILAND

MYANMAR (BURMA)

BHUTAN

NEPAL

BANGLADESH

INDIA

SRI LANKA

MALDIVES

Bay of Bengal

Java Sea

Arctic Ocean

North Pole

Asia–Europe boundary

KAZAKHSTAN

KYRGYZSTAN

TAJIKISTAN

UZBEKISTAN

TURKMENISTAN

AFGHANISTAN

PAKISTAN

ARMENIA

AZERBAIJAN

GEORGIA

IRAN

TURKEY

SYRIA

IRAQ

LEBANON

ISRAEL

JORDAN

SAUDI ARABIA

KUWAIT

QATAR

BAHRAIN

UNITED ARAB EMIRATES

YEMEN

OMAN

Arabian Sea

Indian Ocean

EUROPE

AFRICA

Asia–Africa boundary

Mediterranean Sea

800 Miles

800 Kilometers

Two-point Equidistant Projection

GLOBAL CONTAINER PORTS

FACTS & FIGURES

○ **World Container Shipping Fleet, 2018:**
6,104 active ships

○ **Total World Trade, 2018:**
22,067,177 TEUs

World's Largest Container Fleets, 2018
(number of ships owned or chartered)

APM-Maersk (Denmark)	778
Mediterranean Shipping Co. (Italy)	511
CMA CGM (France)	494
COSCO Shipping Co. (China)	341
Hapag-Lloyd (Germany)	212
Evergreen Line (Taiwan)	194
OOCL (Hong Kong)	100
Yang Ming Marine Transport (Taiwan)	101
MOL (Japan)	80

Leading Exporters of Containerized Cargo (million TEUs), 2014

China	36.0
United States	11.9
South Korea	5.9
Japan	5.3
Indonesia	4.0
Thailand	3.9
Germany	3.3
Taiwan	3.3
India	3.1
Vietnam	2.9

Leading Importers of Containerized Cargo (million TEUs), 2014

United States	19.6
China	14.7
Japan	6.6
South Korea	5.1
Indonesia	3.2
Germany	3.0
United Kingdom	2.6
Taiwan	2.5
Australia	2.5
Vietnam	2.5

East Asia Ports

Since the mid-20th century, the world's economy has expanded to a truly global scale, made possible, in large part, by the growth of containerized shipping. The first container ship, a converted oil tanker, set sail from Newark, New Jersey, U.S.A., in 1956 carrying 58 containers. Today, more than 6,000 container vessels move manufactured goods cheaply and efficiently among ports around the world.

Container ships range in size up to 1,312 feet (400 m) long and 193 feet (59 m) wide—bigger than four football fields. The capacity of a container ship is measured in TEUs—a unit of measure equivalent to a 20-foot (6-m) standard container. The largest container vessels can carry more than 21,000 20-foot containers, each loaded with as much as 100 tons (91 t) of cargo. Container ports are equipped with giant cranes, more than 400 feet (122 m) tall and weighing as much as 2,000 tons (1,814 t), that can move 30 to 40 containers on and off a ship each hour. With the world's 10 busiest container ports, Asia has become a major player in the global economy.

○ **WAIGAOQIAO TERMINAL,** the largest container terminal at China's Shanghai Port, appears as a colorful mosaic when viewed from above. Shanghai leads all container ports in tonnage handled, moving some 700 million tons (635 million t) of goods and material each year.

○ **SHIPPING CONTAINERS** are ready to be loaded onto trucks in the busy port of Busan, which opened in 2004, 280 miles (450 km) southeast of Seoul, South Korea.

○ **OLD MEETS NEW** in Ho Chi Minh City's harbor. Vendors steer a sampan near a container vessel in this network of ports that contributes to more than two-thirds of Vietnam's economy.

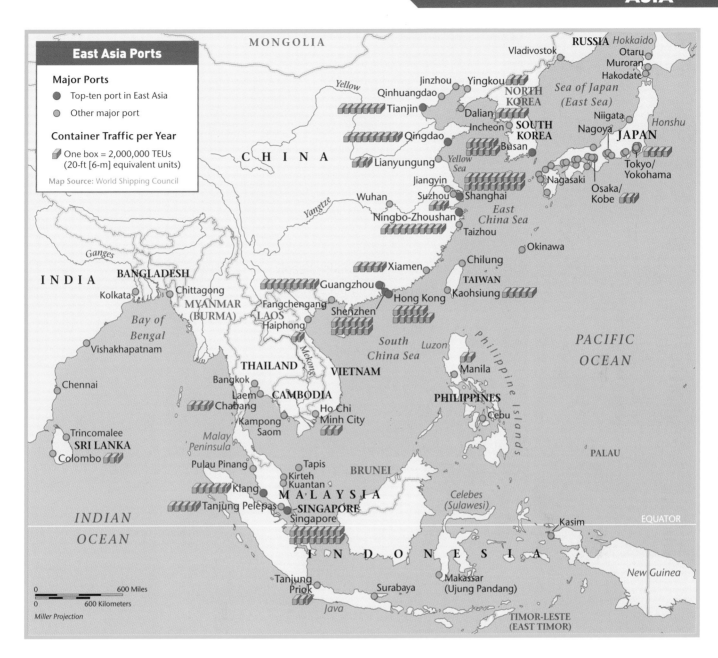

East Asia Ports

Major Ports
- Top-ten port in East Asia
- Other major port

Container Traffic per Year
One box = 2,000,000 TEUs
(20-ft [6-m] equivalent units)
Map Source: World Shipping Council

MONGOLIA

RUSSIA · Hokkaido
Vladivostok · Otaru · Muroran · Hakodate

Yellow · Jinzhou · Yingkou
Qinhuangdao · Tianjin · Dalian · NORTH KOREA
Sea of Japan (East Sea)
Niigata · Honshu
Incheon · SOUTH KOREA · Nagoya · JAPAN
Qingdao · Busan · Tokyo/Yokohama

CHINA

Lianyungung · Yellow Sea
Jiangyin · Osaka/Kobe
Wuhan · Suzhou · Shanghai · Nagasaki
Ningbo-Zhoushan · East China Sea
Taizhou

Ganges · Okinawa
Chilung
INDIA · BANGLADESH
Kolkata · Chittagong · Xiamen · TAIWAN
MYANMAR (BURMA) · Guangzhou · Kaohsiung
Fangchengang · Hong Kong
LAOS · Shenzhen
Haiphong

Bay of Bengal
Vishakhapatnam · South China Sea · Luzon
PACIFIC OCEAN
Chennai · THAILAND · VIETNAM · Manila
Bangkok · PHILIPPINES
Laem Chabang · CAMBODIA · Cebu
Trincomalee · Kampong Saom · Ho Chi Minh City
SRI LANKA
Colombo
Malay Peninsula
Pulau Pinang · Tapis · BRUNEI · PALAU
Kirteh · Kuantan
Klang · MALAYSIA · Celebes (Sulawesi)
Tanjung Pelepas · SINGAPORE · Kasim
Singapore · EQUATOR
INDIAN OCEAN · INDONESIA
New Guinea
Tanjung Priok · Surabaya · Makassar (Ujung Pandang)
Java · TIMOR-LESTE (EAST TIMOR)

Philippine Islands

Mekong
Yangtze

0 ___ 600 Miles
0 ___ 600 Kilometers
Miller Projection

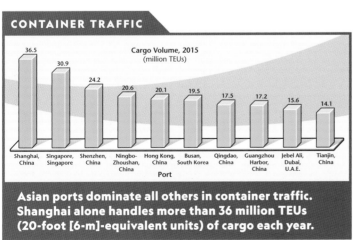

CONTAINER TRAFFIC

Cargo Volume, 2015
(million TEUs)

Port	TEUs
Shanghai, China	36.5
Singapore, Singapore	30.9
Shenzhen, China	24.2
Ningbo-Zhoushan, China	20.6
Hong Kong, China	20.1
Busan, South Korea	19.5
Qingdao, China	17.5
Guangzhou Harbor, China	17.2
Jebel Ali, Dubai, U.A.E.	15.6
Tianjin, China	14.1

Asian ports dominate all others in container traffic. Shanghai alone handles more than 36 million TEUs (20-foot [6-m]-equivalent units) of cargo each year.

REMOTE CONTROL. This crane operator moves containers off a ship in Manila, Philippines.

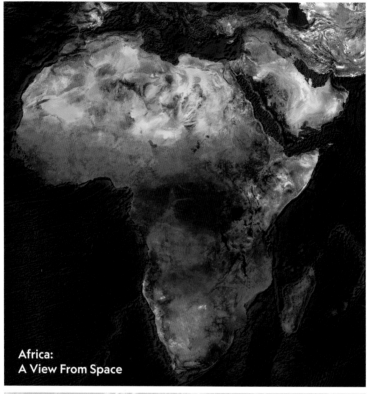

Africa:
A View From Space

From space, Africa appears to be divided into three regions: the north, dominated by the Sahara, the largest hot desert in the world; central bands of tropical grasslands and rain forests; and more dry land to the south. The Great Rift Valley may be splitting Africa apart. The valley runs from the Red Sea through the Afar Triangle to the southern lake district.

PHYSICAL

Land area 11,608,000 sq mi (30,065,000 sq km)	**Lowest point** Lake Assal, Djibouti -509 ft (-155 m)	**Largest lake** Victoria 26,800 sq mi (69,500 sq km)
Highest point Kilimanjaro, Tanzania 19,340 ft (5,895 m)	**Longest river** Nile 4,400 mi (7,081 km)	

POLITICAL

Population 1,215,763,000 **Number of independent countries** 54	**Largest country** Algeria 919,595 sq mi (2,381,741 sq km)	**Most populous country** Nigeria Pop. 190,632,000
	Smallest country Seychelles 176 sq mi (455 sq km)	**Least populous country** Seychelles Pop. 94,000

Africa

An elephant and calf walk in Kenya's Amboseli National Park. Kilimanjaro, in neighboring Tanzania, rises in the distance.

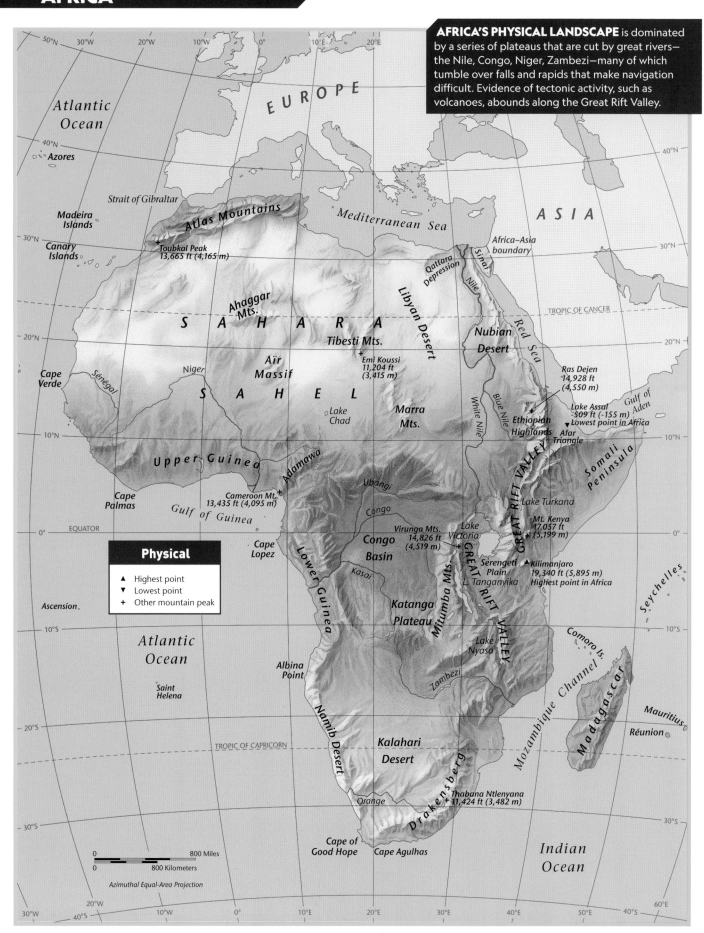

AFRICA'S PHYSICAL LANDSCAPE is dominated by a series of plateaus that are cut by great rivers—the Nile, Congo, Niger, Zambezi—many of which tumble over falls and rapids that make navigation difficult. Evidence of tectonic activity, such as volcanoes, abounds along the Great Rift Valley.

EUROPE

ASIA

Atlantic Ocean

Azores

Strait of Gibraltar

Madeira Islands

Canary Islands

Cape Verde

Mediterranean Sea

Atlas Mountains

Toubkal Peak
13,665 ft (4,165 m)

Africa–Asia boundary

Qattara Depression

Sinai

Nile

Libyan Desert

Nubian Desert

Red Sea

TROPIC OF CANCER

S A H A R A

Ahaggar Mts.

Tibesti Mts.

Emi Koussi
11,204 ft
(3,415 m)

Aïr Massif

S A H E L

Niger

Sénégal

Lake Chad

Marra Mts.

White Nile

Blue Nile

Ethiopian Highlands

Ras Dejen
14,928 ft
(4,550 m)

Lake Assal
-509 ft (-155 m)
Lowest point in Africa

Gulf of Aden

Afar Triangle

Somali Peninsula

Upper Guinea

Adamawa

Cameroon Mt.
13,435 ft (4,095 m)

Cape Palmas

Gulf of Guinea

EQUATOR

Ubangi

Congo

Lower Guinea

Cape Lopez

Kasai

Congo Basin

Virunga Mts.
14,826 ft
(4,519 m)

Lake Victoria

Lake Turkana

Mt. Kenya
17,057 ft
(5,199 m)

GREAT RIFT VALLEY

Serengeti Plain

L. Tanganyika

Kilimanjaro
19,340 ft (5,895 m)
Highest point in Africa

Seychelles

Physical

▲ Highest point
▼ Lowest point
+ Other mountain peak

Ascension

Mitumba Mts.

Katanga Plateau

GREAT RIFT VALLEY

Lake Nyasa

Comoro Is.

Atlantic Ocean

Saint Helena

Albina Point

Namib Desert

Zambezi

Mozambique Channel

Madagascar

Mauritius

Réunion

TROPIC OF CAPRICORN

Kalahari Desert

Orange

Drakensberg

Thabana Ntlenyana
11,424 ft (3,482 m)

Cape of Good Hope

Cape Agulhas

Indian Ocean

0   800 Miles
0   800 Kilometers

Azimuthal Equal-Area Projection

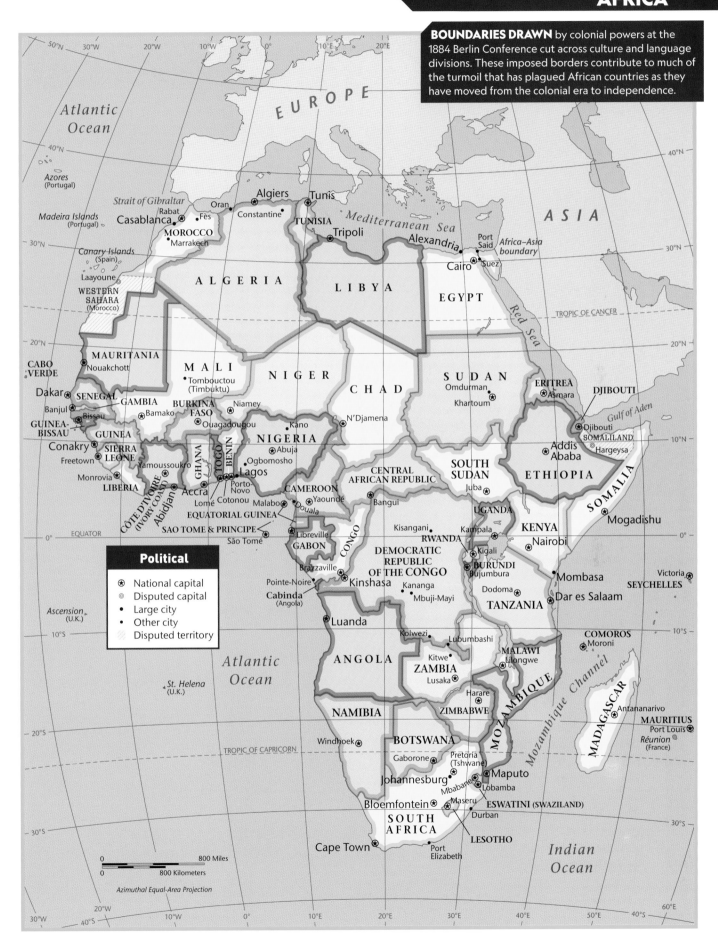

BOUNDARIES DRAWN by colonial powers at the 1884 Berlin Conference cut across culture and language divisions. These imposed borders contribute to much of the turmoil that has plagued African countries as they have moved from the colonial era to independence.

EUROPE

ASIA

Atlantic Ocean

Mediterranean Sea

Azores (Portugal)

Madeira Islands (Portugal)

Strait of Gibraltar

Algiers • Tunis

Oran • Constantine

Rabat • Fès
Casablanca
MOROCCO
Marrakech

TUNISIA
Tripoli

Alexandria
Port Said
Cairo • Suez

Africa–Asia boundary

TROPIC OF CANCER

Canary Islands (Spain)

Laayoune
WESTERN SAHARA (Morocco)

ALGERIA

LIBYA

EGYPT

Red Sea

MAURITANIA
Nouakchott

MALI
• Tombouctou (Timbuktu)

NIGER

CHAD

SUDAN
Omdurman
Khartoum

ERITREA
Asmara

DJIBOUTI
Djibouti
SOMALILAND
Hargeysa

Gulf of Aden

CABO VERDE

Dakar
SENEGAL
GAMBIA
Banjul
Bissau
GUINEA-BISSAU
GUINEA
Conakry
SIERRA LEONE
Freetown
Monrovia
LIBERIA

Niamey
BURKINA FASO
Bamako
Ouagadougou

Kano
N'Djamena

NIGERIA
• Abuja
Ogbomosho
GHANA
TOGO
BENIN
Yamoussoukro
Accra
CÔTE D'IVOIRE (IVORY COAST)
Abidjan
Porto-Novo
Lomé Cotonou
Lagos

CENTRAL AFRICAN REPUBLIC

Bangui

SOUTH SUDAN
Juba

Addis Ababa
ETHIOPIA

SOMALIA

CAMEROON
Yaoundé
Malabo
Douala
EQUATORIAL GUINEA
SAO TOME & PRINCIPE
São Tomé
Libreville
GABON
CONGO
Brazzaville
Pointe-Noire
Cabinda (Angola)

Kisangani
DEMOCRATIC REPUBLIC OF THE CONGO
Kinshasa
Kananga
Mbuji-Mayi

UGANDA
Kampala
RWANDA
Kigali
BURUNDI
Bujumbura

KENYA
Nairobi

Mogadishu

Mombasa

Dodoma
TANZANIA
Dar es Salaam

SEYCHELLES
Victoria

EQUATOR

Luanda

Kolwezi
Lubumbashi
Kitwe
ZAMBIA
Lusaka

ANGOLA

MALAWI
Lilongwe

COMOROS
Moroni

MADAGASCAR

Antananarivo
MAURITIUS
Port Louis
Réunion (France)

Harare
ZIMBABWE

MOZAMBIQUE

Mozambique Channel

NAMIBIA

Windhoek

BOTSWANA

TROPIC OF CAPRICORN

Gaborone
Pretoria (Tshwane)
Johannesburg
Mbabane
Lobamba
Maputo
Maseru
ESWATINI (SWAZILAND)
Durban
LESOTHO
Bloemfontein

SOUTH AFRICA

Cape Town
Port Elizabeth

Atlantic Ocean

Ascension (U.K.)

St. Helena (U.K.)

Indian Ocean

Political
- ⊛ National capital
- ◎ Disputed capital
- • Large city
- • Other city
- ▨ Disputed territory

0 — 800 Miles
0 — 800 Kilometers

Azimuthal Equal-Area Projection

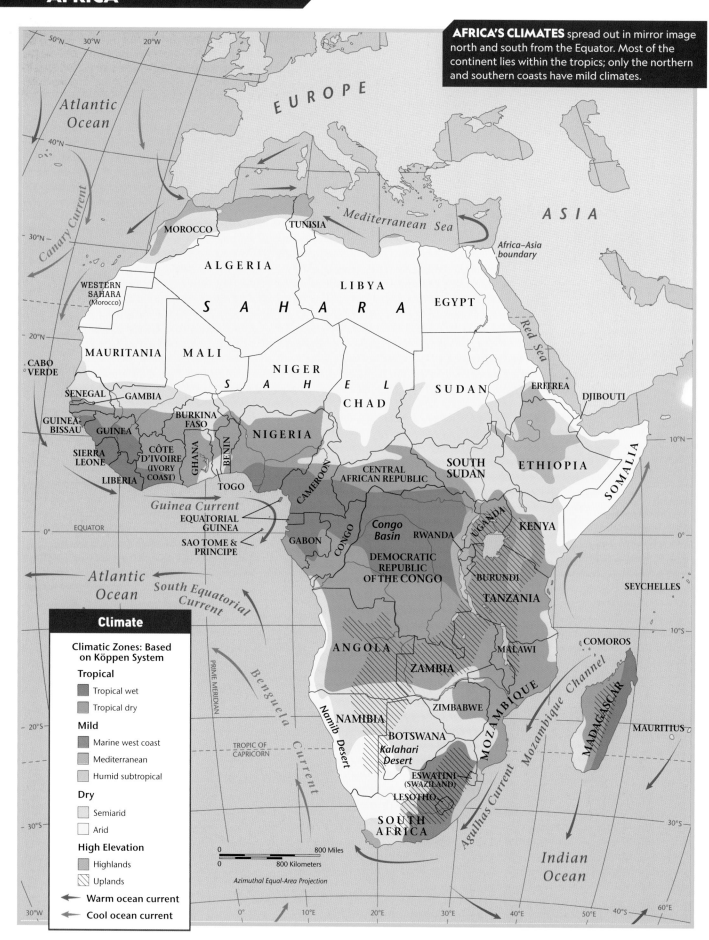

AFRICA'S CLIMATES spread out in mirror image north and south from the Equator. Most of the continent lies within the tropics; only the northern and southern coasts have mild climates.

Climate

Climatic Zones: Based on Köppen System

Tropical
- Tropical wet
- Tropical dry

Mild
- Marine west coast
- Mediterranean
- Humid subtropical

Dry
- Semiarid
- Arid

High Elevation
- Highlands
- Uplands

← Warm ocean current
← Cool ocean current

0   800 Miles
0   800 Kilometers

Azimuthal Equal-Area Projection

EUROPE

ASIA

Atlantic Ocean

Canary Current

Mediterranean Sea

Africa–Asia boundary

MOROCCO
TUNISIA
ALGERIA
LIBYA
EGYPT
WESTERN SAHARA (Morocco)
S A H A R A
MAURITANIA
MALI
NIGER
CHAD
SUDAN
ERITREA
DJIBOUTI
CABO VERDE
SENEGAL
GAMBIA
S A H E L
GUINEA-BISSAU
GUINEA
BURKINA FASO
NIGERIA
SOUTH SUDAN
ETHIOPIA
SIERRA LEONE
CÔTE D'IVOIRE (IVORY COAST)
GHANA
BENIN
TOGO
CAMEROON
CENTRAL AFRICAN REPUBLIC
SOMALIA
LIBERIA

Red Sea

Guinea Current
EQUATORIAL GUINEA
SAO TOME & PRINCIPE
GABON
CONGO
Congo Basin
RWANDA
UGANDA
KENYA
DEMOCRATIC REPUBLIC OF THE CONGO
BURUNDI
TANZANIA

EQUATOR

SEYCHELLES

Atlantic Ocean
South Equatorial Current

ANGOLA
ZAMBIA
MALAWI
COMOROS
Mozambique Channel
MADAGASCAR
MAURITIUS

PRIME MERIDIAN

Benguela Current

ZIMBABWE
MOZAMBIQUE

TROPIC OF CAPRICORN

Namib Desert
NAMIBIA
BOTSWANA
Kalahari Desert

ESWATINI (SWAZILAND)
LESOTHO
SOUTH AFRICA

Agulhas Current

Indian Ocean

50°N
40°N
30°N
20°N
10°N
0°
10°S
20°S
30°S
40°S

30°W
20°W
0°
10°E
20°E
30°E
40°E
50°E
60°E

HEAVY RAINS near the Equator give way to the seasonal wet and dry patterns of the tall grass savanna that is home to Africa's big game animals. As rainfall decreases, short grass yields to desert—the Sahara in the north, the Kalahari and the Namib in the south.

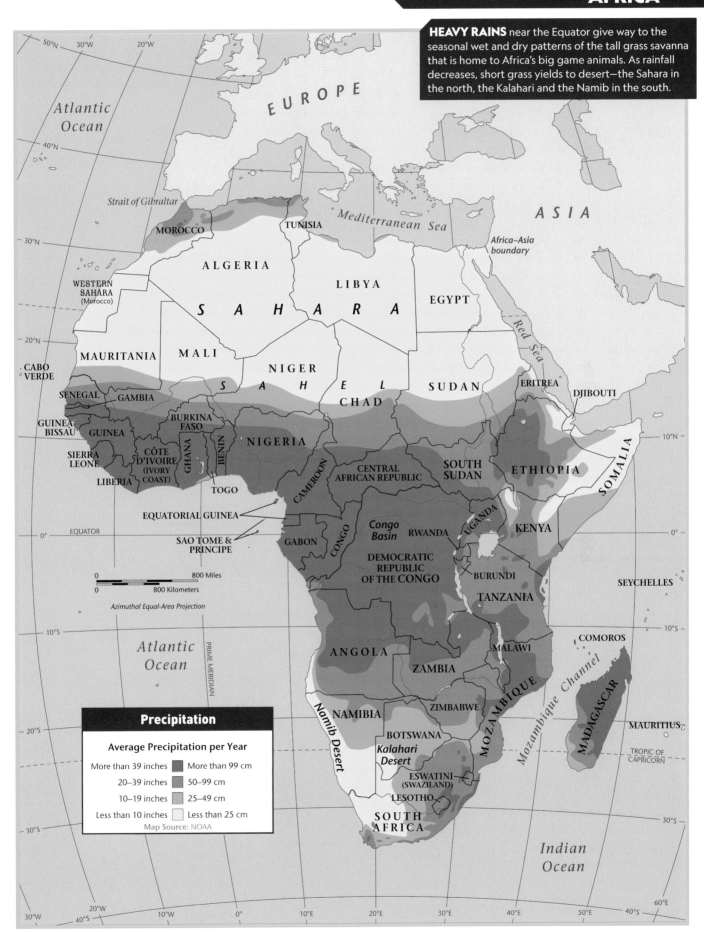

Atlantic Ocean

EUROPE

ASIA

Strait of Gibraltar

Mediterranean Sea

Africa–Asia boundary

MOROCCO

TUNISIA

ALGERIA

LIBYA

EGYPT

WESTERN SAHARA (Morocco)

S A H A R A

Red Sea

MAURITANIA

MALI

NIGER

SUDAN

ERITREA

CABO VERDE

S

A

H

E

L

DJIBOUTI

SENEGAL

GAMBIA

CHAD

GUINEA-BISSAU

BURKINA FASO

GUINEA

NIGERIA

SOUTH SUDAN

ETHIOPIA

SOMALIA

SIERRA LEONE

CÔTE D'IVOIRE (IVORY COAST)

GHANA

BENIN

LIBERIA

TOGO

CAMEROON

CENTRAL AFRICAN REPUBLIC

EQUATORIAL GUINEA

SAO TOME & PRINCIPE

GABON

CONGO

Congo Basin

RWANDA

UGANDA

KENYA

EQUATOR

DEMOCRATIC REPUBLIC OF THE CONGO

BURUNDI

TANZANIA

SEYCHELLES

0   800 Miles
0   800 Kilometers

Azimuthal Equal-Area Projection

MALAWI

COMOROS

Atlantic Ocean

PRIME MERIDIAN

ANGOLA

ZAMBIA

MOZAMBIQUE

Mozambique Channel

MADAGASCAR

Namib Desert

NAMIBIA

ZIMBABWE

MAURITIUS

BOTSWANA

Kalahari Desert

TROPIC OF CAPRICORN

Precipitation

Average Precipitation per Year

More than 39 inches	More than 99 cm
20–39 inches	50–99 cm
10–19 inches	25–49 cm
Less than 10 inches	Less than 25 cm

Map Source: NOAA

ESWATINI (SWAZILAND)

LESOTHO

SOUTH AFRICA

Indian Ocean

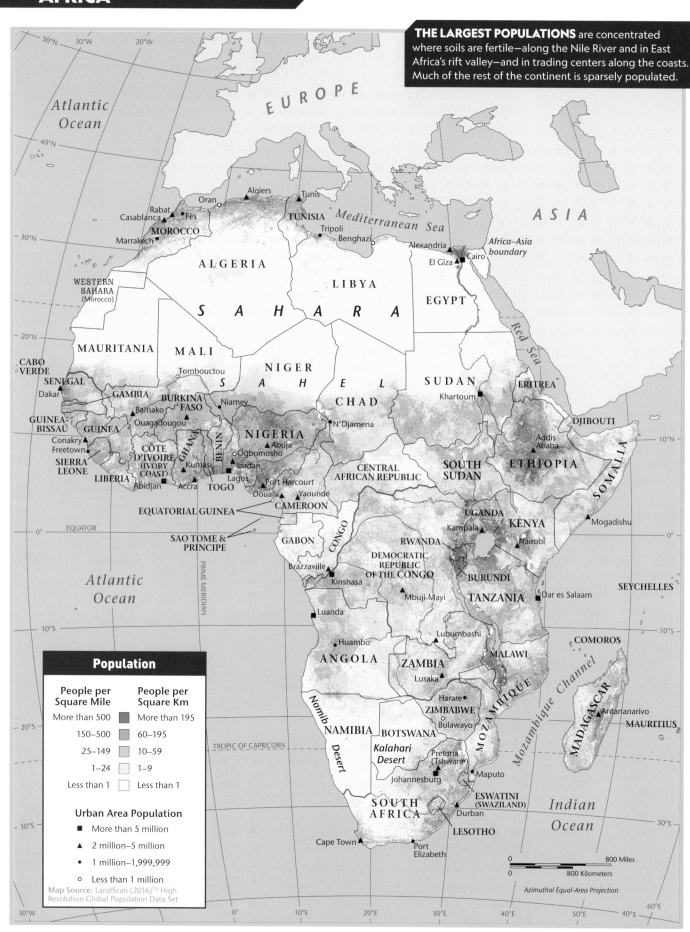

THE LARGEST POPULATIONS are concentrated where soils are fertile—along the Nile River and in East Africa's rift valley—and in trading centers along the coasts. Much of the rest of the continent is sparsely populated.

EUROPE

Atlantic Ocean

ASIA

Mediterranean Sea

Oran
Algiers
Tunis
Rabat
Casablanca   Fes
TUNISIA
MOROCCO
Tripoli
Marrakech
Benghazi
Alexandria   *Africa–Asia boundary*
El Giza   Cairo

ALGERIA
LIBYA
EGYPT

WESTERN SAHARA (Morocco)

S A H A R A

Red Sea

MAURITANIA
MALI
NIGER
SUDAN
ERITREA

Tombouctou
S A H E L
Khartoum

CABO VERDE
SENEGAL
Dakar
GAMBIA
BURKINA FASO
Niamey
CHAD
DJIBOUTI

GUINEA-BISSAU
Bamako
Ouagadougou
N'Djamena
Addis Ababa
Conakry
GUINEA
CÔTE D'IVOIRE (IVORY COAST)
GHANA
BENIN
NIGERIA
Abuja
Ogbomosho
CENTRAL AFRICAN REPUBLIC
SOUTH SUDAN
ETHIOPIA
SOMALIA
Freetown
SIERRA LEONE
Kumasi
Ibadan
LIBERIA
Abidjan
Accra
TOGO
Lagos
Port Harcourt
Douala
Yaoundé
Mogadishu
EQUATORIAL GUINEA
CAMEROON

EQUATOR
SAO TOME & PRINCIPE
GABON
CONGO
UGANDA
KENYA
Kampala
Nairobi
RWANDA
DEMOCRATIC REPUBLIC OF THE CONGO
Brazzaville
Kinshasa
BURUNDI
SEYCHELLES
Mbuji-Mayi
TANZANIA
Dar es Salaam

Atlantic Ocean
Luanda
Lubumbashi
COMOROS
Huambo
MALAWI
Mozambique Channel
ANGOLA
ZAMBIA
Lusaka
Antananarivo
MAURITIUS
MADAGASCAR
Harare
ZIMBABWE
Bulawayo
MOZAMBIQUE
Namib Desert
NAMIBIA
BOTSWANA
Kalahari Desert
Pretoria (Tshwane)
Maputo
TROPIC OF CAPRICORN
Johannesburg
ESWATINI (SWAZILAND)
Indian Ocean
Cape Town
SOUTH AFRICA
Durban
LESOTHO
Port Elizabeth

Population

People per Square Mile	People per Square Km
More than 500	More than 195
150–500	60–195
25–149	10–59
1–24	1–9
Less than 1	Less than 1

Urban Area Population
- ■ More than 5 million
- ▲ 2 million–5 million
- • 1 million–1,999,999
- ○ Less than 1 million

Map Source: LandScan (2016)™ High Resolution Global Population Data Set

Azimuthal Equal-Area Projection

0   800 Miles
0   800 Kilometers

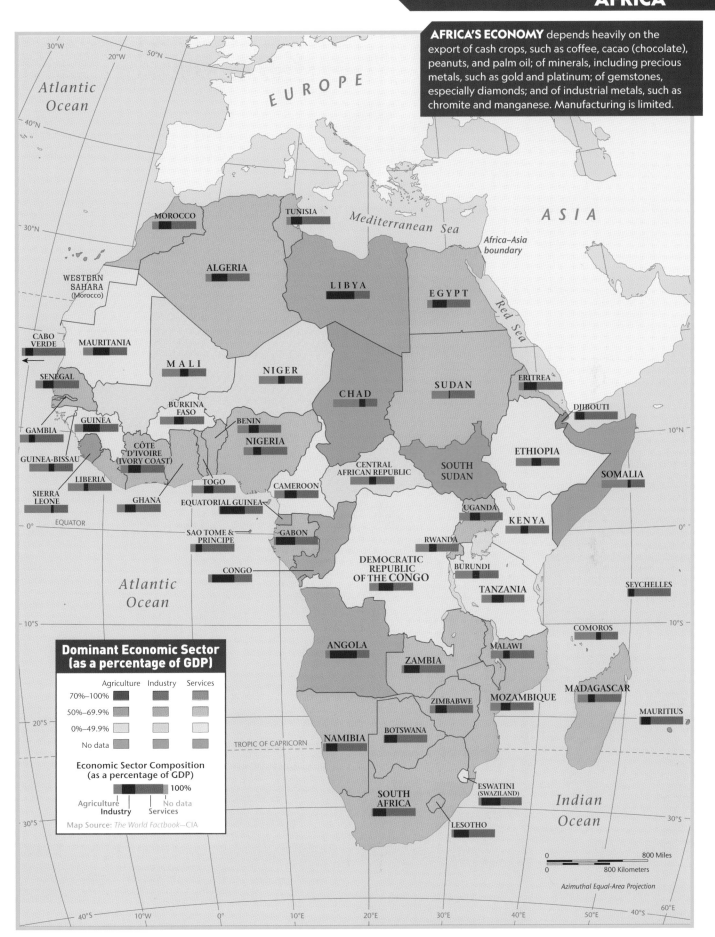

AFRICA'S ECONOMY depends heavily on the export of cash crops, such as coffee, cacao (chocolate), peanuts, and palm oil; of minerals, including precious metals, such as gold and platinum; of gemstones, especially diamonds; and of industrial metals, such as chromite and manganese. Manufacturing is limited.

Atlantic Ocean

EUROPE

ASIA

Mediterranean Sea

Africa–Asia boundary

MOROCCO

TUNISIA

ALGERIA

LIBYA

EGYPT

Red Sea

WESTERN SAHARA (Morocco)

CABO VERDE

MAURITANIA

MALI

NIGER

CHAD

SUDAN

ERITREA

DJIBOUTI

SENEGAL

BURKINA FASO

GAMBIA

GUINEA

BENIN

NIGERIA

CÔTE D'IVOIRE (IVORY COAST)

GUINEA-BISSAU

ETHIOPIA

CENTRAL AFRICAN REPUBLIC

SOUTH SUDAN

SOMALIA

SIERRA LEONE

LIBERIA

TOGO

GHANA

CAMEROON

EQUATORIAL GUINEA

UGANDA

KENYA

SAO TOME & PRINCIPE

GABON

RWANDA

EQUATOR

CONGO

DEMOCRATIC REPUBLIC OF THE CONGO

BURUNDI

TANZANIA

SEYCHELLES

Atlantic Ocean

ANGOLA

ZAMBIA

MALAWI

COMOROS

MADAGASCAR

ZIMBABWE

MOZAMBIQUE

MAURITIUS

NAMIBIA

BOTSWANA

TROPIC OF CAPRICORN

ESWATINI (SWAZILAND)

SOUTH AFRICA

LESOTHO

Indian Ocean

Dominant Economic Sector (as a percentage of GDP)

	Agriculture	Industry	Services
70%–100%			
50%–69.9%			
0%–49.9%			
No data			

Economic Sector Composition (as a percentage of GDP)

100%

Agriculture
Industry
Services
No data

Map Source: *The World Factbook*—CIA

800 Miles

800 Kilometers

Azimuthal Equal-Area Projection

THE CONTINENT:
AFRICA

PROTECTED AREAS

FACTS & FIGURES

Land Protected in Africa (2016)
1,676,169 square miles
(4,341,259 sq km)

**Percentage of Land Protected
in Africa (2016): 16.96%**

**Number of Protected Areas
in Africa (2016): 8,431**

**Countries With Highest Percentage
of Protected Land (2016)**

Seychelles	42.09%
Rep. of Congo	40.59%
Tanzania	38.15%
Namibia	37.89%
Zambia	37.87%
Guinea	35.65%
Morocco	30.78%

Species at Risk Globally (2017)

	Critically endangered	Endangered
Mammals	202	476
Birds	222	461
Reptiles	266	484
Fish	468	676
Plants	2,722	4,123

Selected African Species at Risk
African elephant, northern white
rhino, black rhino, mountain gorilla,
Rothschild's giraffe, Ethiopian wolf,
Grévy's zebra, African wild dog,
African penguin, chimpanzee,
cheetah, blue crane, vulture

⬭ FOREST DWELLER.
A critically endangered
mountain gorilla in Rwanda
stares intently. Native to
the Virunga Mountains of
central Africa, fewer than
900 mountain gorillas
remain in the wild.

Protected Areas

Africa is home to many different animals. Some are
familiar, such as the giraffe and rhinoceros; others
are rare. All are part of Earth's valuable storehouse of biodiversity, but many are at risk due
to a variety of pressures. Natural changes,
such as periodic drought, may put stress on
both plant and animal populations, but human
activity is the main threat. Africa's human
population is growing on average at a rate
of 2.6 percent each year. Converting land for
agricultural use, hunting animals for food, and
cutting trees for fuel, as well as expanding
commercial logging and building roads have led
to loss of natural habitat for many of Africa's
animals. Some, such as the mountain gorilla, are
even at risk of extinction.

To reverse this trend of biodiversity loss, many
countries have created protected areas (see map
at right), which include nature reserves, wilderness areas, and national parks. Protected areas
allow animals to live in a natural environment.
They also provide a source of income for
African countries, many of which are very
poor, as tourists come on photo safaris
to view these unique animals.

⬭ STANDING TALL. At an average height
of more than 18 feet (5.7 m), giraffes are the
world's tallest mammal. This giraffe stands
on the grassy plain of Kenya's Maasai Mara.

BIODIVERSITY THREATENED

Madagascar	746 / 789
Tanzania	485 / 631
South Africa	452 / 151
Cameroon	287 / 535
Kenya	256 / 234

Animal species
Plant species

2017 data

**Madagascar, an island country off the southeast coast,
leads all countries in Africa in number of species that are
critically endangered, endangered, or vulnerable.**

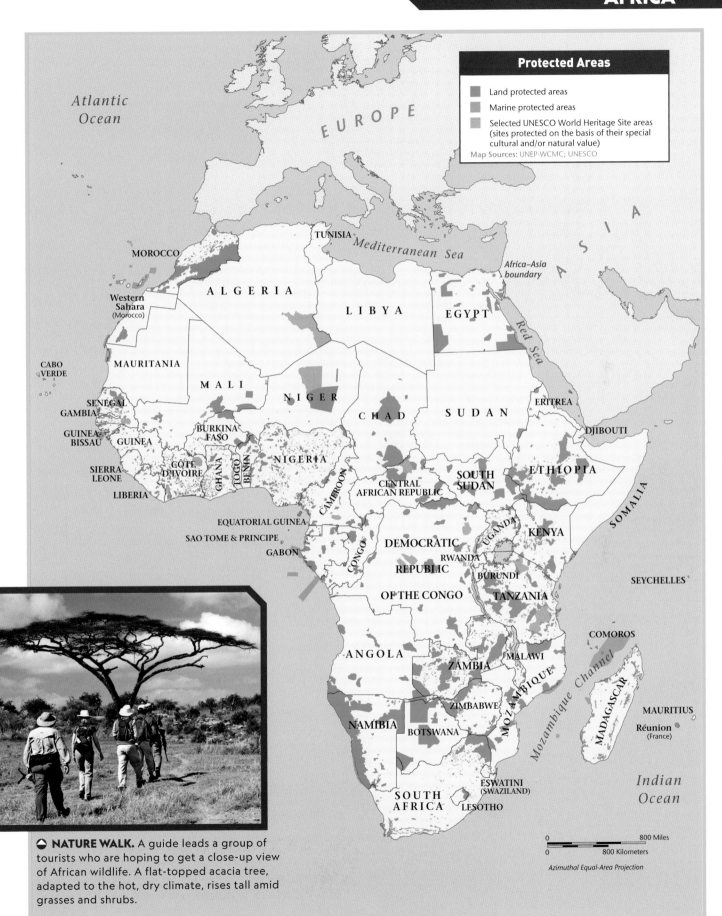

Atlantic Ocean

EUROPE

ASIA

Protected Areas

Land protected areas

Marine protected areas

Selected UNESCO World Heritage Site areas
(sites protected on the basis of their special
cultural and/or natural value)

Map Sources: UNEP-WCMC; UNESCO

TUNISIA

Mediterranean Sea

MOROCCO

Africa–Asia
boundary

ALGERIA

LIBYA

EGYPT

Western
Sahara
(Morocco)

Red Sea

CABO
VERDE

MAURITANIA

MALI

NIGER

CHAD

SUDAN

ERITREA

SENEGAL

GAMBIA

BURKINA
FASO

DJIBOUTI

GUINEA-
BISSAU

GUINEA

NIGERIA

ETHIOPIA

SIERRA
LEONE

CÔTE
D'IVOIRE

GHANA

TOGO

BENIN

CAMEROON

CENTRAL
AFRICAN REPUBLIC

SOUTH
SUDAN

LIBERIA

EQUATORIAL GUINEA

SAO TOME & PRINCIPE

GABON

CONGO

DEMOCRATIC

REPUBLIC

OF THE CONGO

UGANDA

RWANDA

BURUNDI

KENYA

SOMALIA

TANZANIA

SEYCHELLES

ANGOLA

ZAMBIA

MALAWI

MOZAMBIQUE

COMOROS

Mozambique Channel

MADAGASCAR

MAURITIUS

Réunion
(France)

ZIMBABWE

NAMIBIA

BOTSWANA

ESWATINI
(SWAZILAND)

*Indian
Ocean*

SOUTH
AFRICA

LESOTHO

0   800 Miles
0   800 Kilometers

Azimuthal Equal-Area Projection

🔺 **NATURE WALK.** A guide leads a group of tourists who are hoping to get a close-up view of African wildlife. A flat-topped acacia tree, adapted to the hot, dry climate, rises tall amid grasses and shrubs.

Australia:
A View From Space

Smallest of Earth's great landmasses, Australia is the only one that is both a continent and a country. It is part of the greater region of Oceania, which includes New Zealand, the eastern part of New Guinea, and hundreds of smaller islands scattered across the Pacific Ocean. Although Hawai'i is politically part of the United States, geographically and culturally it is part of Oceania.

The opera house in Sydney, Australia

THE REGION:
AUSTRALIA & OCEANIA

Australia & Oceania

PHYSICAL			POLITICAL		
Area and population totals are for the independent countries in the region only.	Highest point **Mount Wilhelm, Papua New Guinea** **14,793 ft (4,509 m)**	Longest river **Murray-Darling, Australia** **2,282 mi (3,672 km)**	Population **38,004,000** Number of independent countries **14**	Largest country **Australia** **2,988,901 sq mi** **(7,741,220 sq km)**	Most populous country **Australia** **Pop. 23,232,000**
Land area **3,278,000 sq mi** **(8,490,000 sq km)**	Lowest point **Lake Eyre, Australia** **-49 ft (-15 m)**	Largest lake **Lake Eyre, Australia** **3,430 sq mi** **(8,884 sq km)**		Smallest country **Nauru** **8 sq mi (21 sq km)**	Least populous country **Nauru** **Pop. 11,000**

THE REGION:
AUSTRALIA & OCEANIA

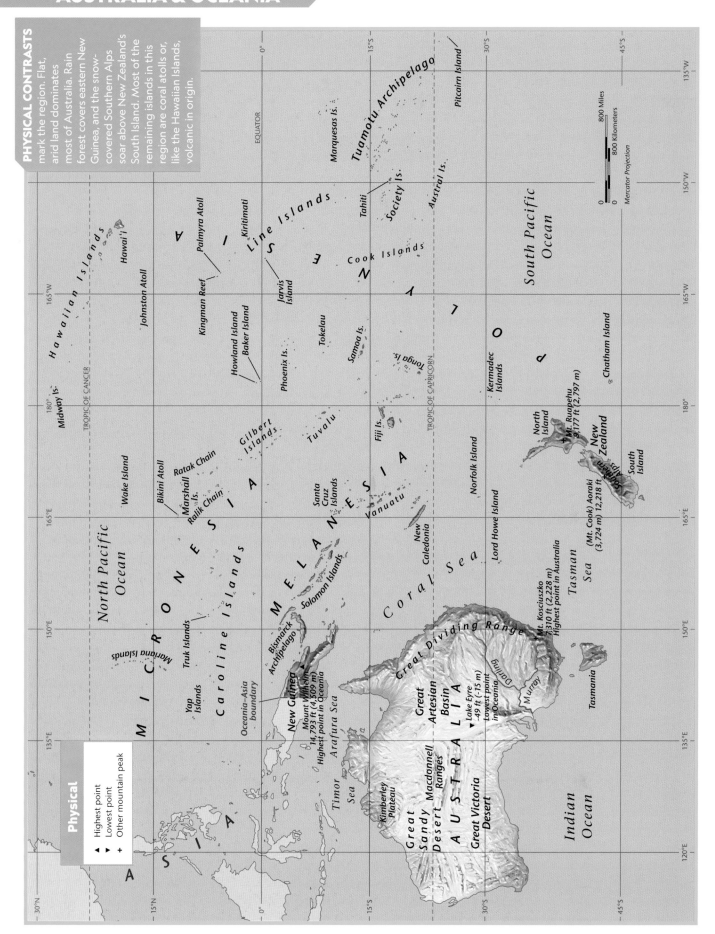

PHYSICAL CONTRASTS mark the region. Flat, arid land dominates most of Australia. Rain forest covers eastern New Guinea, and the snow-covered Southern Alps soar above New Zealand's South Island. Most of the remaining islands in this region are coral atolls or, like the Hawaiian Islands, volcanic in origin.

Physical

◄ Highest point
► Lowest point
+ Other mountain peak

800 Miles
800 Kilometers
Mercator Projection

Hawaiian Islands

Hawai'i

Midway Is.

Johnston Atoll

TROPIC OF CANCER

Palmyra Atoll

Kiritimati

Line Islands

Kingman Reef

Jarvis Island

Howland Island
Baker Island

Phoenix Is.

Tokelau

Samoa Is.

Marquesas Is.

Tuamotu Archipelago

Pitcairn Island

Tahiti
Society Is.

Austral Is.

Cook Islands

P O L Y N E S I A

EQUATOR

Wake Island

Bikini Atoll

Ratak Chain
Marshall Is.
Ralik Chain

Gilbert Islands

Tuvalu

Fiji Is.

Tonga Is.

TROPIC OF CAPRICORN

Kermadec Islands

South Pacific Ocean

North Pacific Ocean

M I C R O N E S I A

Caroline Islands

Mariana Islands

Truk Islands

Yap Islands

Santa Cruz Islands

M E L A N E S I A

Vanuatu

New Caledonia

Norfolk Island

Lord Howe Island

Chatham Island

North Island

Mt. Ruapehu
9,177 ft (2,797 m)

New Zealand

South Island

Southern Alps

(Mt. Cook) Aoraki
(3,724 m) 12,218 ft

Tasman Sea

Bismarck Archipelago

New Guinea

Mount Wilhelm
14,793 ft (4,509 m)
Highest point in Oceania

Solomon Islands

Coral Sea

Great Dividing Range

Mt. Kosciuszko
7,310 ft (2,228 m)
Highest point in Australia

Darling

Murray

Tasmania

Oceania–Asia boundary

A S I A

Timor Sea

Arafura Sea

Great Sandy Desert

Kimberley Plateau

Macdonnell Ranges

Great Artesian Basin

A U S T R A L I A

Great Victoria Desert

Lake Eyre
-49 ft (-15 m)
Lowest point in Oceania

Indian Ocean

30°N
15°N
0°
15°S
30°S
45°S

120°E
135°E
150°E
165°E
180°
165°W
150°W
135°W

180° Is.

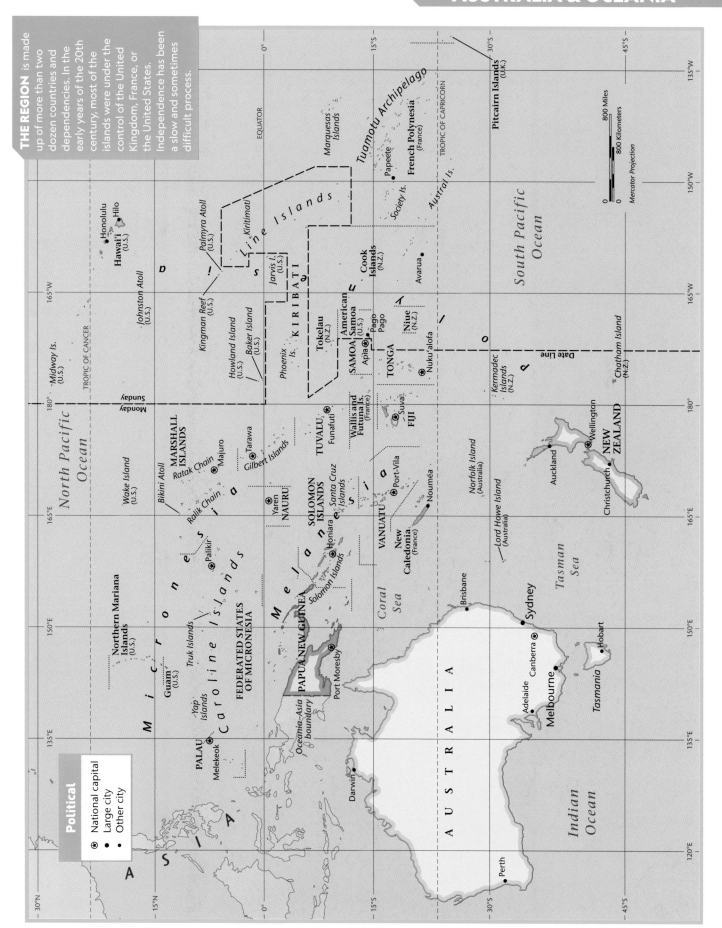

THE REGION is made up of more than two dozen countries and dependencies. In the early years of the 20th century, most of the islands were under the control of the United Kingdom, France, or the United States. Independence has been a slow and sometimes difficult process.

Political

⊛ National capital
● Large city
· Other city

800 Miles
800 Kilometers
Mercator Projection

EQUATOR

Marquesas Islands

Tuamotu Archipelago

Papeete
French Polynesia (France)
TROPIC OF CAPRICORN
Pitcairn Islands (U.K.)

Society Is.
Austral Is.

South Pacific Ocean

Honolulu
Hilo
Hawai'i (U.S.)

Palmyra Atoll (U.S.)
Line Islands
Kiritimati

Johnston Atoll (U.S.)

Kingman Reef (U.S.)
Jarvis I. (U.S.)
KIRIBATI

Cook Islands (N.Z.)
Avarua

North Pacific Ocean

TROPIC OF CANCER

Midway Is. (U.S.)

Howland Island (U.S.)
Baker Island (U.S.)
Phoenix Is.
Tokelau (N.Z.)
American Samoa (U.S.)
Pago Pago
Niue (N.Z.)

Monday
Sunday

SAMOA
Apia
TONGA
Nuku'alofa

Kermadec Islands (N.Z.)

Date Line

Chatham Island (N.Z.)

Wake Island (U.S.)

MARSHALL ISLANDS
Ratak Chain
Majuro
Tarawa
Gilbert Islands

Bikini Atoll
Ralik Chain

Yaren
NAURU

TUVALU
Funafuti

Wallis and Futuna Is. (France)
Suva
FIJI

Norfolk Island (Australia)

New Zealand
Wellington
Auckland
NEW ZEALAND
Christchurch

Micronesia

Northern Mariana Islands (U.S.)

Guam (U.S.)
Truk Islands

Caroline Islands

FEDERATED STATES OF MICRONESIA
Palikir

Melanesia

SOLOMON ISLANDS
Honiara
Solomon Islands
Santa Cruz Islands

VANUATU
Port-Vila

New Caledonia (France)
Nouméa

Lord Howe Island (Australia)

Coral Sea

Tasman Sea

PALAU
Melekeok

Yap Islands

ASIA

PAPUA NEW GUINEA
Port Moresby

Oceania-Asia boundary

Darwin

AUSTRALIA

Brisbane

Sydney
Canberra
Adelaide
Melbourne
Hobart
Tasmania

Perth

Indian Ocean

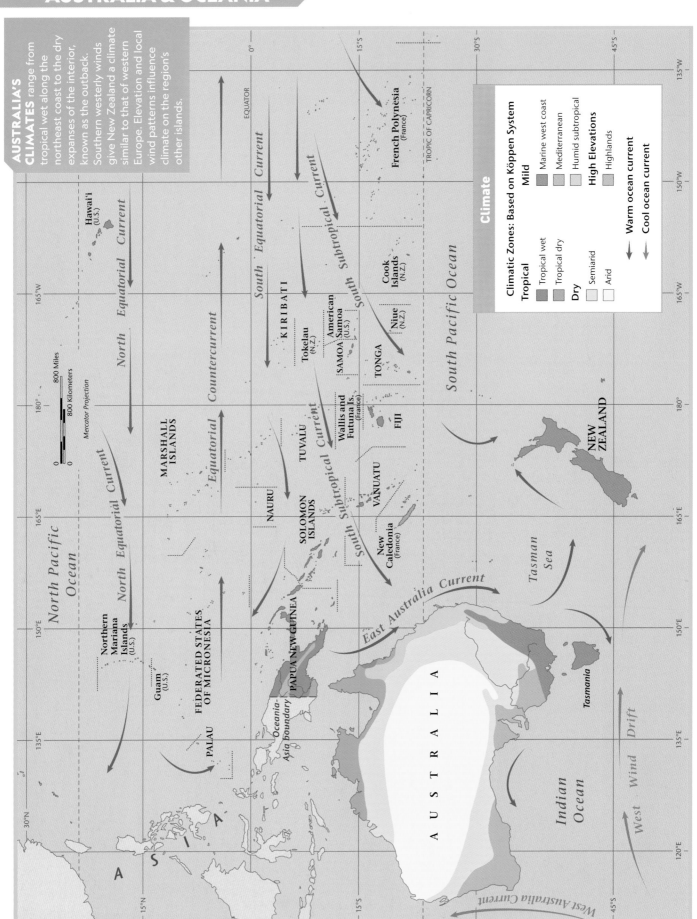

Climate

Climatic Zones: Based on Köppen System

Tropical
- Tropical wet
- Tropical dry

Dry
- Semiarid
- Arid

Mild
- Marine west coast
- Mediterranean
- Humid subtropical

High Elevations
- Highlands

→ Warm ocean current
→ Cool ocean current

North Pacific Ocean

South Pacific Ocean

Indian Ocean

North Equatorial Current

North Equatorial Current

Equatorial Countercurrent

South Equatorial Current

South Subtropical Current

South Subtropical Current

East Australia Current

Tasman Sea

West Australia Current

West Wind Drift

EQUATOR

TROPIC OF CAPRICORN

Hawai'i (U.S.)

Northern Mariana Islands (U.S.)

Guam (U.S.)

PALAU

FEDERATED STATES OF MICRONESIA

MARSHALL ISLANDS

NAURU

KIRIBATI

Tokelau (N.Z.)

American Samoa (U.S.)

SAMOA

TONGA

Niue (N.Z.)

Cook Islands (N.Z.)

French Polynesia (France)

TUVALU

Wallis and Futuna Is. (France)

FIJI

VANUATU

New Caledonia (France)

SOLOMON ISLANDS

PAPUA NEW GUINEA

Oceania-Asia Boundary

ASIA

AUSTRALIA

Tasmania

NEW ZEALAND

800 Miles
800 Kilometers
0
0

Mercator Projection

30°N
15°N
15°S
45°S

120°E
135°E
150°E
165°E
180°
165°W
150°W
135°W

0°
15°S
30°S
45°S

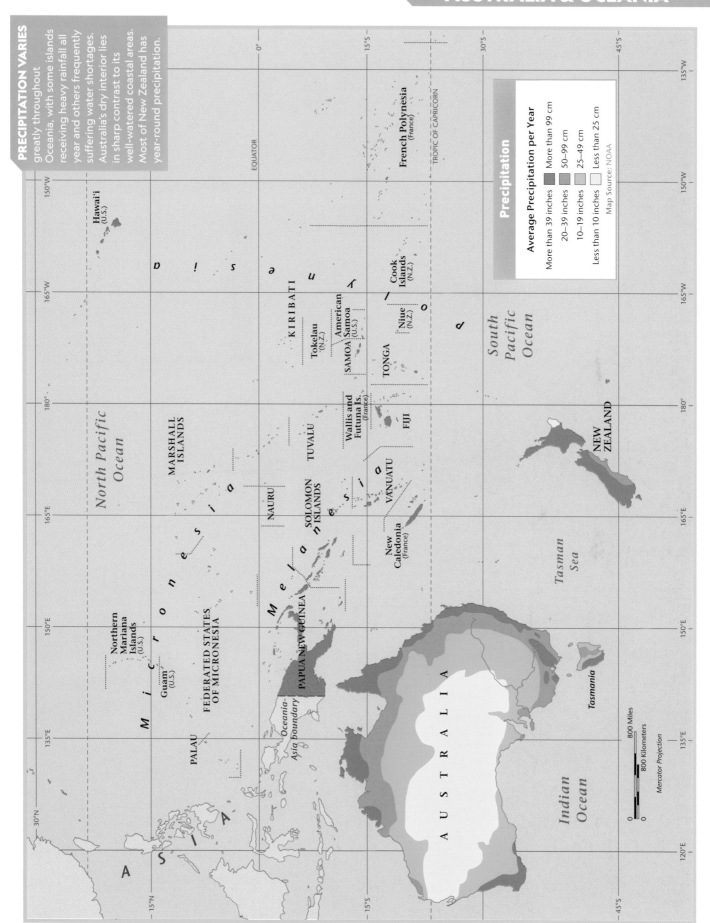

PRECIPITATION VARIES greatly throughout Oceania, with some islands receiving heavy rainfall all year and others frequently suffering water shortages. Australia's dry interior lies in sharp contrast to its well-watered coastal areas. Most of New Zealand has year-round precipitation.

Precipitation

Average Precipitation per Year

More than 39 inches	More than 99 cm
20–39 inches	50–99 cm
10–19 inches	25–49 cm
Less than 10 inches	Less than 25 cm

Map Source: NOAA

Hawai'i (U.S.)

French Polynesia (France)

TROPIC OF CAPRICORN

EQUATOR

North Pacific Ocean

Micronesia

Melanesia

Polynesia

KIRIBATI

Tokelau (N.Z.)

American Samoa (U.S.)

SAMOA

TONGA

Niue (N.Z.)

Cook Islands (N.Z.)

South Pacific Ocean

MARSHALL ISLANDS

NAURU

TUVALU

Wallis and Futuna Is. (France)

FIJI

SOLOMON ISLANDS

VANUATU

New Caledonia (France)

NEW ZEALAND

Tasman Sea

Northern Mariana Islands (U.S.)

Guam (U.S.)

FEDERATED STATES OF MICRONESIA

PALAU

Oceania-Asia Boundary

PAPUA NEW GUINEA

ASIA

AUSTRALIA

Tasmania

Indian Ocean

800 Miles

800 Kilometers

Mercator Projection

THE REGION:
AUSTRALIA & OCEANIA

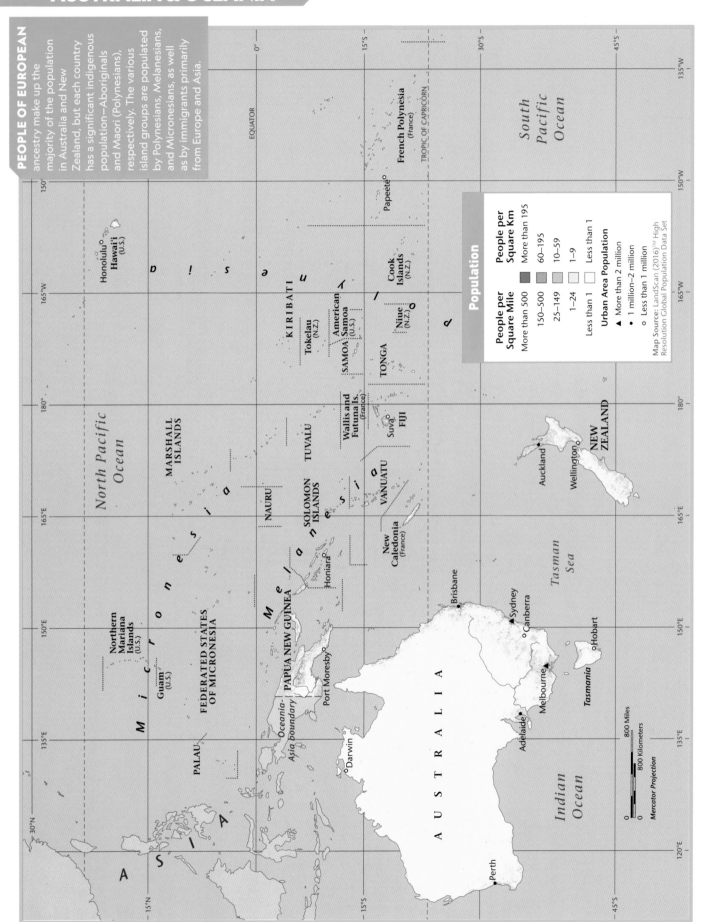

PEOPLE OF EUROPEAN ancestry make up the majority of the population in Australia and New Zealand, but each country has a significant indigenous population—Aboriginals and Maori (Polynesians), respectively. The various island groups are populated by Polynesians, Melanesians, and Micronesians, as well as by immigrants primarily from Europe and Asia.

Population

People per Square Mile
- More than 500
- 150–500
- 25–149
- 1–24
- Less than 1

People per Square Km
- More than 195
- 60–195
- 10–59
- 1–9
- Less than 1

Urban Area Population
- ▲ More than 2 million
- ● 1 million–2 million
- ○ Less than 1 million

Map Source: LandScan (2016)™ High Resolution Global Population Data Set

South Pacific Ocean

North Pacific Ocean

Indian Ocean

Tasman Sea

AUSTRALIA

NEW ZEALAND

Tasmania

PAPUA NEW GUINEA

FEDERATED STATES OF MICRONESIA

MARSHALL ISLANDS

SOLOMON ISLANDS

VANUATU

New Caledonia (France)

FIJI

TUVALU

NAURU

KIRIBATI

TONGA

SAMOA
American Samoa (U.S.)

Tokelau (N.Z.)

Niue (N.Z.)

Cook Islands (N.Z.)

French Polynesia (France)

Wallis and Futuna Is. (France)

Hawai'i (U.S.)

PALAU

Guam (U.S.)

Northern Mariana Islands (U.S.)

Micronesia

Melanesia

Polynesia

A S I A

Oceania-Asia Boundary

EQUATOR

TROPIC OF CAPRICORN

Darwin

Perth

Adelaide

Melbourne

Hobart

Canberra

Sydney

Brisbane

Port Moresby

Honiara

Suva

Papeete

Honolulu

Auckland

Wellington

0   800 Miles
0   800 Kilometers

Mercator Projection

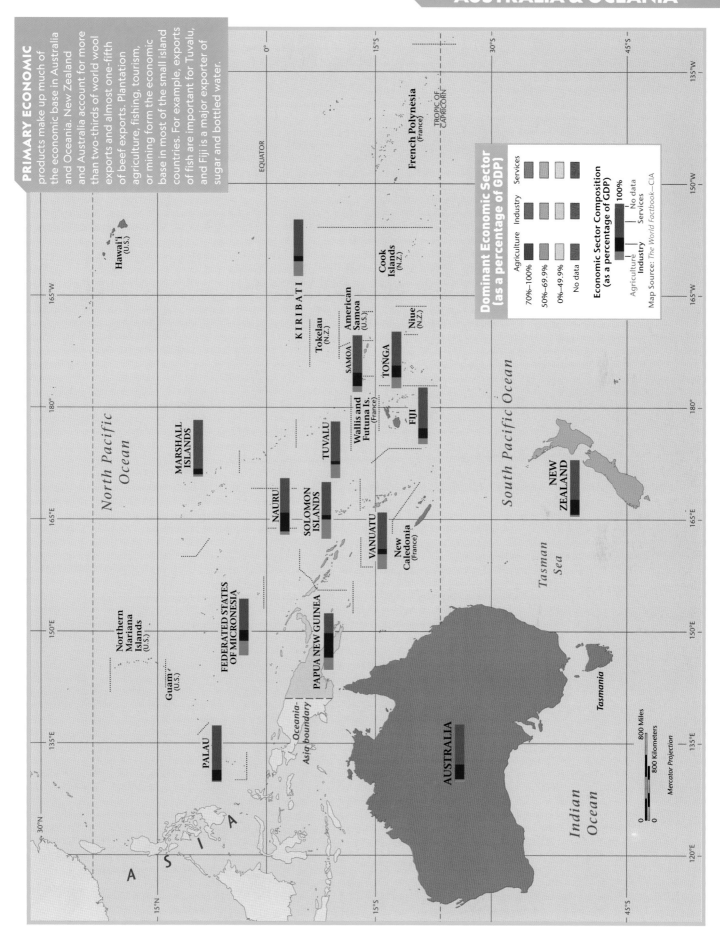

PRIMARY ECONOMIC products make up much of the economic base in Australia and Oceania. New Zealand and Australia account for more than two-thirds of world wool exports and almost one-fifth of beef exports. Plantation agriculture, fishing, tourism, or mining form the economic base in most of the small island countries. For example, exports of fish are important for Tuvalu, and Fiji is a major exporter of sugar and bottled water.

Dominant Economic Sector
(as a percentage of GDP)

Agriculture   Industry   Services

70%–100%

50%–69.9%

0%–49.9%

No data

Economic Sector Composition
(as a percentage of GDP)

100%

Agriculture
Industry
Services
No data

Agriculture
Industry
Services

Map Source: *The World Factbook*—CIA

North Pacific Ocean

South Pacific Ocean

Indian Ocean

Tasman Sea

Hawai'i
(U.S.)

KIRIBATI

Tokelau
(N.Z.)

American
Samoa
(U.S.)

Cook
Islands
(N.Z.)

SAMOA

Niue
(N.Z.)

TONGA

Wallis and
Futuna Is.
(France)

FIJI

MARSHALL
ISLANDS

TUVALU

NAURU

SOLOMON
ISLANDS

VANUATU

New
Caledonia
(France)

NEW
ZEALAND

Northern
Mariana
Islands
(U.S.)

Guam
(U.S.)

FEDERATED STATES
OF MICRONESIA

PAPUA NEW GUINEA

PALAU

Oceania
Asia boundary

AUSTRALIA

Tasmania

A S I A

EQUATOR

TROPIC OF
CAPRICORN

Mercator Projection

0   800 Miles

0   800 Kilometers

THE REGION:
AUSTRALIA & OCEANIA

CORAL REEFS

SELECTED FACTS

Most coral reefs are between 5,000 and 10,000 years old, but some may have begun growing as much as 50 million years ago.

Types of Reefs

Fringing reefs form near coastlines of islands and continents.

Barrier reefs form parallel to coastlines but are separated by deep lagoons.

Atolls form as circular reefs around the fringe of sunken volcanic islands.

Patch reefs grow from a continental shelf to form isolated reefs.

Growing Conditions

Corals grow best in

○ **the tropics (30° N to 30° S),** where sunlight is consistent year-round.

○ **shallow, warm water,** ranging in temperature from 70° to 85°F (21° to 29°C).

○ **clear, clean water** that is free of pollutants or sediments that may block sunlight or smother the coral.

○ **salt water** where there is a constant salt-to-water ratio.

Great Barrier Reef

Stretching like intricate necklaces along the edges of landmasses in the warm ocean waters of the tropics, coral reefs form one of nature's most complex ecosystems. Corals are tiny marine animals that thrive in shallow coastal waters of the tropics. One type of coral, called a "hard coral," produces a limestone skeleton. When the tiny animal dies, its stone-like skeleton is left behind. The accumulation of millions of these skeletons over thousands of years has produced the large reef formations found in many coastal waters of the tropics.

ANEMONE FISH swim among the waving polyps of one of the reef's sea anemones. These fish are specially adapted to live safely among the venom-filled tentacles that can inject a paralyzing neurotoxin into unsuspecting prey when disturbed.

Most coral reefs are found between 30 degrees N and 30 degrees S latitude in waters with a temperature between 70 and 85 degrees Fahrenheit (21° and 29°C). It is estimated that Earth's coral reefs cover 110,000 square miles (284,900 sq km). Coral reefs are important because they form a habitat for such marine animals as fish, sea turtles, lobsters, and sea stars. They also protect fragile coastlines from damaging ocean waves and may be a source of valuable medicines.

The world's largest coral reef, the Great Barrier Reef, lies off the northeast coast of Australia (see large-scale map). This reef, which is made up of more than 600 different types of corals and is home to more than 1,600 species of fish, is a popular tourist destination. People visit to snorkel and dive along the reef and view the great diversity of marine life living among the corals.

BRILLIANTLY COLORED CORALS and the fish that live among them attract divers and snorkelers to the Great Barrier Reef every year.

GREAT BARRIER REEF BIODIVERSITY

Number of selected species, 2016

Mollusks	Fish	Corals	Rays & Sharks	Marine Turtles
more than 3,000	1,625	more than 600	133	6

The Great Barrier Reef, one of the seven wonders of the natural world and Earth's largest living structure, is home to almost 9,000 species of marine life.

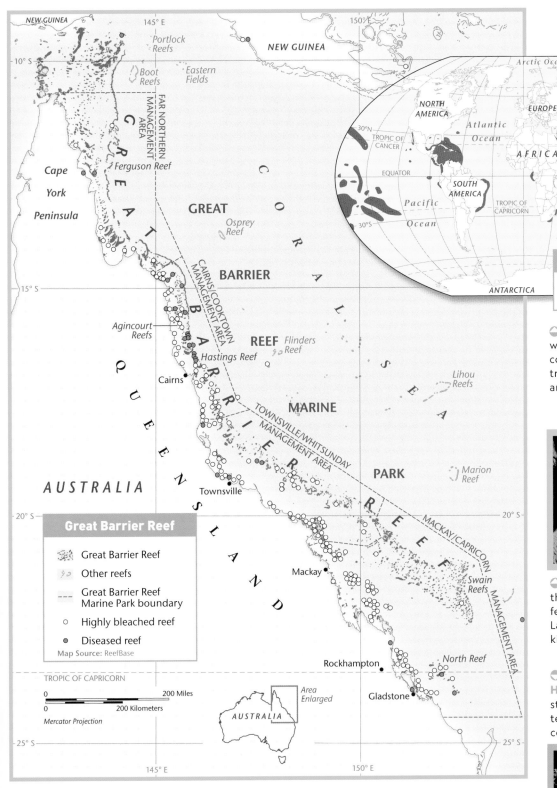

NEW GUINEA

145° E

150° E

NEW GUINEA

Portlock
Reefs

10° S

Boot
Reefs

Eastern
Fields

Arctic Ocean

NORTH
AMERICA

EUROPE

ASIA

Pacific
Ocean

30°N

TROPIC OF
CANCER

Atlantic
Ocean

AFRICA

EQUATOR

SOUTH
AMERICA

Indian
Ocean

Pacific
Ocean

TROPIC OF
CAPRICORN

AUSTRALIA

30°S

ANTARCTICA

FAR NORTHERN MANAGEMENT AREA

Cape
York
Peninsula

Ferguson Reef

GREAT

C
O
R
A
L

GREAT

Osprey
Reef

BARRIER

CAIRNS/COOKTOWN MANAGEMENT AREA

15° S

Agincourt
Reefs

REEF

Flinders
Reef

Hastings Reef

Cairns

B
A
R
R
I
E
R

S
E
A

MARINE

Lihou
Reefs

Q
U
E
E
N
S
L
A
N
D

TOWNSVILLE/WHITSUNDAY MANAGEMENT AREA

PARK

Marion
Reef

AUSTRALIA

Townsville

R
E
E
F

20° S

20° S

MACKAY/CAPRICORN MANAGEMENT AREA

Great Barrier Reef

Great Barrier Reef

Other reefs

Great Barrier Reef
Marine Park boundary

○ Highly bleached reef

● Diseased reef

Map Source: ReefBase

Mackay

Swain
Reefs

TROPIC OF CAPRICORN

0   200 Miles

0   200 Kilometers

Mercator Projection

Area
Enlarged

AUSTRALIA

Rockhampton

North Reef

Gladstone

25° S

25° S

145° E

150° E

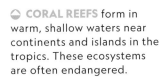

■ Area with coral
present

⬭ **CORAL REEFS** form in
warm, shallow waters near
continents and islands in the
tropics. These ecosystems
are often endangered.

⬭ **PREDATORS,** such as
this crown-of-thorns sea star,
feed on the coral polyps.
Large numbers of sea stars can
kill the coral.

⬭ **ENVIRONMENTAL
HAZARDS,** such as pollution,
storms, and changes in water
temperature and salinity, put
corals at risk.

⬭ **THE GREAT BARRIER REEF** stretches along the northeast coast of Australia for 1,429 miles
(2,300 km), from the tip of the Cape York Peninsula to south of Rockhampton. The reef is actually
a collection of more than 3,000 individual reef systems and is home to many different species of
fish, mollusks, rays, dolphins, reptiles, and birds. There are even giant clams more than 120 years
old. The reef is habitat for several endangered species, including the dugong (sea cow) and four
species of sea turtles. UNESCO recognized the Great Barrier Reef as a World Heritage site in 1981.

Antarctica:
A View From Space

About 180 million years ago, Antarctica broke away from the ancient super-continent Gondwana (see page 16). Slowly the continent drifted to its present location at Earth's southernmost point. Antarctica has no permanent human population, but it does have many types of wildlife. Seals, whales, and birds such as penguins, albatrosses, petrels, and terns have adapted to the continent's bitter-cold climate and long, dark winters.

Gentoo penguins nest and raise their young in large colonies along the coastal margins of Antarctica.

PHYSICAL

Land area **5,100,000 sq mi** **(13,209,000 sq km)**	**Lowest point** **Byrd Glacier (Depression)** **-9,416 ft (-2,870 m)**	**Average precipitation on the polar plateau** **Less than 2 in (5 cm) per year**
Highest point **Vinson Massif** **16,067 ft (4,897 m)**	**Coldest place** **Annual average temperature** **Ridge A -94°F (-70°C)**	

POLITICAL

Population **There are no permanent inhabitants, but there are staff at both year-round and summer-only research stations.**	**Number of independent countries** **0**	**Number of countries operating year-round research stations** **21**
	Number of countries claiming land **7**	**Number of year-round research stations** **40**

Antarctica

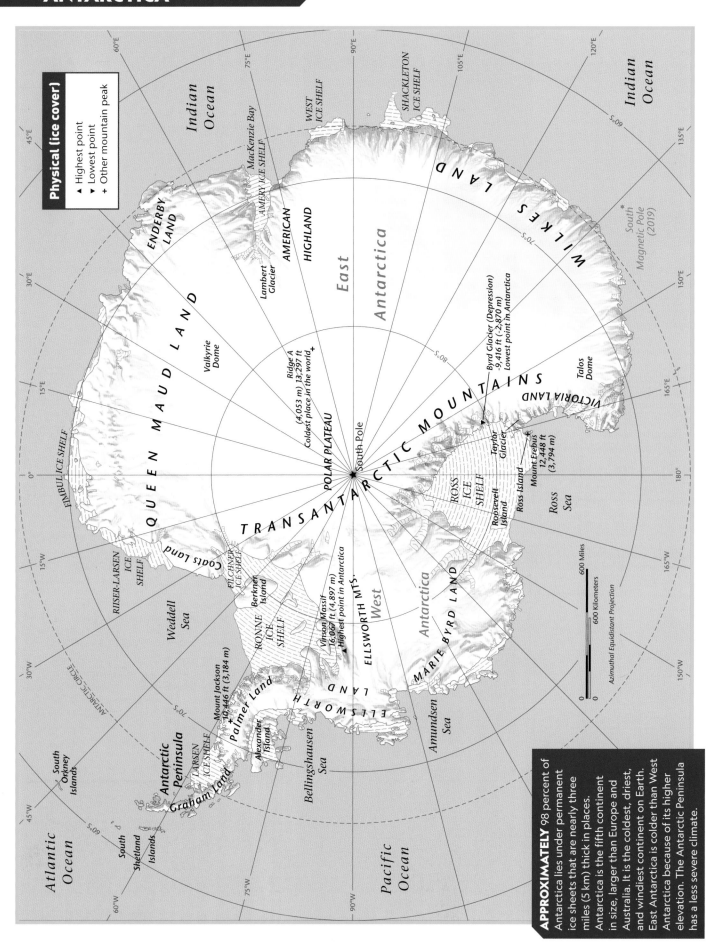

Physical (ice cover)
- ▲ Highest point
- ▼ Lowest point
- + Other mountain peak

Indian Ocean

Indian Ocean

MacKenzie Bay

WEST ICE SHELF

SHACKLETON ICE SHELF

AMERY ICE SHELF

ENDERBY LAND

AMERICAN HIGHLAND

WILKES LAND

South Magnetic Pole (2019)

Lambert Glacier

East Antarctica

QUEEN MAUD LAND

Valkyrie Dome

Ridge A (4,053 m) 13,297 ft Coldest place in the world +

Byrd Glacier (Depression) -9,416 ft (-2,870 m) Lowest point in Antarctica

Talos Dome

VICTORIA LAND

FIMBUL ICE SHELF

POLAR PLATEAU

South Pole

T R A N S A N T A R C T I C   M O U N T A I N S

Taylor Glacier

Mount Erebus 12,448 ft (3,794 m)

ROSS ICE SHELF

Roosevelt Island

Ross Island

Ross Sea

RIISER-LARSEN ICE SHELF

Coats Land

FILCHNER ICE SHELF

Berkner Island

Weddell Sea

RONNE ICE SHELF

Vinson Massif 16,067 ft (4,897 m) ▲ Highest point in Antarctica

ELLSWORTH MTS.

West Antarctica

MARIE BYRD LAND

600 Miles

600 Kilometers

Azimuthal Equidistant Projection

South Orkney Islands

LARSEN ICE SHELF

Mount Jackson 10,446 ft (3,184 m) +

Palmer Land

Alexander Island

ELLSWORTH LAND

Amundsen Sea

Antarctic Peninsula

Graham Land

Bellingshausen Sea

South Shetland Islands

Atlantic Ocean

Pacific Ocean

ANTARCTIC CIRCLE

APPROXIMATELY 98 percent of Antarctica lies under permanent ice sheets that are nearly three miles (5 km) thick in places. Antarctica is the fifth continent in size, larger than Europe and Australia. It is the coldest, driest, and windiest continent on Earth. East Antarctica is colder than West Antarctica because of its higher elevation. The Antarctic Peninsula has a less severe climate.

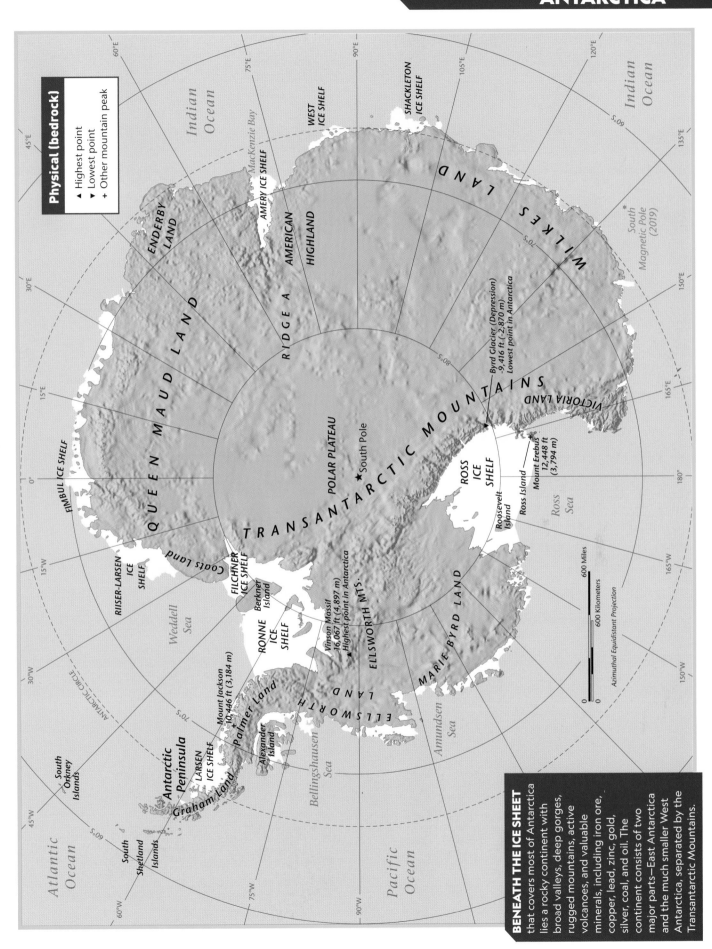

Physical (bedrock)
▲ Highest point
▼ Lowest point
+ Other mountain peak

Indian Ocean

60°E

75°E

MacKenzie Bay

WEST ICE SHELF

SHACKLETON ICE SHELF

90°E

Indian Ocean

45°E

ENDERBY LAND

AMERY ICE SHELF

WILKES LAND

60°S

105°E

30°E

RIDGE A AMERICAN HIGHLAND

QUEEN MAUD LAND

South Magnetic Pole (2019)

120°E

15°E

70°S

135°E

Byrd Glacier (Depression) -9,416 ft (-2,870 m) Lowest point in Antarctica

VICTORIA LAND

80°S

FIMBUL ICE SHELF

POLAR PLATEAU

★ South Pole

TRANSANTARCTIC MOUNTAINS

150°E

0°

TRANSANTARCTIC MOUNTAINS

Mount Erebus 12,448 ft (3,794 m)

165°E

RIISER-LARSEN ICE SHELF

Coats Land

FILCHNER ICE SHELF

ROSS ICE SHELF

Ross Island

Ross Sea

180°

15°W

Weddell Sea

Berkner Island

Roosevelt Island

RONNE ICE SHELF

Vinson Massif 16,067 ft (4,897 m) ▲ Highest point in Antarctica

ELLSWORTH MTS.

MARIE BYRD LAND

165°W

30°W

ANTARCTIC CIRCLE

Mount Jackson 10,446 ft (3,184 m) +

Palmer Land

ELLSWORTH LAND

600 Miles

600 Kilometers

Azimuthal Equidistant Projection

150°W

45°W

70°S

LARSEN ICE SHELF

Alexander Island

Antarctic Peninsula

Graham Land

Bellingshausen Sea

Amundsen Sea

South Orkney Islands

60°S

Atlantic Ocean

South Shetland Islands

75°W

90°W

Pacific Ocean

BENEATH THE ICE SHEET

that covers most of Antarctica lies a rocky continent with broad valleys, deep gorges, rugged mountains, active volcanoes, and valuable minerals, including iron ore, copper, lead, zinc, gold, silver, coal, and oil. The continent consists of two major parts—East Antarctica and the much smaller West Antarctica, separated by the Transantarctic Mountains.

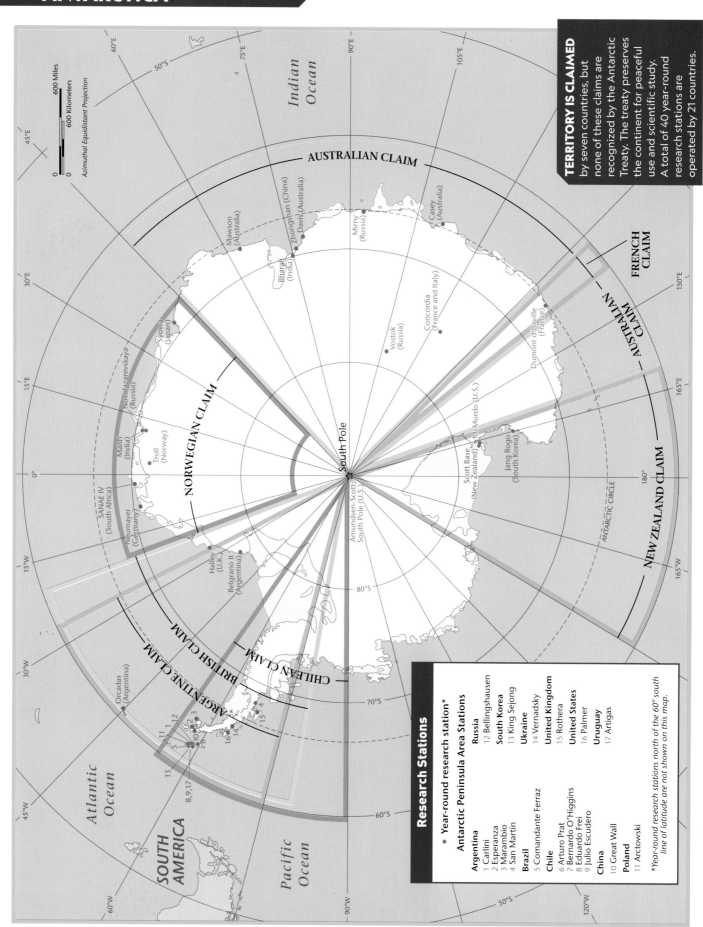

600 Miles
600 Kilometers
Azimuthal Equidistant Projection

Indian Ocean

AUSTRALIAN CLAIM

Mawson (Australia)
Zhongshan (China)
Davis (Australia)
Mirny (Russia)
Casey (Australia)
Bharati (India)
Concordia (France and Italy)
Vostok (Russia)

FRENCH CLAIM
AUSTRALIAN CLAIM
Dumont d'Urville (France)

Syowa (Japan)

NORWEGIAN CLAIM

Novolazarevskaya (Russia)
Maitri (India)
Troll (Norway)
SANAE IV (South Africa)
Neumayer (Germany)

McMurdo (U.S.)
Jang Bogo (South Korea)
Scott Base (New Zealand)

NEW ZEALAND CLAIM

ANTARCTIC CIRCLE

South Pole
Amundsen-Scott South Pole (U.S.)

80°S

Halley (U.K.)
Belgrano II (Argentina)

ARGENTINE CLAIM
BRITISH CLAIM
CHILEAN CLAIM

70°S

Orcadas (Argentina)

60°S

Atlantic Ocean

SOUTH AMERICA

Pacific Ocean

50°S

TERRITORY IS CLAIMED by seven countries, but none of these claims are recognized by the Antarctic Treaty. The treaty preserves the continent for peaceful use and scientific study. A total of 40 year-round research stations are operated by 21 countries.

Research Stations

• Year-round research station*

Antarctic Peninsula Area Stations

Argentina
1 Carlini
2 Esperanza
3 Marambio
4 San Martín

Brazil
5 Comandante Ferraz

Chile
6 Arturo Prat
7 Bernardo O'Higgins
8 Eduardo Frei
9 Julio Escudero

China
10 Great Wall

Poland
11 Arctowski

Russia
12 Bellingshausen

South Korea
13 King Sejong

Ukraine
14 Vernadsky

United Kingdom
15 Rothera

United States
16 Palmer

Uruguay
17 Artigas

Year-round research stations north of the 60° south line of latitude are not shown on this map.

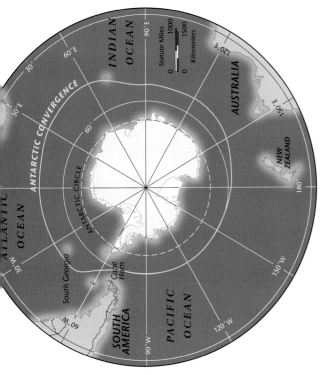

Extreme Environment

Antarctica, located at Earth's southernmost point, is one of the planet's most extreme environments. This ice-covered landmass experiences average temperatures ranging from a mild 22.5°F (-5.3°C) on the Antarctic Peninsula to a bitter -67.2°F (-55.1°C) on the high interior plateau. During the Antarctic winter, pack ice (frozen sea water) forms around the continent, making it even colder. The waters surrounding Antarctica are colder and less salty than Earth's major oceans. This results in a marine boundary called the Antarctic Convergence, where the water temperature changes sharply in a short distance (see graph). The mixing of waters along the convergence creates a zone extremely rich in nutrients—especially krill, which supports seals, penguins, whales, and other marine life that have adapted to the continent's extreme conditions.

FROZEN CONTINENT
FACTS & FIGURES

o One of the largest icebergs ever—more than 2,200 square miles (5,698 sq km) and weighing one trillion pounds (453.6 billion kg)—broke free from the Larsen Ice Shelf in 2017.

o The lowest temperature ever recorded in Antarctica—minus 135.8°F (-93.2°C)—was in East Antarctica.

o At the beginning of the Antarctic winter, sea ice advances at a rate of 40,000 square miles (104,000 sq km) each day.

o It is estimated that if all of Antarctica's ice were to melt, the global ocean level would rise more than 200 feet (60 m). The continent itself would rise more than 1,600 feet (500 m) because of lost weight—a process known as isostasy.

◑ **THE ANTARCTIC CONVERGENCE** (approximately 55° S–60° S) is an important climate and marine boundary where cold, slightly less saline Antarctic waters meet the southern extremes of the Atlantic, Pacific, and Indian Oceans. The waters south of the Antarctic Convergence are sometimes referred to as the Southern Ocean.

ANTARCTIC CONVERGENCE

Waters surrounding Antarctica south of the Antarctic Convergence are marked by a sharp change in temperature and salinity as well as by different marine life.

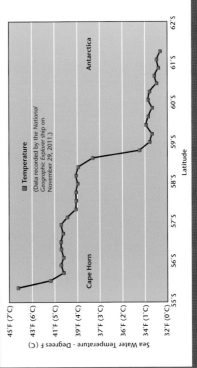

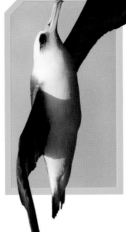

◑ **THE ALBATROSS** is the largest of all sea birds. Found mainly north of the Antarctic Convergence, the albatross often stays at sea for more than five years at a time.

◑ **ANTARCTIC KRILL,** small (about two-inch [5-cm]-long) shrimplike creatures that thrive in the cold Antarctic waters, are critical to the food chain around the continent.

◑ **THE EMPEROR PENGUIN,** tallest of these flightless birds, is the only large animal that remains in Antarctica through the long, dark winter.

Flags & Stats

These flags and factoids represent the world's 195 independent countries—those with national governments that are recognized as having the highest legal authority over the land and people within their boundaries. Capital city populations (2018) are from the United Nations Population Division and sometimes include the surrounding area. All other data are based on the CIA's 2017 *World Factbook*.

All flags are national flags recognized by the United Nations. Area figures include land and water bodies. Languages are those most commonly spoken within a country or official languages, which are marked with an asterisk (*).

Argentina
CONTINENT: South America
AREA: 1,073,518 sq mi (2,780,400 sq km)
POPULATION: 44,293,000
CAPITAL: Buenos Aires 14,967,000
LANGUAGE: Spanish*, English, Italian, German, French

Bahamas
CONTINENT: North America
AREA: 5,359 sq mi (13,880 sq km)
POPULATION: 330,000
CAPITAL: Nassau 280,000
LANGUAGE: English*

Belgium
CONTINENT: Europe
AREA: 11,787 sq mi (30,528 sq km)
POPULATION: 11,491,000
CAPITAL: Brussels 2,050,000
LANGUAGE: Dutch*, French*, German*

Armenia
CONTINENT: Asia
AREA: 11,484 sq mi (29,743 sq km)
POPULATION: 3,045,000
CAPITAL: Yerevan 1,080,000
LANGUAGE: Armenian*

Bahrain
CONTINENT: Asia
AREA: 293 sq mi (760 sq km)
POPULATION: 1,411,000
CAPITAL: Manama 565,000
LANGUAGE: Arabic*, English

Belize
CONTINENT: North America
AREA: 8,867 sq mi (22,966 sq km)
POPULATION: 360,000
CAPITAL: Belmopan 23,000
LANGUAGE: English*, Spanish, Creole, Mayan

Afghanistan
CONTINENT: Asia
AREA: 251,827 sq mi (652,230 sq km)
POPULATION: 34,125,000
CAPITAL: Kabul 4,012,000
LANGUAGE: Dari*, Pashto*, Turkic languages

Andorra
CONTINENT: Europe
AREA: 181 sq mi (468 sq km)
POPULATION: 86,000
CAPITAL: Andorra la Vella 23,000
LANGUAGE: Catalan*, French, Spanish, Portuguese

Australia
REGION: Australia/Oceania
AREA: 2,988,901 sq mi (7,741,220 sq km)
POPULATION: 23,232,000
CAPITAL: Canberra 448,000
LANGUAGE: English

Bangladesh
CONTINENT: Asia
AREA: 57,321 sq mi (148,460 sq km)
POPULATION: 157,827,000
CAPITAL: Dhaka 19,578,000
LANGUAGE: Bengali*

Benin
CONTINENT: Africa
AREA: 43,484 sq mi (112,622 sq km)
POPULATION: 11,039,000
CAPITAL: Cotonou (seat of government) 685,000; Porto-Novo (official) 285,000
LANGUAGE: French*, Fon, Yoruba

Albania
CONTINENT: Europe
AREA: 11,100 sq mi (28,748 sq km)
POPULATION: 3,048,000
CAPITAL: Tirana 476,000
LANGUAGE: Albanian*

Angola
CONTINENT: Africa
AREA: 481,353 sq mi (1,246,700 sq km)
POPULATION: 29,310,000
CAPITAL: Luanda 7,774,000
LANGUAGE: Portuguese*, Bantu, other indigenous languages

Austria
CONTINENT: Europe
AREA: 32,383 sq mi (83,871 sq km)
POPULATION: 8,754,000
CAPITAL: Vienna 1,901,000
LANGUAGE: German*

Barbados
CONTINENT: North America
AREA: 166 sq mi (430 sq km)
POPULATION: 292,000
CAPITAL: Bridgetown 89,000
LANGUAGE: English*, Creole

Bhutan
CONTINENT: Asia
AREA: 14,824 sq mi (38,394 sq km)
POPULATION: 758,000
CAPITAL: Thimphu 203,000
LANGUAGE: Sharchhopka, Dzongkha*, Lhotshamkha

Algeria
CONTINENT: Africa
AREA: 919,595 sq mi (2,381,741 sq km)
POPULATION: 40,969,000
CAPITAL: Algiers 2,694,000
LANGUAGE: Arabic*, French, Berber*

Antigua and Barbuda
CONTINENT: North America
AREA: 171 sq mi (443 sq km)
POPULATION: 95,000
CAPITAL: St. John's 21,000
LANGUAGE: English*, Creole

Azerbaijan
CONTINENT: Asia/Europe
AREA: 33,436 sq mi (86,600 sq km)
POPULATION: 9,961,000
CAPITAL: Baku 2,286,000
LANGUAGE: Azerbaijani*

Belarus
CONTINENT: Europe
AREA: 80,155 sq mi (207,600 sq km)
POPULATION: 9,550,000
CAPITAL: Minsk 2,005,000
LANGUAGE: Russian*, Belarusian*

Bolivia
CONTINENT: South America
AREA: 424,164 sq mi (1,098,581 sq km)
POPULATION: 11,138,000
CAPITAL: La Paz (administrative) 1,814,000; Sucre (legal) 278,000
LANGUAGE: Spanish*, Quechua*, Aymara*, other indigenous languages

Bosnia and Herzegovina
CONTINENT: Europe
AREA: 19,767 sq mi
(51,197 sq km)
POPULATION: 3,856,000
CAPITAL: Sarajevo 343,000
LANGUAGE: Bosnian*, Serbian*, Croatian*

Burkina Faso
CONTINENT: Africa
AREA: 105,869 sq mi
(274,200 sq km)
POPULATION: 20,108,000
CAPITAL: Ouagadougou 2,531,000
LANGUAGE: French*, indigenous languages

Canada
CONTINENT: North America
AREA: 3,855,101 sq mi
(9,984,670 sq km)
POPULATION: 35,624,000
CAPITAL: Ottawa 1,363,000
LANGUAGE: English*, French*

Colombia
CONTINENT: South America
AREA: 439,735 sq mi
(1,138,910 sq km)
POPULATION: 47,699,000
CAPITAL: Bogotá 10,574,000
LANGUAGE: Spanish*

Côte d'Ivoire
(Ivory Coast)
CONTINENT: Africa
AREA: 124,504 sq mi
(322,463 sq km)
POPULATION: 24,185,000
CAPITAL: Abidjan 4,921,000 (administrative); Yamoussoukro (legislative) 231,000
LANGUAGE: French*, Dioula, other indigenous languages

Botswana
CONTINENT: Africa
AREA: 224,607 sq mi
(581,730 sq km)
POPULATION: 2,215,000
CAPITAL: Gaborone 269,000
LANGUAGE: Setswana, English*

Burundi
CONTINENT: Africa
AREA: 10,745 sq mi
(27,830 sq km)
POPULATION: 11,467,000
CAPITAL: Bujumbura 899,000
LANGUAGE: Kirundi*, French*, English*

Central African Republic
CONTINENT: Africa
AREA: 240,535 sq mi
(622,984 sq km)
POPULATION: 5,625,000
CAPITAL: Bangui 851,000
LANGUAGE: French*, Sangho

Comoros
CONTINENT: Africa
AREA: 863 sq mi
(2,235 sq km)
POPULATION: 808,000
CAPITAL: Moroni 62,000
LANGUAGE: Arabic*, French*, Shikomoro*

Croatia
CONTINENT: Europe
AREA: 21,851 sq mi
(56,594 sq km)
POPULATION: 4,292,000
CAPITAL: Zagreb 686,000
LANGUAGE: Croatian*

Brazil
CONTINENT: South America
AREA: 3,287,956 sq mi
(8,515,770 sq km)
POPULATION: 207,353,000
CAPITAL: Brasília 4,470,000
LANGUAGE: Portuguese*

Cabo Verde
(Cape Verde)
CONTINENT: Africa
AREA: 1,557 sq mi
(4,033 sq km)
POPULATION: 561,000
CAPITAL: Praia 168,000
LANGUAGE: Portuguese*, Creole

Chad
CONTINENT: Africa
AREA: 495,755 sq mi
(1,284,000 sq km)
POPULATION: 12,076,000
CAPITAL: N'Djamena 1,323,000
LANGUAGE: French*, Arabic*, indigenous languages

Congo
CONTINENT: Africa
AREA: 132,047 sq mi
(342,000 sq km)
POPULATION: 4,955,000
CAPITAL: Brazzaville 2,230,000
LANGUAGE: French*, Lingala, Monokutuba, other indigenous languages

Cuba
CONTINENT: North America
AREA: 42,803 sq mi
(110,860 sq km)
POPULATION: 11,147,000
CAPITAL: Havana 2,136,000
LANGUAGE: Spanish*

Brunei
CONTINENT: Asia
AREA: 2,226 sq mi
(5,765 sq km)
POPULATION: 444,000
CAPITAL: Bandar Seri Begawan 41,000
LANGUAGE: Malay*, English

Cambodia
CONTINENT: Asia
AREA: 69,898 sq mi
(181,035 sq km)
POPULATION: 16,204,000
CAPITAL: Phnom Penh 1,952,000
LANGUAGE: Khmer*

Chile
CONTINENT: South America
AREA: 291,932 sq mi
(756,102 sq km)
POPULATION: 17,789,000
CAPITAL: Santiago 6,680,000
LANGUAGE: Spanish*, English

Congo, Democratic Republic of the
CONTINENT: Africa
AREA: 905,354 sq mi
(2,344,858 sq km)
POPULATION: 83,301,000
CAPITAL: Kinshasa 13,171,000
LANGUAGE: French*, Lingala, other indigenous languages

Cyprus
CONTINENT: Europe
AREA: 3,572 sq mi
(9,251 sq km)
POPULATION: 1,222,000
CAPITAL: Nicosia 269,000
LANGUAGE: Greek*, Turkish*

Bulgaria
CONTINENT: Europe
AREA: 42,811 sq mi
(110,879 sq km)
POPULATION: 7,102,000
CAPITAL: Sofia 1,272,000
LANGUAGE: Bulgarian*

Cameroon
CONTINENT: Africa
AREA: 183,568 sq mi
(475,440 sq km)
POPULATION: 24,995,000
CAPITAL: Yaoundé 3,656,000
LANGUAGE: English*, French*, indigenous languages

China
CONTINENT: Asia
AREA: 3,705,405 sq mi
(9,596,960 sq km)
POPULATION: 1,379,303,000
CAPITAL: Beijing 19,618,000
LANGUAGE: Mandarin*

Costa Rica
CONTINENT: North America
AREA: 19,730 sq mi
(51,100 sq km)
POPULATION: 4,930,000
CAPITAL: San José 1,358,000
LANGUAGE: Spanish*, English

Czechia
(Czech Republic)
CONTINENT: Europe
AREA: 30,451 sq mi
(78,867 sq km)
POPULATION: 10,675,000
CAPITAL: Prague 1,292,000
LANGUAGE: Czech*

Denmark
CONTINENT: Europe
AREA: 16,639 sq mi
(43,094 sq km)
POPULATION: 5,606,000
CAPITAL: Copenhagen 1,321,000
LANGUAGE: Danish, English

Egypt
CONTINENT: Africa
AREA: 386,662 sq mi
(1,001,450 sq km)
POPULATION: 97,041,000
CAPITAL: Cairo 20,076,000
LANGUAGE: Arabic*, English,
French

Eswatini
(Swaziland)
CONTINENT: Africa
AREA: 6,704 sq mi (17,364 sq km)
POPULATION: 1,467,000
CAPITAL: Lobamba
(legislative and royal) 11,000;
Mbabane (administrative)
68,000
LANGUAGE: English*, siSwati*

Gabon
CONTINENT: Africa
AREA: 103,347 sq mi
(267,667 sq km)
POPULATION: 1,772,000
CAPITAL: Libreville 813,000
LANGUAGE: French*,
indigenous languages

Greece
CONTINENT: Europe
AREA: 50,949 sq mi
(131,957 sq km)
POPULATION: 10,768,000
CAPITAL: Athens 3,156,000
LANGUAGE: Greek*

Djibouti
CONTINENT: Africa
AREA: 8,958 sq mi
(23,200 sq km)
POPULATION: 865,000
CAPITAL: Djibouti 562,000
LANGUAGE: French*, Arabic*,
Somali, Afar

El Salvador
CONTINENT: North America
AREA: 8,124 sq mi
(21,041 sq km)
POPULATION: 6,172,000
CAPITAL: San Salvador 1,107,000
LANGUAGE: Spanish*

Ethiopia
CONTINENT: Africa
AREA: 426,372 sq mi
(1,104,300 sq km)
POPULATION: 105,350,000
CAPITAL: Addis Ababa
4,400,000
LANGUAGE: Oromo, Amharic*,
Somali, Tigrinya, Afar

Gambia
CONTINENT: Africa
AREA: 4,363 sq mi
(11,300 sq km)
POPULATION: 2,051,000
CAPITAL: Banjul 437,000
LANGUAGE: English*,
indigenous languages

Grenada
CONTINENT: North America
AREA: 133 sq mi (344 sq km)
POPULATION: 112,000
CAPITAL: St. George's 39,000
LANGUAGE: English*, Creole

Dominica
CONTINENT: North America
AREA: 290 sq mi (751 sq km)
POPULATION: 74,000
CAPITAL: Roseau 15,000
LANGUAGE: English*, Creole

Equatorial Guinea
CONTINENT: Africa
AREA: 10,831 sq mi
(28,051 sq km)
POPULATION: 778,000
CAPITAL: Malabo 297,000
LANGUAGE: Spanish*, French*,
Portuguese*, indigenous
languages

Fiji
REGION: Australia/Oceania
AREA: 7,056 sq mi
(18,274 sq km)
POPULATION: 921,000
CAPITAL: Suva 178,000
LANGUAGE: English*, Fijian*,
Hindi

Georgia
CONTINENT: Asia/Europe
AREA: 26,911 sq mi
(69,700 sq km)
POPULATION: 4,926,000
CAPITAL: Tbilisi 1,077,000
LANGUAGE: Georgian*

Guatemala
CONTINENT: North America
AREA: 42,042 sq mi
(108,889 sq km)
POPULATION: 15,461,000
CAPITAL: Guatemala City
2,851,000
LANGUAGE: Spanish*,
indigenous languages

Dominican
Republic
CONTINENT: North America
AREA: 18,792 sq mi
(48,670 sq km)
POPULATION: 10,734,000
CAPITAL: Santo Domingo
3,172,000
LANGUAGE: Spanish*

Eritrea
CONTINENT: Africa
AREA: 45,406 sq mi
(117,600 sq km)
POPULATION: 5,919,000
CAPITAL: Asmara 896,000
LANGUAGE: Tigrinya*, Arabic*,
English*, indigenous languages

Finland
CONTINENT: Europe
AREA: 130,558 sq mi
(338,145 sq km)
POPULATION: 5,518,000
CAPITAL: Helsinki 1,279,000
LANGUAGE: Finnish*, Swedish*

Germany
CONTINENT: Europe
AREA: 137,847 sq mi
(357,022 sq km)
POPULATION: 80,594,000
CAPITAL: Berlin 3,552,000
LANGUAGE: German*

Guinea
CONTINENT: Africa
AREA: 94,926 sq mi
(245,857 sq km)
POPULATION: 12,414,000
CAPITAL: Conakry 1,843,000
LANGUAGE: French*,
indigenous languages

Ecuador
CONTINENT: South America
AREA: 109,483 sq mi
(283,561 sq km)
POPULATION: 16,291,000
CAPITAL: Quito 1,822,000
LANGUAGE: Spanish*,
indigenous languages

Estonia
CONTINENT: Europe
AREA: 17,463 sq mi
(45,228 sq km)
POPULATION: 1,252,000
CAPITAL: Tallinn 437,000
LANGUAGE: Estonian*, Russian

France
CONTINENT: Europe
AREA: 248,573 sq mi
(643,801 sq km)
POPULATION: 67,106,000
CAPITAL: Paris 10,901,000
LANGUAGE: French*

Ghana
CONTINENT: Africa
AREA: 92,098 sq mi
(238,533 sq km)
POPULATION: 27,500,000
CAPITAL: Accra 2,439,000
LANGUAGE: Assanta, Ewe,
Fante, English*

Guinea-Bissau
CONTINENT: Africa
AREA: 13,948 sq mi
(36,125 sq km)
POPULATION: 1,792,000
CAPITAL: Bissau 558,000
LANGUAGE: Creole,
Portuguese*

Guyana
CONTINENT: South America
AREA: 83,000 sq mi
(214,969 sq km)
POPULATION: 738,000
CAPITAL: Georgetown 110,000
LANGUAGE: English*, Creole

India
CONTINENT: Asia
AREA: 1,269,219 sq mi
(3,287,263 sq km)
POPULATION: 1,281,936,000
CAPITAL: New Delhi 28,514,000
LANGUAGE: Hindi*, English*,
state languages

Israel
CONTINENT: Asia
AREA: 8,019 sq mi
(20,770 sq km)
POPULATION: 8,300,000
CAPITAL: Jerusalem 907,000
LANGUAGE: Hebrew*, Arabic,
English

Kazakhstan
CONTINENT: Asia/Europe
AREA: 1,052,089 sq mi
(2,724,900 sq km)
POPULATION: 18,557,000
CAPITAL: Astana 1,068,000
LANGUAGE: Kazakh*, Russian*

Kyrgyzstan
CONTINENT: Asia
AREA: 77,201 sq mi
(199,951 sq km)
POPULATION: 5,789,000
CAPITAL: Bishkek 996,000
LANGUAGE: Kyrgyz*, Uzbek,
Russian*

Haiti
CONTINENT: North America
AREA: 10,714 sq mi
(27,750 sq km)
POPULATION: 10,647,000
CAPITAL: Port-au-Prince
2,637,000
LANGUAGE: French*, Creole*

Indonesia
CONTINENT: Asia
AREA: 735,358 sq mi
(1,904,569 sq km)
POPULATION: 260,581,000
CAPITAL: Jakarta 10,517,000
LANGUAGE: Indonesian*,
indigenous languages

Italy
CONTINENT: Europe
AREA: 116,348 sq mi
(301,340 sq km)
POPULATION: 62,138,000
CAPITAL: Rome 4,210,000
LANGUAGE: Italian*

Kenya
CONTINENT: Africa
AREA: 224,081 sq mi
(580,367 sq km)
POPULATION: 47,616,000
CAPITAL: Nairobi 4,386,000
LANGUAGE: English*, Kiswahili*,
indigenous languages

Laos
CONTINENT: Asia
AREA: 91,429 sq mi
(236,800 sq km)
POPULATION: 7,127,000
CAPITAL: Vientiane 665,000
LANGUAGE: Lao*, French,
indigenous languages

Honduras
CONTINENT: North America
AREA: 43,278 sq mi
(112,090 sq km)
POPULATION: 9,039,000
CAPITAL: Tegucigalpa 1,363,000
LANGUAGE: Spanish*,
indigenous languages

Iran
CONTINENT: Asia
AREA: 636,371 sq mi
(1,648,195 sq km)
POPULATION: 82,022,000
CAPITAL: Tehran 8,896,000
LANGUAGE: Persian (Farsi)*

Jamaica
CONTINENT: North America
AREA: 4,244 sq mi
(10,991 sq km)
POPULATION: 2,991,000
CAPITAL: Kingston 589,000
LANGUAGE: English*, Creole

Kiribati
REGION: Australia/Oceania
AREA: 313 sq mi (811 sq km)
POPULATION: 108,000
CAPITAL: Tarawa 64,000
LANGUAGE: I-Kiribati, English*

Latvia
CONTINENT: Europe
AREA: 24,938 sq mi
(64,589 sq km)
POPULATION: 1,945,000
CAPITAL: Riga 637,000
LANGUAGE: Latvian*, Russian

Hungary
CONTINENT: Europe
AREA: 35,918 sq mi
(93,028 sq km)
POPULATION: 9,851,000
CAPITAL: Budapest 1,759,000
LANGUAGE: Hungarian*,
English, German

Iraq
CONTINENT: Asia
AREA: 169,235 sq mi
(438,317 sq km)
POPULATION: 39,192,000
CAPITAL: Baghdad 6,812,000
LANGUAGE: Arabic*, Kurdish*

Japan
CONTINENT: Asia
AREA: 145,914 sq mi
(377,915 sq km)
POPULATION: 126,451,000
CAPITAL: Tokyo 37,468,000
LANGUAGE: Japanese

Kosovo
CONTINENT: Europe
AREA: 4,203 sq mi
(10,887 sq km)
POPULATION: 1,895,000
CAPITAL: Pristina 205,000
LANGUAGE: Albanian*, Serbian*

Lebanon
CONTINENT: Asia
AREA: 4,015 sq mi
(10,400 sq km)
POPULATION: 6,230,000
CAPITAL: Beirut 2,385,000
LANGUAGE: Arabic*, French,
English

Iceland
CONTINENT: Europe
AREA: 39,769 sq mi
(103,000 sq km)
POPULATION: 340,000
CAPITAL: Reykjavík 216,000
LANGUAGE: Icelandic, English,
Nordic languages

Ireland
CONTINENT: Europe
AREA: 27,133 sq mi
(70,273 sq km)
POPULATION: 5,011,000
CAPITAL: Dublin 1,201,000
LANGUAGE: English*, Irish
(Gaelic)*

Jordan
CONTINENT: Asia
AREA: 34,495 sq mi
(89,342 sq km)
POPULATION: 10,248,000
CAPITAL: Amman 2,065,000
LANGUAGE: Arabic*, English

Kuwait
CONTINENT: Asia
AREA: 6,880 sq mi
(17,818 sq km)
POPULATION: 4,200,000
CAPITAL: Kuwait City 2,989,000
LANGUAGE: Arabic*, English

Lesotho
CONTINENT: Africa
AREA: 11,720 sq mi
(30,355 sq km)
POPULATION: 1,958,000
CAPITAL: Maseru 202,000
LANGUAGE: Sesotho*, English*

Liberia
CONTINENT: Africa
AREA: 43,000 sq mi
(111,369 sq km)
POPULATION: 4,689,000
CAPITAL: Monrovia 1,418,000
LANGUAGE: English*,
indigenous languages

Macedonia
CONTINENT: Europe
AREA: 9,928 sq mi
(25,713 sq km)
POPULATION: 2,104,000
CAPITAL: Skopje 584,000
LANGUAGE: Macedonian*,
Albanian*

Mali
CONTINENT: Africa
AREA: 478,841 sq mi
(1,240,192 sq km)
POPULATION: 17,885,000
CAPITAL: Bamako 2,447,000
LANGUAGE: French*, Bambara,
other indigenous languages

Mexico
CONTINENT: North America
AREA: 758,449 sq mi
(1,964,375 sq km)
POPULATION: 124,575,000
CAPITAL: Mexico City 21,581,000
LANGUAGE: Spanish

Montenegro
CONTINENT: Europe
AREA: 5,333 sq mi
(13,812 sq km)
POPULATION: 643,000
CAPITAL: Podgorica 177,000
LANGUAGE: Serbian,
Montenegrin*

Libya
CONTINENT: Africa
AREA: 679,362 sq mi
(1,759,540 sq km)
POPULATION: 6,653,000
CAPITAL: Tripoli 1,158,000
LANGUAGE: Arabic*, Italian,
English

Madagascar
CONTINENT: Africa
AREA: 226,658 sq mi
(587,041 sq km)
POPULATION: 25,054,000
CAPITAL: Antananarivo
3,058,000
LANGUAGE: French*, Malagasy*

Malta
CONTINENT: Europe
AREA: 122 sq mi (316 sq km)
POPULATION: 416,000
CAPITAL: Valletta 213,000
LANGUAGE: Maltese*, English*

Micronesia,
Federated States of
REGION: Australia/Oceania
AREA: 271 sq mi (702 sq km)
POPULATION: 104,000
CAPITAL: Palikir 7,000
LANGUAGE: English*,
indigenous languages

Morocco
CONTINENT: Africa
AREA: 172,414 sq mi
(446,550 sq km)
POPULATION: 33,987,000
CAPITAL: Rabat 1,847,000
LANGUAGE: Arabic*,
Tamazight*, French

Liechtenstein
CONTINENT: Europe
AREA: 62 sq mi (160 sq km)
POPULATION: 38,000
CAPITAL: Vaduz 5,500
LANGUAGE: German*

Malawi
CONTINENT: Africa
AREA: 45,747 sq mi
(118,484 sq km)
POPULATION: 19,196,000
CAPITAL: Lilongwe 1,030,000
LANGUAGE: English*,
Chichewa, other
indigenous languages

Marshall Islands
REGION: Australia/Oceania
AREA: 70 sq mi (181 sq km)
POPULATION: 75,000
CAPITAL: Majuro 31,000
LANGUAGE: Marshallese*,
English*

Moldova
CONTINENT: Europe
AREA: 13,070 sq mi
(33,851 sq km)
POPULATION: 3,474,000
CAPITAL: Chisinau 510,000
LANGUAGE: Romanian
(Moldovan)*, Russian

Mozambique
CONTINENT: Africa
AREA: 308,642 sq mi
(799,380 sq km)
POPULATION: 26,574,000
CAPITAL: Maputo 1,102,000
LANGUAGE: Emakhuwa,
Portuguese*, Xichangana, other
indigenous languages

Lithuania
CONTINENT: Europe
AREA: 25,212 sq mi
(65,300 sq km)
POPULATION: 2,824,000
CAPITAL: Vilnius 536,000
LANGUAGE: Lithuanian*

Malaysia
CONTINENT: Asia
AREA: 127,355 sq mi
(329,847 sq km)
POPULATION: 31,382,000
CAPITAL: Kuala Lumpur
7,564,000
LANGUAGE: Malaysian*, English

Mauritania
CONTINENT: Africa
AREA: 397,955 sq mi
(1,030,700 sq km)
POPULATION: 3,759,000
CAPITAL: Nouakchott 1,205,000
LANGUAGE: Arabic*,
indigenous languages

Monaco
CONTINENT: Europe
AREA: 0.8 sq mi (2.0 sq km)
POPULATION: 40,000
CAPITAL: Monaco 39,000
LANGUAGE: French*, English,
Italian, Monégasque

Myanmar (Burma)
CONTINENT: Asia
AREA: 261,228 sq mi
(676,578 sq km)
POPULATION: 55,124,000
CAPITAL: Nay Pyi Taw 500,000
LANGUAGE: Burmese*

Luxembourg
CONTINENT: Europe
AREA: 998 sq mi (2,586 sq km)
POPULATION: 594,000
CAPITAL: Luxembourg 120,000
LANGUAGE: Luxembourgish*,
French*, German*

Maldives
CONTINENT: Asia
AREA: 115 sq mi (298 sq km)
POPULATION: 393,000
CAPITAL: Male 177,000
LANGUAGE: Dhivehi*, English

Mauritius
CONTINENT: Africa
AREA: 788 sq mi (2,040 sq km)
POPULATION: 1,356,000
CAPITAL: Port Louis 149,000
LANGUAGE: Creole, English*

Mongolia
CONTINENT: Asia
AREA: 603,908 sq mi
(1,564,116 sq km)
POPULATION: 3,068,000
CAPITAL: Ulaanbaatar 1,520,000
LANGUAGE: Mongolian*

Namibia
CONTINENT: Africa
AREA: 318,261 sq mi
(824,292 sq km)
POPULATION: 2,485,000
CAPITAL: Windhoek 404,000
LANGUAGE: Indigenous lan-
guages, Afrikaans, English*

Nauru
REGION: Australia/Oceania
AREA: 8 sq mi (21 sq km)
POPULATION: 11,000
CAPITAL: Yaren 11,000
LANGUAGE: Nauruan*, English

Niger
CONTINENT: Africa
AREA: 489,191 sq mi
(1,267,000 sq km)
POPULATION: 19,245,000
CAPITAL: Niamey 1,214,000
LANGUAGE: French*,
indigenous languages

Pakistan
CONTINENT: Asia
AREA: 307,374 sq mi
(796,095 sq km)
POPULATION: 204,925,000
CAPITAL: Islamabad 1,061,000
LANGUAGE: Punjabi, Sindhi,
Saraiki, Pashto, Urdu*, English*

Peru
CONTINENT: South America
AREA: 496,224 sq mi
(1,285,216 sq km)
POPULATION: 31,037,000
CAPITAL: Lima 10,391,000
LANGUAGE: Spanish*,
Quechua*, Aymara*

Romania
CONTINENT: Europe
AREA: 92,043 sq mi
(238,391 sq km)
POPULATION: 21,530,000
CAPITAL: Bucharest 1,821,000
LANGUAGE: Romanian*

Nepal
CONTINENT: Asia
AREA: 56,827 sq mi
(147,181 sq km)
POPULATION: 29,384,000
CAPITAL: Kathmandu 1,330,000
LANGUAGE: Nepali*, Maithali

Nigeria
CONTINENT: Africa
AREA: 356,669 sq mi
(923,768 sq km)
POPULATION: 190,632,000
CAPITAL: Abuja 2,919,000
LANGUAGE: English*,
indigenous languages

Palau
REGION: Australia/Oceania
AREA: 177 sq mi (459 sq km)
POPULATION: 21,000
CAPITAL: Melekeok, 11,000
LANGUAGE: Palauan*, English*,
Filipino

Philippines
CONTINENT: Asia
AREA: 115,831 sq mi
(300,000 sq km)
POPULATION: 104,256,000
CAPITAL: Manila 13,482,000
LANGUAGE: Filipino (Tagalog)*,
English*, indigenous languages

Russia
CONTINENT: Europe/Asia
AREA: 6,601,665 sq mi
(17,098,242 sq km)
POPULATION: 142,258,000
CAPITAL: Moscow 12,410,000
LANGUAGE: Russian*

Netherlands
CONTINENT: Europe
AREA: 16,040 sq mi
(41,543 sq km)
POPULATION: 17,085,000
CAPITAL: Amsterdam (official)
1,132,000; The Hague (adminis-
trative) 685,000
LANGUAGE: Dutch*

North Korea
CONTINENT: Asia
AREA: 46,540 sq mi
(120,538 sq km)
POPULATION: 25,248,000
CAPITAL: Pyongyang 3,038,000
LANGUAGE: Korean

Panama
CONTINENT: North America
AREA: 29,120 sq mi
(75,420 sq km)
POPULATION: 3,753,000
CAPITAL: Panama City 1,783,000
LANGUAGE: Spanish*,
indigenous languages

Poland
CONTINENT: Europe
AREA: 120,728 sq mi
(312,685 sq km)
POPULATION: 38,476,000
CAPITAL: Warsaw 1,768,000
LANGUAGE: Polish*

Rwanda
CONTINENT: Africa
AREA: 10,169 sq mi
(26,338 sq km)
POPULATION: 11,901,000
CAPITAL: Kigali 1,058,000
LANGUAGE: Kinyarwanda*,
Kiswahili, French*, English*

New Zealand
REGION: Australia/Oceania
AREA: 103,799 sq mi
(268,838 sq km)
POPULATION: 4,510,000
CAPITAL: Wellington 411,000
LANGUAGE: English*, Maori*

Norway
CONTINENT: Europe
AREA: 125,021 sq mi
(323,802 sq km)
POPULATION: 5,320,000
CAPITAL: Oslo 1,012,000
LANGUAGE: Norwegian*, Sami

Papua New Guinea
REGION: Australia/Oceania
AREA: 178,703 sq mi
(462,840 sq km)
POPULATION: 6,910,000
CAPITAL: Port Moresby 367,000
LANGUAGE: Tok Pisin*, English*,
Hiri Motu*, other indigenous
languages

Portugal
CONTINENT: Europe
AREA: 35,556 sq mi
(92,090 sq km)
POPULATION: 10,840,000
CAPITAL: Lisbon 2,927,000
LANGUAGE: Portuguese*,
Mirandese*

Samoa
REGION: Australia/Oceania
AREA: 1,093 sq mi
(2,831 sq km)
POPULATION: 200,000
CAPITAL: Apia 36,000
LANGUAGE: Samoan*, English

Nicaragua
CONTINENT: North America
AREA: 50,336 sq mi
(130,370 sq km)
POPULATION: 6,026,000
CAPITAL: Managua 1,048,000
LANGUAGE: Spanish*

Oman
CONTINENT: Asia
AREA: 119,499 sq mi
(309,500 sq km)
POPULATION: 3,424,000
CAPITAL: Muscat 1,447,000
LANGUAGE: Arabic*, English

Paraguay
CONTINENT: South America
AREA: 157,048 sq mi
(406,752 sq km)
POPULATION: 6,944,000
CAPITAL: Asunción 3,222,000
LANGUAGE: Spanish*, Guarani*

Qatar
CONTINENT: Asia
AREA: 4,473 sq mi
(11,586 sq km)
POPULATION: 2,314,000
CAPITAL: Doha 633,000
LANGUAGE: Arabic*, English

San Marino
CONTINENT: Europe
AREA: 24 sq mi (61 sq km)
POPULATION: 34,000
CAPITAL: San Marino 4,500
LANGUAGE: Italian

Sao Tome and Principe
CONTINENT: Africa
AREA: 372 sq mi (964 sq km)
POPULATION: 201,000
CAPITAL: São Tomé 80,000
LANGUAGE: Portuguese*, Forro

Sierra Leone
CONTINENT: Africa
AREA: 27,699 sq mi (71,740 sq km)
POPULATION: 6,163,000
CAPITAL: Freetown 1,136,000
LANGUAGE: English*, Mende, Temne, Krio

Somalia
CONTINENT: Africa
AREA: 246,201 sq mi (637,657 sq km)
POPULATION: 11,031,000
CAPITAL: Mogadishu 2,082,000
LANGUAGE: Somali*, Arabic*, Italian, English

Sri Lanka
CONTINENT: Asia
AREA: 25,332 sq mi (65,610 sq km)
POPULATION: 22,409,000
CAPITAL: Colombo (administrative) 600,000; Sri Jayewardenepura Kotte (legislative) 103,000
LANGUAGE: Sinhala*, Tamil*, English

Suriname
CONTINENT: South America
AREA: 63,251 sq mi (163,820 sq km)
POPULATION: 592,000
CAPITAL: Paramaribo 239,000
LANGUAGE: Dutch*, Sranan, English

Saudi Arabia
CONTINENT: Asia
AREA: 830,000 sq mi (2,149,690 sq km)
POPULATION: 28,572,000
CAPITAL: Riyadh 6,907,000
LANGUAGE: Arabic*

Singapore
CONTINENT: Asia
AREA: 269 sq mi (697 sq km)
POPULATION: 5,889,000
CAPITAL: Singapore 5,792,000
LANGUAGE: Mandarin*, English*, Malay*, Tamil*

South Africa
CONTINENT: Africa
AREA: 470,693 sq mi (1,219,090 sq km)
POPULATION: 54,842,000
CAPITAL: Bloemfontein (judicial) 546,000; Cape Town (legislative) 4,430,000; Pretoria (Tshwane) (administrative) 2,378,000
LANGUAGE: IsiZulu*, IsiXhosa*, other indigenous languages*, Afrikaans*, English*

St. Kitts and Nevis
CONTINENT: North America
AREA: 101 sq mi (261 sq km)
POPULATION: 53,000
CAPITAL: Basseterre 14,000
LANGUAGE: English*

Sweden
CONTINENT: Europe
AREA: 173,860 sq mi (450,295 sq km)
POPULATION: 9,960,000
CAPITAL: Stockholm 1,583,000
LANGUAGE: Swedish*

Senegal
CONTINENT: Africa
AREA: 75,955 sq mi (196,722 sq km)
POPULATION: 14,669,000
CAPITAL: Dakar 2,978,000
LANGUAGE: French*, Wolof, other indigenous languages

Slovakia
CONTINENT: Europe
AREA: 18,933 sq mi (49,035 sq km)
POPULATION: 5,446,000
CAPITAL: Bratislava 430,000
LANGUAGE: Slovak*

South Korea
CONTINENT: Asia
AREA: 38,502 sq mi (99,720 sq km)
POPULATION: 51,181,000
CAPITAL: Seoul 9,963,000
LANGUAGE: Korean, English

St. Lucia
CONTINENT: North America
AREA: 238 sq mi (616 sq km)
POPULATION: 165,000
CAPITAL: Castries 22,000
LANGUAGE: English*, Creole

Switzerland
CONTINENT: Europe
AREA: 15,937 sq mi (41,277 sq km)
POPULATION: 8,236,000
CAPITAL: Bern 422,000
LANGUAGE: German*, French*, Italian*, Romansch*

Serbia
CONTINENT: Europe
AREA: 29,913 sq mi (77,474 sq km)
POPULATION: 7,111,000
CAPITAL: Belgrade 1,389,000
LANGUAGE: Serbian*

Slovenia
CONTINENT: Europe
AREA: 7,827 sq mi (20,273 sq km)
POPULATION: 1,972,000
CAPITAL: Ljubljana 286,000
LANGUAGE: Slovenian*

South Sudan
CONTINENT: Africa
AREA: 248,777 sq mi (644,329 sq km)
POPULATION: 13,026,000
CAPITAL: Juba 369,000
LANGUAGE: English*, Arabic, indigenous languages

St. Vincent and the Grenadines
CONTINENT: North America
AREA: 150 sq mi (389 sq km)
POPULATION: 102,000
CAPITAL: Kingstown 27,000
LANGUAGE: English*, Creole

Syria
CONTINENT: Asia
AREA: 71,498 sq mi (185,180 sq km)
POPULATION: 18,029,000
CAPITAL: Damascus 2,320,000
LANGUAGE: Arabic*, Kurdish, English, French

Seychelles
CONTINENT: Africa
AREA: 176 sq mi (455 sq km)
POPULATION: 94,000
CAPITAL: Victoria 28,000
LANGUAGE: Creole*, English*, French*

Solomon Islands
REGION: Australia/Oceania
AREA: 11,157 sq mi (28,896 sq km)
POPULATION: 648,000
CAPITAL: Honiara 82,000
LANGUAGE: Melanesian pidgin, English*, indigenous languages

Spain
CONTINENT: Europe
AREA: 195,124 sq mi (505,370 sq km)
POPULATION: 48,958,000
CAPITAL: Madrid 6,497,000
LANGUAGE: Spanish*, Catalan, Galician, Basque

Sudan
CONTINENT: Africa
AREA: 718,723 sq mi (1,861,484 sq km)
POPULATION: 37,346,000
CAPITAL: Khartoum 5,534,000
LANGUAGE: Arabic*, English*

Tajikistan
CONTINENT: Asia
AREA: 55,637 sq mi (144,100 sq km)
POPULATION: 8,469,000
CAPITAL: Dushanbe 873,000
LANGUAGE: Tajik*, Russian

Tanzania
CONTINENT: Africa
AREA: 365,754 sq mi (947,300 sq km)
POPULATION: 53,951,000
CAPITAL: Dar es Salaam (administrative) 6,048,000; Dodoma (official) 262,000
LANGUAGE: Kiswahili*, English*, indigenous languages

Thailand
CONTINENT: Asia
AREA: 198,117 sq mi (513,120 sq km)
POPULATION: 68,414,000
CAPITAL: Bangkok 10,156,000
LANGUAGE: Thai*

Timor-Leste (East Timor)
CONTINENT: Asia
AREA: 5,743 sq mi (14,874 sq km)
POPULATION: 1,291,000
CAPITAL: Dili 281,000
LANGUAGE: Tetum*, Portuguese*, Indonesian, English

Togo
CONTINENT: Africa
AREA: 21,925 sq mi (56,785 sq km)
POPULATION: 7,965,000
CAPITAL: Lomé 1,746,000
LANGUAGE: French*, Ewe, Mina, Kabye, Dagomba

Tonga
REGION: Australia/Oceania
AREA: 288 sq mi (747 sq km)
POPULATION: 106,000
CAPITAL: Nuku'alofa 23,000
LANGUAGE: Tongan*, English*

Trinidad and Tobago
CONTINENT: North America
AREA: 1,980 sq mi (5,128 sq km)
POPULATION: 1,218,000
CAPITAL: Port of Spain 544,000
LANGUAGE: English*, Creole

Tunisia
CONTINENT: Africa
AREA: 63,170 sq mi (163,610 sq km)
POPULATION: 11,404,000
CAPITAL: Tunis 2,291,000
LANGUAGE: Arabic*, French, Berber

Turkey
CONTINENT: Asia/Europe
AREA: 302,535 sq mi (783,562 sq km)
POPULATION: 80,845,000
CAPITAL: Ankara 4,919,000
LANGUAGE: Turkish*, Kurdish

Turkmenistan
CONTINENT: Asia
AREA: 188,456 sq mi (488,100 sq km)
POPULATION: 5,351,000
CAPITAL: Ashgabat 810,000
LANGUAGE: Turkmen*, Russian

Tuvalu
REGION: Australia/Oceania
AREA: 10 sq mi (26 sq km)
POPULATION: 11,000
CAPITAL: Funafuti 7,000
LANGUAGE: Tuvaluan*, English*

Uganda
CONTINENT: Africa
AREA: 93,065 sq mi (241,038 sq km)
POPULATION: 39,570,000
CAPITAL: Kampala 2,986,000
LANGUAGE: English*, Swahili*, Ganda (Luganda)

Ukraine
CONTINENT: Europe
AREA: 233,032 sq mi (603,550 sq km)
POPULATION: 44,034,000
CAPITAL: Kiev 2,957,000
LANGUAGE: Ukrainian*, Russian

United Arab Emirates
CONTINENT: Asia
AREA: 32,278 sq mi (83,600 sq km)
POPULATION: 6,072,000
CAPITAL: Abu Dhabi 1,420,000
LANGUAGE: Arabic*, Persian, English

United Kingdom
CONTINENT: Europe
AREA: 94,058 sq mi (243,610 sq km)
POPULATION: 64,769,000
CAPITAL: London 9,046,000
LANGUAGE: English, regional languages

United States
CONTINENT: North America
AREA: 3,796,741 sq mi (9,833,517 sq km)
POPULATION: 326,626,000
CAPITAL: Washington, D.C. 5,207,000
LANGUAGE: English, Spanish

Uruguay
CONTINENT: South America
AREA: 68,037 sq mi (176,215 sq km)
POPULATION: 3,360,000
CAPITAL: Montevideo 1,737,000
LANGUAGE: Spanish*

Uzbekistan
CONTINENT: Asia
AREA: 172,742 sq mi (447,400 sq km)
POPULATION: 29,749,000
CAPITAL: Tashkent 2,464,000
LANGUAGE: Uzbek*, Russian

Vanuatu
REGION: Australia/Oceania
AREA: 4,706 sq mi (12,189 sq km)
POPULATION: 283,000
CAPITAL: Port-Vila 53,000
LANGUAGE: Bislama*, English*, French*, indigenous languages

Vatican City (Holy See)
CONTINENT: Europe
AREA: 0.2 sq mi (0.4 sq km)
POPULATION: 1,000
CAPITAL: Vatican City 1,000
LANGUAGE: Italian, Latin, French

Venezuela
CONTINENT: South America
AREA: 352,144 sq mi (912,050 sq km)
POPULATION: 31,304,000
CAPITAL: Caracas 2,935,000
LANGUAGE: Spanish*, indigenous languages

Vietnam
CONTINENT: Asia
AREA: 127,881 sq mi (331,210 sq km)
POPULATION: 96,160,000
CAPITAL: Hanoi 4,283,000
LANGUAGE: Vietnamese*, English

Yemen
CONTINENT: Asia
AREA: 203,850 sq mi (527,968 sq km)
POPULATION: 28,037,000
CAPITAL: Sanaa 2,779,000
LANGUAGE: Arabic*

Zambia
CONTINENT: Africa
AREA: 290,587 sq mi (752,618 sq km)
POPULATION: 15,972,000
CAPITAL: Lusaka 2,524,000
LANGUAGE: Bembe, Nyanja, Tonga, other indigenous languages, English*

Zimbabwe
CONTINENT: Africa
AREA: 150,872 sq mi (390,757 sq km)
POPULATION: 13,805,000
CAPITAL: Harare 1,515,000
LANGUAGE: Shona*, Ndebele*, English*, indigenous languages*

METRIC CONVERSION TABLES
CONVERSION TO METRIC MEASURES

SYMBOL	WHEN YOU KNOW	MULTIPLY BY	TO FIND	SYMBOL
LENGTH				
in	inches	2.54	centimeters	cm
ft	feet	0.30	meters	m
yd	yards	0.91	meters	m
mi	miles	1.61	kilometers	km
AREA				
in²	square inches	6.45	square centimeters	cm²
ft²	square feet	0.09	square meters	m²
yd²	square yards	0.84	square meters	m²
mi²	square miles	2.59	square kilometers	km²
—	acres	0.40	hectares	ha
MASS				
oz	ounces	28.35	grams	g
lb	pounds	0.45	kilograms	kg
—	short tons	0.91	metric tons	t
VOLUME				
in³	cubic inches	16.39	milliliters	mL
liq oz	liquid ounces	29.57	milliliters	mL
pt	pints	0.47	liters	L
qt	quarts	0.95	liters	L
gal	gallons	3.79	liters	L
ft³	cubic feet	0.03	cubic meters	m³
yd³	cubic yards	0.76	cubic meters	m³
TEMPERATURE				
°F	degrees Fahrenheit	5/9 after subtracting 32	degrees Celsius (centigrade)	°C

CONVERSION FROM METRIC MEASURES

SYMBOL	WHEN YOU KNOW	MULTIPLY BY	TO FIND	SYMBOL
LENGTH				
cm	centimeters	0.39	inches	in
m	meters	3.28	feet	ft
m	meters	1.09	yards	yd
km	kilometers	0.62	miles	mi
AREA				
cm²	square centimeters	0.16	square inches	in²
m²	square meters	10.76	square feet	ft²
m²	square meters	1.20	square yards	yd²
km²	square kilometers	0.39	square miles	mi²
ha	hectares	2.47	acres	—
MASS				
g	grams	0.04	ounces	oz
kg	kilograms	2.20	pounds	lb
t	metric tons	1.10	short tons	—
VOLUME				
mL	milliliters	0.06	cubic inches	in³
mL	milliliters	0.03	liquid ounces	liq oz
L	liters	2.11	pints	pt
L	liters	1.06	quarts	qt
L	liters	0.26	gallons	gal
m³	cubic meters	35.31	cubic feet	ft³
m³	cubic meters	1.31	cubic yards	ft³
TEMPERATURE				
°C	degrees Celsius (centigrade)	9/5 then add 32	degrees Fahrenheit	°F

ABBREVIATIONS
COUNTRY NAMES

ARM. ....Armenia
AZERB. ....Azerbaijan
B. & H.; BOSN. & HERZG. ...... Bosnia and Herzegovina
BELG. ....Belgium
CRO. ....Croatia
EST. ....Estonia
HUNG. ....Hungary
KOS. ....Kosovo
LATV. ....Latvia
LIECH. ....Liechtenstein
LITH. ....Lithuania
LUX. ....Luxembourg
MACED. ....Macedonia
MOLD. .... Moldova
MONT. .... Montenegro
N.Z. .... New Zealand
NETH. .... Netherlands
SLOV. .... Slovenia
SWITZ. ....Switzerland
U.A.E. ....United Arab Emirates
U.K. ....United Kingdom
U.S. ....United States

PHYSICAL FEATURES

I.-s. .... Island-s
L. .... Lake
Mt.-s. .... Mont, Mount-ain-s
R. .... River

OTHER

ALA. ....Alabama
ARK. ....Arkansas
CONN. .... Connecticut
D.C. ....District of Columbia
Eq. ....Equatorial
FLA. ....Florida
ILL. .... Illinois
IND. ....Indiana
KY. ....Kentucky
LA. ....Louisiana
MASS. ....Massachusetts
MD. .... Maryland
MINN. ....Minnesota
MISS. ....Mississippi
N.H. ....New Hampshire
N.Y. .... New York
PA. ....Pennsylvania
P.E.I. .... Prince Edward Island
Pop. ....Population
Rep. ....Republic
R.I. .... Rhode Island
St.-e. .... Saint-e
TENN. .... Tennessee
VA. .... Virginia
VT. .... Vermont
WASH. .... Washington
WIS. .... Wisconsin
W. VA. ....West Virginia
& .... and

SELECTED WORLD FACTS

THE EARTH

AREA: 196,938,000 sq mi
(510,066,000 sq km)

LAND: 57,393,000 sq mi
(148,647,000 sq km)— 29.1%

WATER: 139,545,000 sq mi
(361,419,000 sq km)— 70.9%

POPULATION: 7,533,036,000 people

DEEPEST POINT IN EACH OCEAN

	FEET	METERS
Challenger Deep, Mariana Trench, Pacific	-36,037	-10,984
Puerto Rico Trench, Atlantic	-28,232	-8,605
Java Trench, Indian	-23,376	-7,125
Molloy Deep, Arctic	-18,599	-5,669

THE OCEANS

	AREA (sq mi)	AREA (sq km)	PERCENTAGE OF EARTH'S OCEANS
Pacific	69,000,000	178,800,000	49.5
Atlantic	35,400,000	91,700,000	25.4
Indian	29,400,000	76,200,000	21.0
Arctic	5,600,000	14,700,000	4.1

10 LARGEST ISLANDS

	AREA (sq mi)	AREA (sq km)
Greenland, North America	836,000	2,166,000
New Guinea, Asia-Oceania	306,000	792,500
Borneo, Asia	280,100	725,500
Madagascar, Africa	226,600	587,000
Baffin, North America	196,000	507,500
Sumatra, Asia	165,000	427,300
Honshu, Asia	87,800	227,400
Great Britain, Europe	84,200	218,100
Victoria, North America	83,900	217,300
Ellesmere, North America	75,800	196,200

10 LARGEST SEAS

	AREA (sq mi)	AREA (sq km)	AVERAGE DEPTH (feet)	AVERAGE DEPTH (meters)
Coral Sea	1,615,500	4,184,000	8,107	2,471
South China Sea	1,388,400	3,596,000	3,871	1,180
Caribbean Sea	1,094,200	2,834,000	8,517	2,596
Bering Sea	973,000	2,520,000	6,010	1,832
Mediterranean Sea	953,300	2,469,000	5,157	1,572
Sea of Okhotsk	627,400	1,625,000	2,671	814
Gulf of Mexico	591,500	1,532,000	5,066	1,544
Norwegian Sea	550,200	1,425,000	5,801	1,768
Greenland Sea	447,100	1,158,000	4,734	1,443
Sea of Japan (East Sea)	389,200	1,008,000	5,404	1,647

WEBSITES

Antarctica: coolantarctica.com

Cultural Diffusion: lightworld.okstate.edu

Earth's Climates: worldclimate.com

Earth's Vegetation: thecanadianencyclopedia.ca/en/article/vegetation-regions

Environmental Hot Spots: Quiz for Students: myfootprint.org

Flags of the World: crwflags.com/fotw/flags

Globalization: globalization101.org

Natural Hazards:
Earthquakes: earthquake.usgs.gov
Hurricanes: nhc.noaa.gov
Tornadoes: nssl.noaa.gov/education/svrwx101/tornadoes/types/
Tsunamis: tsunami.noaa.gov
Volcanoes: www.geo.mtu.edu/volcanoes/world.html

Political World: cia.gov/library/publications/resources/the-world-factbook/index.htm

Quality of Life: hdr.undp.org/en/2016-report

Species at Risk: iucnredlist.org

UNESCO World Heritage Sites: whc.unesco.org/en/list

World Cities: esa.un.org/unpd/wup

World Energy: bp.com/en/global/corporate/energy-economics/statistical-review-of-world-energy/downloads

World Food: www.fao.org/worldfoodsituation/en/
apps.fas.usda.gov/psdonline/app/index.html#/app/downloads

World Languages: ethnologue.com

World Population: census.gov/data-tools/demo/idb/informationGateway.php
prb.org/wp-content/uploads/2017/08/2017_World_Population.pdf

World Refugees: unhcr.org/en-us/figures-at-a-glance.html

World Religions: adherents.com

World Water: worldbank.org/en/topic/watersupply
wri.org/our-work/topics/water

Note: All websites were viable as of publication date. In the event that a site has been discontinued, a reliable search engine can lead you to new sites with helpful information.

Glossary

Note: Terms defined within the main body of the atlas text generally are not listed below. Atlas page references are in bold (125).

AFAR TRIANGLE hot, dry, low-lying area located in eastern Africa where the Great Rift Valley joins the southern end of the Red Sea (**100, 102**)

ANTARCTIC CONVERGENCE climate and marine boundary (roughly 55° S–60° S) where cold, slightly less saline Antarctic waters meet the southern extremes of the Atlantic, Pacific, and Indian Oceans; waters south of the Antarctic Convergence are sometimes referred to as the Southern Ocean (**125**)

ARID CLIMATE type of dry climate in which annual precipitation is often less than 10 inches (25 cm); experiences great daily variations in day-night temperatures (**20–21**)

ASYLUM place where a person can go to find safety; to offer asylum means to offer protection in a safe country to people who fear being persecuted or who have been persecuted in their own country (**34–35**)

BATHYMETRY measurement of depth at various places in the ocean or other body of water (**11**)

BIODIVERSITY biological diversity in an environment as indicated by numbers of different species of plants and animals (**108, 118**)

BOREAL FOREST *see* Northern coniferous forest

BOUNDARY line established by people to separate one political or mapped area from another; physical features, such as mountains and rivers, or latitude and longitude lines sometimes act as boundaries (**10, 30**)

BREADBASKET geographic region that is a principal source of grain (**64**)

CANADIAN SHIELD region containing the oldest rock in North America; areas are exposed in much of eastern Canada and some bordering U.S. regions (**56, 62**)

CLIMATE CHANGE any significant change in the measures of climate, such as temperature, precipitation, or wind patterns, resulting from natural variability or human activity and lasting for an extended period of time (**29**)

COASTAL PLAIN any comparatively level land of low elevation that borders the ocean (**64**)

CONTINENTAL CLIMATE midlatitude climate zone occurring on large landmasses in the Northern Hemisphere and characterized by great variations of temperature, both seasonally and between day and night; continental cool summer climates are influenced by nearby colder subarctic climates; continental warm summer climates are influenced by nearby mild or dry climates (**20–21**)

CONTINENTAL SHELF submerged edge of a continent where the ocean is relatively shallow (**118**)

COORDINATED UNIVERSAL TIME (UTC) basis for the current worldwide system of civil (versus military) time determined by highly precise atomic clocks; also known as Universal Time; formerly known as Greenwich Mean Time (**13**)

CULTURE HEARTH center from which major cultural traditions spread and are adopted by people in a wide geographic area (**90**)

CYBERCAFE café that has a collection of computers that customers can use to access the internet (**52**)

DEGRADED FOREST forested area severely damaged by overharvesting, repeated fires, overgrazing, poor management practices, or other abuse that delays or prevents forest regrowth (**28**)

DESERT AND DRY SHRUB vegetation region with either hot or cold temperatures that annually receives 10 inches (25 cm) or less of precipitation (**24–25**)

DIFFUSE BOUNDARY evolving boundary zone between two or more tectonic plates with edges that are not clearly defined (**17**)

ECOSYSTEM term for classifying Earth's natural communities according to how all things in an environment, such as a forest or a coral reef, interact with each other (**10, 15, 29, 68, 79, 118**)

FAULT break in Earth's crust along which movement up, down, or sideways occurs (**16–17**)

FLOODED GRASSLAND wetland dominated by grasses and covered by water (**24–25**)

FOSSIL FUEL fuel, such as coal, petroleum, and natural gas, derived from the remains of ancient plants and animals (**48**)

GEOTHERMAL ENERGY heat energy generated within Earth (**48**)

GLACIER large, slow-moving mass of ice that forms over time from snow (**26**)

GLOBAL WARMING theory about the increase of Earth's average global temperature due to a buildup of so-called greenhouse gases, such as carbon dioxide and methane, released by human activities (**78**)

GLOBALIZATION purposeful spread of activities, technology, goods, and values throughout the world through the expansion of global links, such as trade, media, and the internet (**50**)

GONDWANA name given to the southern part of the supercontinent Pangaea; made up of what we now call Africa, South America, Australia, Antarctica, and India (**16, 120**)

GREENWICH MEAN TIME *see* Coordinated Universal Time

GROSS DOMESTIC PRODUCT (GDP) gross national product, excluding the value of net income earned abroad (**10, 44**)

GROSS NATIONAL INCOME PER CAPITA a country's annual earned income divided by its population (**36–37**)

GROSS NATIONAL PRODUCT (GNP) total value of the goods and services produced by the residents of a country during a specified period, such as a year (**44**)

GROUNDWATER water, primarily from rain or melted snow, that collects beneath Earth's surface, in saturated soil or in underground reservoirs, or aquifers, and that supplies springs and wells (**27, 28**)

HEMISPHERE one-half of the globe; the Equator divides Earth into Northern and Southern Hemispheres; the prime meridian and the 180-degree meridian divide it into Eastern and Western Hemispheres (**5**)

HIGHLAND/UPLAND CLIMATE region associated with mountains or plateaus that varies depending on elevation, latitude, continental location, and exposure to sun and wind; in general, temperature decreases and precipitation increases with elevation (**20–21**)

HOST COUNTRY country where a refugee goes to find asylum (**34**)

HOT SPOT in geology, an extremely hot region beneath the lithosphere that stays relatively stationary while plates of Earth's outer crust move over it; environmentally, an ecological trouble spot (**28**)

HUMAN DEVELOPMENT INDEX (HDI) way of measuring development that combines both social and economic factors to rank the world's countries based on health, education, and income level (**36–37**)

HUMID SUBTROPICAL CLIMATE region characterized by hot summers, mild to cool winters, and year-round precipitation that is heaviest in summer; generally located on the southeastern margins of continents (**20–21**)

ICE CAP CLIMATE one of two kinds of polar climate; summer temperatures rarely rise above freezing and what little precipitation occurs is mostly in the form of snow (**20–21**)

INDIGENOUS native to or occurring naturally in a specific area or environment (**42, 116**)

INFILTRATION process that occurs in the water, or hydrologic, cycle when gravity causes surface water to seep down through the soil (**26**)

INTERNALLY DISPLACED PERSON (IDP) person who has fled his or her home to escape armed conflict, generalized violence, human rights abuses, or natural or human-made disasters; unlike a refugee, such a person has not crossed an international border but remains in his or her own country (**34**)

LANDFORM physical feature shaped by uplifting, weathering, or erosion; mountains, plateaus, hills, and plains are the four major types (**18, 22**)

LANGUAGE FAMILY group of languages that share a common ancestry (**40-41**)

LATIN AMERICA cultural region generally considered to include Mexico, Central America, South America, and the West Indies; Portuguese and Spanish are the principal languages (**33**)

LIFE EXPECTANCY average number of years a person can expect to live, based on current mortality rates and health conditions (**36**)

LLANOS extensive, mostly treeless grasslands in the Orinoco River basin of northern South America (**72**)

LOWLANDS fairly level land at a lower elevation than surrounding areas (**14**)

MANGROVE VEGETATION tropical trees and shrubs with dense root systems that grow in tidal mudflats and extend coastlines by trapping soil (**24-25**)

MARGINAL LAND land that has little value for growing crops or for commercial or residential development (**28**)

MARINE WEST COAST type of mild climate common on the west coasts of continents in midlatitude regions; characterized by small variations in annual temperature range and wet, foggy winters (**20-21**)

MEDIAN AGE midpoint of a population's age; half the population is older than this age; half is younger (**32**)

MEDITERRANEAN CLIMATE mild climate common on the west coasts of continents, named for the dominant climate along the Mediterranean coast; characterized by mild, rainy winters and hot, dry summers (**20-21**)

MEDITERRANEAN SHRUB low-growing, mostly small-leaf evergreen vegetation, such as chaparral, that thrives in Mediterranean climate regions (**24-25**)

MELANESIA one of three major island groups that make up Oceania; includes the Fiji Islands, New Guinea, Vanuatu, the Solomon Islands, and New Caledonia (**112-113**)

MELANESIAN indigenous to Melanesia (**116**)

MICROCLIMATE climate of a very limited area that varies from the overall climate of the surrounding region (**22**)

MICRONESIA one of three major island groups that make up Oceania; made up of some 2,000 mostly coral islands, including Guam, Kiribati, the Mariana Islands, Palau, and the Federated States of Micronesia (**112-113**)

MICRONESIAN indigenous to Micronesia (**116**)

MONSOON seasonal change in the direction of the prevailing winds that causes wet and dry seasons in some tropical areas (**94**)

MOUNTAIN GRASSLAND vegetation region characterized by clumps of long grass that grow beyond the limit of forests at high elevations (**24-25**)

NONRENEWABLE RESOURCES elements of the natural environment, such as metals, minerals, and fossil fuels, that form within Earth by geological processes over millions of years and thus cannot readily be replaced (**48-49**)

NORTHERN CONIFEROUS FOREST vegetation region composed primarily of cone-bearing, needle- or scale-leaf evergreen trees that grow in regions with long winters and moderate to high annual precipitation; also called boreal forest or taiga (**24-25**)

OCEANIA name for the widely scattered islands of Polynesia, Micronesia, and Melanesia; often includes Australia and New Zealand (**110-119**)

PAMPAS temperate grassland primarily in Argentina between the Andes and the Atlantic Ocean; one of the world's most productive agricultural regions (**70, 72**)

PATAGONIA cool, windy, arid plateau region primarily in southern Argentina between the Andes and the Atlantic Ocean (**72**)

PER CAPITA INCOME total national income divided by the number of people in the country (**36-37**)

PLAIN large area of relatively flat land; one of the four major kinds of landforms (**18**)

PLATE TECTONICS study of the interaction of slabs of Earth's crust as molten rock within Earth causes them to slowly move across the surface (**16-17**)

PLATEAU large, relatively flat area that rises above the surrounding landscape; one of the four major kinds of landforms (**18-19**)

POLAR CLIMATES climates that occur at very high latitudes; generally too cold to support tree growth; include tundra and ice cap (**20-21**)

POLYNESIA one of three major regions in Oceania made up mostly of volcanic and coral islands, including the Hawaiian Islands, Samoa, and French Polynesia (**112-113**)

POLYNESIAN indigenous to Polynesia (**116**)

PREDOMINANT ECONOMY main type of work that most people do to meet their wants and needs in a particular country (**44-45, 61, 77, 87, 97, 107, 117**)

PROVINCE land governed as a political or administrative unit of a country or empire; Canadian provinces, like U.S. states, have substantial powers of self-government (**63**)

RAIN FOREST see Tropical moist broadleaf forest

RENEWABLE FRESHWATER water that is replenished naturally; the supply of freshwater can be endangered by overuse and pollution (**26**)

RIVER BASIN area drained by a single river and its tributaries (**72**)

RURAL pertaining to the countryside, where most of the economic activity centers on agriculture-related work (**38-39**)

SAHEL in Africa, the semiarid region of short, tropical grassland that lies between the dry Sahara and the humid savanna and that is prone to frequent droughts (**102, 104**)

SALINE/SALINITY measure of all salts contained in water; average ocean salinity is 35 parts per thousand (**125**)

SAMPAN flat-bottomed boat used in eastern Asia and usually propelled by two short oars (**98**)

SAVANNA tropical tall grassland with scattered trees (**24-25**)

SELVA Portuguese word referring to tropical rain forests, especially in the Amazon Basin (**78**)

SEMIARID dry climate region with great variation in day-night temperatures; has enough rainfall to support short grasslands (**20-21**)

SILT mineral particles that are larger than grains of clay but smaller than grains of sand (**78**)

STATELESS PEOPLE those who have no recognized country (**35**)

STEPPE Russian word for relatively flat, mostly treeless, temperate grasslands that stretch across much of central Europe and central Asia (**92**)

SUBARCTIC CLIMATE region characterized by short, cool, sometimes freezing summers and long, bitter-cold winters; most precipitation falls in summer (**20-21**)

SUBTROPICAL CLIMATE region between tropical and continental climates characterized by distinct seasons but with milder temperatures than continental climates (**20-21**)

SUBURB residential area on the outskirts of a town or city (**38**)

SUNBELT area of rapid population and economic growth south of the 37th parallel in the United States; its mild climate is attractive to retirees, and a general absence of labor unions has drawn manufacturing to the region (**60**)

TAIGA see Northern coniferous forest

TEMPERATE BROADLEAF FOREST vegetation region with distinct seasons and dependable rainfall; predominant species include oak, maple, and beech, all of which lose their leaves in the cold season (**24-25**)

TEMPERATE CONIFEROUS FOREST vegetation region that has mild winters with heavy precipitation; made up of mostly evergreen, needle-leaf trees that bear seeds in cones (**24-25**)

TEMPERATE GRASSLAND vegetation region where grasses are dominant and the climate is characterized by hot summers, cold winters, and moderate rainfall (**24-25**)

TERRITORY land under the jurisdiction of a country but that is not a state or a province (**57**)

TRANSIT CAMP place where refugees find temporary shelter before moving to a new location (**34**)

TROPICAL CONIFEROUS FOREST vegetation region that occurs in a cooler climate than tropical rain forests; has distinct wet and dry seasons; is made up of mostly evergreen trees with seed-bearing cones (**24-25**)

TROPICAL DRY CLIMATE region characterized by year-round high temperatures and wet and dry seasons (**20-21**)

TROPICAL DRY FOREST vegetation region that has distinct wet and dry seasons and a cooler climate than tropical moist broadleaf forests; has shorter trees than rain forests, and many shed their leaves in the dry season (**24-25**)

TROPICAL GRASS-LAND AND SAVANNA vegetation region characterized by scattered individual trees; occurs in warm or hot climates with annual rainfall of 20 to 50 inches (50–130 cm) (**24-25**)

TROPICAL MOIST BROADLEAF FOREST vegetation region occurring mostly in a belt between the Tropic of Cancer and the Tropic of Capricorn in areas that have at least 80 inches (200 cm) of rain annually and an average annual temperature of 80°F (27°C) (**24-25, 78-79**)

TROPICAL WET CLIMATE region characterized by year-round warm temperatures and rainfall ranging from 20 to 24 inches (50–60 cm) annually (**20-21**)

TROPOSPHERE region of Earth's atmosphere closest to the surface; where weather occurs (**5**)

TUNDRA vegetation region at high latitudes and high elevations characterized by cold temperatures, low vegetation, and a short growing season (**24-25**)

TUNDRA CLIMATE region with one or more months of temperatures slightly above freezing when the ground is free of snow (**20-21**)

UNIVERSALIZING RELIGION a religion that attempts to appeal to all people rather than to just those in a particular region or place (**42**)

UPLAND CLIMATE see Highland/upland climate

URBAN pertaining to a town or city, where most of the economic activity is not based on agriculture (**38-39**)

URBAN AGGLOMERATION a group of several cities and/or towns and their suburbs (**38**)

Thematic Index

Boldface indicates illustrations; *italics* indicates maps.

Place-Name Index

Boldface indicates illustrations; *italics* indicates maps.

Map Data Sources

11 (Satellite Image Maps), NASA Earth Observatory. https://earthobservatory.nasa.gov/

16–17 (Plate Tectonics), USGS Earthquake Hazards Program and USGS National Earthquake Information Center (NEIC). earthquake.usgs.gov; Smithsonian Institution. Global Volcanism Program. volcano.si.edu

26–27 (Water Stress), Gassert, F., M. Landis, M. Luck, P. Reig, and T. Shiao. 2014. "Aqueduct Global Maps 2.1." Washington, DC: World Resources Institute (WRI). http://www.wri.org/publication/aqueduct-metadata-global

28 (Human Footprint), Venter, O., E.W. Sanderson, A. Magrach, J.R. Allan, J. Beher, K.R. Jones, H.P. Possingham, W.F. Laurance, P. Wood, B.M. Fekete, M.A. Levy, and J.E.M. Watson. "Sixteen years of change in the global terrestrial human footprint and implications for biodiversity conservation." *Nature Communications*, doi:10.1038/ncomms12558, 2016; Watson, J.E.M., D.F. Shanahan, M. Di Marco, J. Allan, W.F. Laurance, E.W. Sanderson, B. Mackey, and O. Venter. "Catastrophic Declines in Wilderness Areas Undermine Global Environment Targets." *Current Biology*, doi:10.1016/j.cub.2016.08.049, 26, 2016

28–29 (Fragile Forests), Global Forest Watch. World Resources Institute (WRI)

29 (Failing Fishing), NOAA Fisheries. https://www.fisheries.noaa.gov/welcome; United Nations Environmental World Conservation Monitoring Centre (UNEP-WCMC). https://www.unep-wcmc.org

29 (Climate Change), Lara Hansen, Adam Markham. World Wildlife Fund (WWF)

32–33, 60, 76, 86, 96, 106, 116 (Population Density), This product was made utilizing the LandScan (2016)™ High Resolution Global Population Data Set copyrighted by UT-Battelle, LLC, operator of Oak Ridge National Laboratory under Contract No. DE-AC05-00OR22725 with the United States Department of Energy. The United States Government has certain rights in this Data Set. Neither UT-BATTELLE, LLC NOR THE UNITED STATES DEPARTMENT OF ENERGY, NOR ANY OF THEIR EMPLOYEES, MAKES ANY WARRANTY, EXPRESS OR IMPLIED, OR ASSUMES ANY LEGAL LIABILITY OR RESPONSIBILITY FOR THE ACCURACY, COMPLETENESS, OR USEFULNESS OF THE DATA SET.

34–35 (Refugee Population), The World Bank. World Development Indicators. https://data.worldbank.org/indicator/SM.POP.REFG?name_desc=false; UNHCR. The UN Refugee Agency. http://popstats.unhcr.org/en/overview#_ga=2.262785932.1687030866.1523553155-915436448.1523553155

36–37 (Life Expectancy at Birth, Human Development Index), United Nations Development Programme (UNDP). Human Development Reports. http://hdr.undp.org/en/data#

38–39 (Urban and Rural Population), United Nations (UN). Department of Economic and Social Affairs. Population Division (2014). World Urbanization Prospects: The 2014 Revision, CD-ROM Edition

40–41 (Major Language Families), Global Mapping International (GMI) and SIL International. World Language Mapping System. version 3.2.1

42–43 (Dominant Religion) Johnson, Todd M., and Brian J. Grim, eds. World Religion Database: worldreligiondatabase.org. Leiden/Boston: Brill

44–45, 61, 77, 87, 97, 107, 117 (Predominant Economies), CIA. *The World Factbook*. https://www.cia.gov/library/publications/the-world-factbook

46–47 (Agricultural Land Use), Global Landscapes Initiative. Institute on the Environment. University of Minnesota. Hooke, Roger LeB., and José F. Martín-Duque. "Land Transformation by Humans: A Review." *GSA Today* (2012), Volume 22 (12): 4–10

47 (Low-Income Food-Deficit), Food and Agriculture Organization of the United Nations (FAO). http://www.fao.org/countryprofiles/lifdc/en

48–49 (Exports in Non-Fuel Mineral Resources), World Integrated Trade Solution (WITS). https://wits.worldbank.org/CountryProfile/en/Country/WLD/Year/2016/TradeFlow/Export/Partner/all/Product/25-26_Minerals#

50–51 (Average Continental Globalization Index by Category, Overall Globalization Index), Gygli, Savina, Florian Haelg, and Jan-Egbert Sturm (2018). The KOF Globalisation Index – Revisited. KOF Working Paper. No. 439. https://www.kof.ethz.ch/en/forecasts-and-indicators/indicators/kof-globalisation-index.html; Dreher, Axel (2006). Does Globalization Affect Growth? Evidence from a new Index of Globalization. *Applied Economics* 38, 10: 1091-1110

52–53 (International Tourism), The World Bank. World Development Indicators. https://data.worldbank.org/indicator/ST.INT.ARVL

59, 75, 85, 95, 105, 115 (Precipitation), NOAA. NESDIS. NCEI. Satellite Services Division (SSD). compiled by UNEP-GRID

68–69 (North America Natural Hazards), USGS Earthquake Hazards Program and USGS National Earthquake Information Center (NEIC). earthquake.usgs.gov; Smithsonian Institution. Global Volcanism Program. volcano.si.edu; National Hurricane Center. https://www.nhc.noaa.gov; United States Geological Survey. https://www.usgs.gov

79 (South America Rain Forest Cover), Hansen, M.C., P.V. Potapov, R. Moore, M. Hancher, S.A. Turubanova, A. Tyukavina, D. Thau, S.V. Stehman, S.J. Goetz, T.R. Loveland, A. Kommareddy, A. Egorov, L. Chini, C.O. Justice, and J.R.G. Townshend. 2013. "High-Resolution Global Maps of 21st-Century Forest Cover Change." *Science* 342 (15 November): 850–53. http://earthenginepartners.appspot.com/science-2013-global-forest

99 (East Asia Ports), World Shipping Council. 2013–2015 average. http://www.worldshipping.org/about-the-industry/global-trade/top-50-world-container-ports

109 (Africa Protected Areas), Protected Planet. United Nations Environmental World Conservation Monitoring Centre (UNEP-WCMC). https://www.protectedplanet.net/c/about; UNESCO. https://whc.unesco.org/en/list

119 (Great Barrier Reef, Global Coral Reefs), ReefBase: A Global Information System for Coral Reefs. http://reefgis.reefbase.org

Illustration Credits

National Geographic Kids magazine inspires children to explore their world with fun yet educational articles on animals, science, nature, and more. Using fresh storytelling and amazing photography, *Nat Geo Kids* shows kids ages 6 to 14 the fascinating truth about the world—and why they should care. **kids.nationalgeographic.com/subscribe**

Designed by Rachel Kenny

The publisher would like to thank everyone who worked to make this book come together: Martha Sharma, writer/researcher; Suzanne Patrick Fonda, project manager; Angela Modany, associate editor; Kathryn Robbins, art director; Sarah J. Mock, photo editor; Debbie Gibbons, Mike McNey, and Jon Bowen, map production; Irene Berman-Vaporis, Theodore A. Sickley, Rosemary P. Wardley, Ryan T. Williams, and Scott A. Zillmer, map research and edit; Stuart Armstrong, illustrator; Sean Philpotts, production director; Sally Abbey, managing editor; Joan Gossett, editorial production manager; and Gus Tello and Anne LeongSon, design production assistants.

National Geographic supports K–12 educators with ELA Common Core Resources.
Visit natgeoed.org/commoncore for more information.

Trade paperback ISBN: 978-1-4263-3479-5
Hardcover ISBN: 978-1-4263-3480-1
Reinforced library binding ISBN: 978-1-4263-3481-8

Printed in Malaysia
20/IVM/2

There's MORE ...
TO EXPLORE!

National Geographic Kids has the perfect atlas for kids of every age, from preschool through high school—all with the latest age-appropriate facts, maps, images, and more.

The atlas series is designed to grow as kids grow, adding more depth and relevant material at every level to help them stay curious about the world and to succeed at school and in life!

AGES 7-10

NATIONAL GEOGRAPHIC KIDS
BEGINNER'S
UNITED STATES ATLAS

AGES 11-14

NATIONAL GEOGRAPHIC KIDS
UNITED STATES ATLAS

It's your country. Learn it. Love it. Explore it.

PARENT'S CHOICE AWARD WINNER!

NATIONAL GEOGRAPHIC KiDS

AVAILABLE WHEREVER BOOKS ARE SOLD